CREATORS

ON CREATING

This *New Consciousness Reader* is part of a new series of original and classic writing by renowned experts on leading-edge concepts in personal development, psychology, spiritual growth, and healing. Other books in this series include:

Founding Series Editor: CONNIE ZWEIG, PH.D.

CREATORS
ON CREATING

*Awakening and Cultivating
the Imaginative Mind*

EDITED BY

Frank Barron,
Alfonso Montuori,
and Anthea Barron

Jeremy P. Tarcher/Penguin
a member of
Penguin Group (USA) Inc.
375 Hudson Street
New York, NY 10014
www.penguin.com

Most Tarcher/Penguin books are available at special quantity
discounts for bulk purchase for sales promotions, premiums,
fund-raising, and educational needs. Special books or book excerpts
also can be created to fit specific needs.
For details, write Penguin Group (USA) Inc.
Special Markets, 375 Hudson Street
New York, NY 10014

Jeremy P. Tarcher/Penguin
a member of
Penguin Group (USA) Inc.
375 Hudson Street
New York, NY 10014
www.penguin.com

Library of Congress Cataloging-in-Publication Data

Creators on creating: awakening and cultivating the imaginative mind /
    edited by Frank Barron, Alfonso Montuori, and Anthea Barron
        p.   cm.
    Includes bibliographical references.
    ISBN 0-87477-854-9
        1. Creation (Literary, artistic, etc.). I. Barron, Frank, date.
II. Montuori, Alfonso. III. Barron, Anthea.
BH301.C84C75   1997
153.3'5—dc20   96-38805 CIP

Book design by Lee Fukui
Cover design by Susan Shankin

Printed in the United States of America

20 19 18 17

This book is printed on acid-free paper. ∞

Dedicated to
Nancy and Kitty,
our special singers;
and to the memory of
Chuck Libutski,
a man who played
on heartstrings

contents

My feeling is that the concept of creativeness
and the concept of the healthy, self-actualizing,
fully human person seem to be coming closer
and closer together, and may perhaps turn out
to be the same thing.

ABRAHAM MASLOW

Every man in creating the beautiful appearance
of the dream worlds is a perfect artist.

FRIEDRICH NIETZSCHE

introduction

by Frank Barron

Creativity is a key that opens many doors. It can produce a change for the better in a wide variety of human activities, ranging from the spiritual to the material, the altruistic to the personal, the practical to the idealistic. Throughout human history this has been the case, but creativity has come to the forefront of human consciousness in a new way in the twentieth century, while recent years of rapid and radical social change have made it of compelling importance. As we enter an uncertain future, creativity can do nothing but increase in value.

However, all too often the almost magical yet supremely practical key of creativity is neither recognized nor used. Think how much better off we all might be if government were more creative in dealing with the issues it faces. Consider the possibilities if the established religions shook themselves loose from the straitjacket of jaded creed and ritual and brought a more personal realization of God to the faithful. What if health care and public education opened themselves more to creative collaboration with their clients, as well as to more creative use of their human resources and the new availability of a greatly expanded knowledge base?

Thoughts like these lead you to the realization that creativity is the most hopeful source of transformations for the good of all. It can bring changes for the better in our own families, our workplaces, our streets, our cities; we ourselves, as creative individuals, can make these changes happen. It is no exaggeration at all to say that creativity is the key to a more advanced humanity, a key to the realization of human potential and the control of human destructiveness.

CREATIVITY AS A SEARCH FOR MEANING

This use of creativity as an instrument for personal and social gain is by no means the whole story. In its deeper philosophical implications, creativity is a quest for meaning. It is an attempt to penetrate the mystery of the self, and perhaps the even greater mystery of Being. The very origin of existence is open to creative exploration, and the science of this century has posed new questions, large and small—intriguing, challenging, important questions.

Creativity in science is fearlessly, even presumptuously curious. It has reached for the stars and into the atom. It has brought not just the vast but the very tiny into our ken in a totally improbable way. Particle physics has gone beyond the splitting of the atom and is dealing with the very heart of matter! Think of DNA. The whole story of life may be writ small from the beginning in the DNA code. Can we change the story of life, by design? We dare to attempt to map the human genome, the entire complement of human DNA, while creating and even patenting new genes. Certainly, creativity can be brash in its efforts to be practical.

Science may seem to some to be the enemy of art and religion, but it has much in common with both. Often the correct solution is the most aesthetic solution. And what is more mysterious, more evocative of feelings of awe, than some of the findings of science in the areas of genetics and astrophysics? Science does not diminish the mystery of creation, it augments it.

MY OWN CONVERSATIONS WITH THE CREATIVE

It was my good fortune and sometimes deep pain to take part in research with highly creative people—famous writers, architects, and mathematicians, as well as lesser-known scientists and artists—during my days in the 1950s as a research psychologist at the University of California at Berkeley. A novel and intense method of research, called holistic assessment, involved these notably creative individuals in three crowded days of interviews, experiments, test-taking, and group discussions.

Just who was assessing whom soon became the question. Between "assessments" a few weeks had to be allowed to elapse to give the psychologists a chance to get over what was invariably an extremely intense, sometimes trying experience. If this was a sort of party, as it might have seemed at lunch and dinner and during the social hours, it was a hard-work, overtime party! These were not the captive and docile college sophomores who had served as "subjects" in so many thousands of experiments in psychology. Not at all! They were often outrageous, eccentric, uninhibited, rule-challenging, norm-rejecting cases of self-possession and self-assertion. Picture if you will an intuitive introvert with a lot of dash, a big bank account (except for the poets), a skipping wit, a disrespectful attitude toward true-false questionnaires, and an assured place in cultural history. Do that, and you can imagine what we poor psychologists were up against.

As for my pain, perhaps it was the toothache—and, soon, the heartache—of the 1960s getting ready to announce itself. I was torn within. I sensed that creativity was the way out of the conventional, conforming, and for some people very comforting 1950s. A new possibility beckoned—more freedom of expression, deeper cultivation of the self—more honesty, really.

I entered into this research with enthusiasm, but I sometimes felt that the "objective" study of creativity was conformity getting its weapons ready. Which side was I on? I was director of the first study, of a group of writers, and I found myself imagining myself as the person under study. I assembled all the questionnaires and interview schedules, armed myself with some newly sharpened pencils and a tape recorder, and went into a testing-and-interviewing office to put myself through an "assessment." It is said that a crowd of my fellow psychologists was soon gathered outside the door, listening to my swearing, my shouts, and the sound of papers being ripped up and pencils broken. Should they force the door to see whether I was all right, or just wait circumspectly for me to emerge? To their credit, I was allowed to go to my conclusion.

Soon after that, I wrote my first short story. I wanted to see what this was all about. Writing the story worked for me. I did at least a bit of the suffering-through, the coming to grips with oneself, that the creative process may entail.

The lesson I had learned is one that everyone must learn who plunges into the creative process. It grips you in the depths of the self. You're certainly welcome to try to keep it superficial, but then you pay the cost of over-control. You lose, perhaps forever, the part of your experience that you're choosing not to have.

ASSESSMENTS OR CONVERSATIONS?

The assessments were a fascinating and instructive experience, quite apart from the experiments and the psychological testing. They were organized conversations, revolving around questions the interviewer used as a guide to discovering the relation of the individual's creative work to his or her personal life.

The Questions

Here is a chance for you to have a conversation with yourself. Pick the questions that interest you and give your own answers to them. Do it with a friend, and record it, if you wish.

1. Do you think of yourself as a creative person? If you do, why? If you don't, why not?

2. Do you feel that your maturation as a person has been related in any close way to the maturation of your creative abilities and commitments? Do you grow through your work?

3. What about the act of creation itself? Can you recall some piece of work that meant a lot to you? Try to describe it in detail.

4. In retrospect, did you become aware of anything going on in you that at the time of creation you were unaware of? Think of examples of such periods: what was going on in your life or in your thinking about your work at that time?

5. Are there ebbs and flows in your creativity? Are you suddenly full of ideas, or suddenly without an idea at all? What might cause a sudden spurt of creativity, or a long period of drought? What in particular was going on in your life that you may have been unaware of at the time but in retrospect was highly important in your creative effort? When do you consider the work "finished"? When your work is "finished," do you feel finished with it? How do you feel at the end? Are you most productive when you are feeling happy? Do you suffer if you are not?

6. Is there something creative that you are putting off doing? Do you expect to get to it? What is it? Why must you delay?

These questions may lead you to very serious thinking and feeling about your own creativity. That is one of the goals of this book. It is not just a book to read; it is a book to engage yourself with.

The Value of the Research for You and Me

For the researchers there was always one troubling question: Isn't creativity a sacred matter, a manifestation of humanness that should not be measured, analyzed, anatomized, and made the object of philistine and vulgar scientific-psychological curiosity? Perhaps not; yet where else can these claims, which after all are assertions about the nature of reality, be carefully investigated and evaluated?

The reason for looking at very clear examples of any process in nature is simply this: that the more unmistakable and more organized the specific case, the more it can reveal about the general phenomenon. Specific knowledge transfers into an understanding of a process everywhere.

Creativity is the specifically human resource. It is part of the general human potential, something that we can cultivate in ourselves if we set out to. It is also something that can be nurtured in others who are close to us and perhaps in our care. Teachers can help foster creativity in students, parents in children, and children in parents! Lovers may bring out the creativity in lovers, the pastor in the congregation, the entertainer in the audience. It can work both ways, and it can be an important part of the mutuality that helps make all of us stronger.

Looking back on the Berkeley researches, I am content that they helped somewhat to demystify creativity, specify its conditions, and make it something within our own grasp. The famous people who gave their time and yielded up some of their magic, mystery, and invulnerability for the sake of that enterprise are our benefactors. I think our findings did shed some light on important practical as well as philosophical questions worth everyone's attention (Barron 1963; 1969). The research was a novelty in itself; nothing like it had been done before, and nothing like it has been done since. It remains unique in the history of psychology as well as in the art and science of creativity.

The Point of It All

Why am I telling you about these people that I got to talk to? Because this book is in a sense an opportunity for you yourself to have some conversations, at least in your own mind, with whomever you choose in its ensemble of creative people—some very famous, some less so, but all individualistic, self-possessed, and strong enough to speak out in an idiosyncratic, forceful, yet refined way on the subject of their own creativity. Like the psychologists at Berkeley, you may learn something in a general way about creativity, something in a particular way about these individuals, and something perhaps of use to yourself in finding the way to your own creative potential.

A book is a sort of room, one with many spaces in it. Henry James once responded to the criticism that his writing was like an acre of embroidery on a small square of canvas by agreeing that indeed it was, so long as one understood that the canvas was time (clock or calendar time, but made eternal by the act of art) and the embroidery was consciousness. Still, Henry was addicted to the comma and the subsidiary clause, and clauses within clauses, so his consciousness might not be typical. All of us, however, do think a lot more than we speak or act, and our reservoir of related associations and impressions is money in the bank of our creative consciousness.

Both Freud and Jung, in their different ways, entered into the world of dreams. Fortunately for all of us who may not find any special creativity in our environments some rainy day, we can always turn, as they did, to our own dreams, that revel-room of images in which we can have our personal creativity at our pleasure. Or we can open a book or go to a library or a museum or a gallery or a video rental shop. Each one is an invitation to come to a party. There the works sit, assembled often so long ago, perhaps dusty and long neglected, but waiting for another consciousness to have a ball with. I find that any such participation helps me to hold on to my sanity and to feel myself in good company.

I believe that it is helpful to one's own creativity to bring oneself into close contact with creative people, whether they are living and breathing and walking around or are to be met simply in that other form of existence sometimes found by the creative, that is, the accomplished works themselves: paintings, films, buildings, writings, inventions, discoveries, novel enterprises.

All three editors of this book, in conversations among ourselves, have acknowledged that the work of putting the book together, and the extensive reading that accompanied it, have compelled us once again to look at ourselves and to ask whether we are being our creative best.

WHAT KIND OF PARTY IS THIS?

We have brought some kind of crowd together in this book, that's for sure. The why of each selection becomes clear as the book unfolds. But an interesting question arises that only the editors can answer: Did we learn anything about creativity in general in putting this whole thing together? Yes.

I believe that we learned a few things, one quite unexpected, in doing the literature search for the pieces we have chosen to include. Our criteria were simply that the persons were creative and that they had told the world, in their own words and in an interesting way, how it all happens with them. That was the basis of our search as we drew up lists and began haunting our local libraries and accessing some faraway ones on our computer. I won't say that we began with Homer, or the Buddha, or Lao-tzu, or even Herodotus or Aristotle or Augustine or Sappho or Confucius or Ikhnaton, as perhaps we might have; but we did think we might find something from Michelangelo, or Dante, or Newton, or Queen Elizabeth, or John Donne, or Milton. But alas! These worthies created, yes indeed; but most of them did not speak of their own creating as a subject of special interest to themselves or others. Not that they were unaware of the act of creation; it was just that they did not think to speak of their own creative processes (there are notable exceptions, of course; Leonardo da Vinci was one). Not until the early nineteenth century, with the romantics, do we begin to get hints of self-awareness of the creative process, and not until the twentieth century does it become a defined self-concern. It almost appears that an interest in the creative process in oneself did not become highly articulate until the very end of the nineteenth century, and that it was part of that general movement of mind we call the discovery of the unconscious. This we had not expected.

THE TWENTIETH CENTURY AND THE ENLARGING WORLD

We, the editors, must plead guilty here to a bit of chauvinism, as to both place and time. We decided finally, after much reading and thought, that the twentieth century was the best period to draw from. Even at that, the past two decades are probably underrepresented, largely because many creative individuals have not yet come to the point of telling their own stories for others to read.

Moreover, we know we haven't been able to do justice to the wide world beyond the boundaries of Europe and North America. We have tried hard to make the body of selections representative of human diversity. There perhaps remains too much "whiteness" here for us to claim universal sampling. All we can say in our defense is that in the literature accessible to us, the selections we have chosen seem to mass themselves in a meaningful and interpretable way. The limitations are there, and acknowledged. Let's all keep them in mind, and explore further in whatever way we may be able to.

The Century Takes On a Head of Steam

Whether or not there is an unconscious, and whether or not it was a new discovery, all of a sudden, the twentieth century in Europe did begin with what has been heralded as a vast movement of mind, a revolution of manners and means as well as consciousness. Freud published *The Interpretation of Dreams* in 1900. Jung later said, looking back on his first reading of that seminal work, "I never had an idea until then." He promptly got in touch with the author of those new thoughts; they met together in a hotel soon thereafter and proceeded to talk up a storm. Out of that meeting and the new organization of psychoanalysis came the broadened depth psychology that has so affected human consciousness (and still has a long way to go!). Psychoanalysis in those days can itself be accused of a certain narcissism in its elevation of its own ideas of the unconscious—a seething mass of sexual and violent impulses, yet held captive in a freezing darkness—to universal status. Freud capitalized Sex and Jung capitalized Symbol; Freud emphasized the personally repressed and Jung emphasized the ancestral and collective unconscious, peopled with archetypal images. Psychoanalysis was in part a radical critique of Western culture, expressed most concisely and trenchantly by Freud himself in his monograph *Civilization and Its Discontents*, and elaborated by Jung in his concept of the reality of evil and the explosive threat of the shadow in a science and technology only dimly aware of its negative potentials.

A big century of creativity was on the move in the West. The 20th Century Limited, the newest and fastest train in the world, was its symbol. There was a broadening of consciousness and human enterprise in quite a number of unexampled ways. In 1904 the mathematical physicist Poincaré called for a special theory of relativity, and in 1905 the young Einstein obliged. The imaginable cosmos took on a new dimension, space-time, with hints of others still to come. The archetypes, those forms from the ancestral memory, were coming into their own, that is, were becoming widely recognized in popular psychology and literature. Yet in the twentieth century they were taking on some new and powerful embodiments. In 1902 the Wright brothers were setting sail for the moon, and soon enough for Jupiter, from Kitty Hawk (surely an archetypal place-name for take-off, with its hint of claws and beak and predatory swoop, as well as of the fledgling bird testing its wings). Henry Ford was just starting to clog the highways of America, most of which hadn't yet been built, with his tin lizzie (soon to become a tank to shoot from). "Soon" is a key word for the twentieth century; soon or sooner, the century of speed.

THE NEW QUEST FOR FREEDOM: WOMEN FREEING THEMSELVES

Virginia Woolf proclaimed the need for "a room of one's own," imagining in a moving, personal way the plight of a forever-to-be-unknown female Shakespeare, perhaps sister of the man we know by that name. More and more women did find that priceless freedom that comes with privacy as the century wore on, and in our own compilation we began to find many women's voices, as you shall see. The oppressed were beginning to speak out, in ways that had been denied them. Women had through the ages been creative in traditionally restricted ways: the making of homes, the bearing and bringing up of families, the forming and fostering of humane relationships and personal values, the growing and preparation of the fruits of the earth. But now their denied faculties of scientific and mathematical and artistic thought were finding expression. Virginia Woolf had seen a key issue, privacy and time to oneself, but even more important perhaps was the self-definition and social acceptance of women who chose not to spend their energy on raising a family but on doing other things with their means. Often enough this meant some simple acknowledgment and change of fact: The "man of the house" had to take his turn at cooking the meals, doing the dishes, changing the diapers when that was called for, just as a matter of recognized co-responsibility.

A decisive moment in women's freeing of themselves from bondage came in 1920 in the United States with the passage by Congress and ratification by the states of the Nineteenth Amendment, recognizing the right of women to vote. This was brought about by the thousands of women who organized themselves to make the fight that their menfolk wouldn't or couldn't make. They suffered outrageous physical and mental abuse from the male authorities, but it only stiffened their resolve. (Incidentally, the final and decisive vote cast for ratification was that of a Tennessee assemblyman who had already voted no, in the morning. That very afternoon he received, fortuitously, a letter from his aged mother in rural Tennessee, saying, "I know you're a good boy and will vote what you know is right—Yes!" He immediately changed his vote. There is more than one way to skin a cat.)

CIVIL RIGHTS FOR ETHNIC MINORITIES — A BIT AT A TIME

Another battle was won too in the 1920s in the United States of America. Jazz came into its heyday, or its hi-de-hey day, an indigenous, made-only-in-America creation that combined spirituals with freedom to express the soul of a downtrodden people. Songs and singers played a part. It wasn't always an easy one: Bessie Smith died without medical attention when she was refused admittance to a hospital because she was "colored." Billie Holiday gave a soul-shivering rendition of a song she wrote, "Strange Fruit," about the lynchings of black men. Marian Anderson sang to a vast throng from the steps of the Lincoln Memorial—at the invitation of another brave and creative woman, Eleanor Roosevelt, who cared not a whit for the Daughters of the American Revolution and their thoughtless opposition.

In that historic decade of the thirties, the "forgotten man" was remembered by a great and courageous leader, Franklin Delano Roosevelt. He was a physically crippled but spiritually vibrant counterforce to the collectivism arising in Germany and Italy. As events began to unfold, portentous of destruction as well as creation, he kept alert to what was going on, and he responded for the entire endangered world. But matters were never again to be as simple as they had seemed before. The atom was split in Berlin in 1938, the atomic fission chain reaction was achieved in Chicago in late 1942, and the scientists at Los Alamos exploded their awesome dark feat of intellect in 1945. The heedless, perhaps needless, karmic fire consumed Hiroshima and God knows what else—the fires, after all, are still burning in the ashes of the radioactive waste from all the nuclear explosions the world has known since then. It was perhaps these events that brought us to the historical point in science, psychology, and even the evolution of human consciousness where creativity research became both possible and necessary.

THE NATURE OF CREATIVITY: QUESTIONS AND MAYBE ANSWERS

Answers to the big questions are not all in, not by a long shot. Still, a great deal of headway has been made. A sort of "progress report" published in the *Annual Review of Psychology* summarized the evidence on many issues (Barron and Harrington 1981). There have been many other reviews of scientific findings about creativity in recent years. Books of readings featuring chapters and earlier papers by leaders in the field (often containing the proceedings of important conferences) have been published. And there have been new slants on some of the big issues: factors in intelligence (also known as frames of mind or multitalents); the ecology of creativity; creativity and leadership; the creative career; creativity and mental health; motives and creativity. Much has been done, and much is being done. The field remains a lively one for research and, of course, for new applications.

So what are some of the big questions? Without presuming that we are giving all the final answers, here's a picture of where things stand. Let's begin with the question of creativity and intelligence, and try to frame the matter in a non-technical way.

1. Is a high IQ essential to creativity?

Well, it helps, a bit. Try making a list of the ten most intelligent people you know, and then make a list of the ten most creative. How much overlap is there? (Be careful, of course, that the overlap is not just in your definition of the terms.) Maybe try it another way. Make a list of the people you know who are not outstandingly intelligent but are outstandingly creative. Ponder those lists for a while; they will soon get you thinking.

There are some kinds of creative work that absolutely require high intelligence in order even to come to grips with the problem. Only when that point has been reached does creativity come into play (although sensitivity to problems is also an aspect of creative thinking). But often a modest IQ is quite sufficient when coupled with an openness to creative solutions. Our assessment depends to a large degree on how novel or how original we require a product or action to be in order to call it creative. Recently I read a doctoral dissertation that dealt with "the living experience of creativity in the nursing profession." The author (Davis 1995) interviewed nurses who had been nominated by their supervisors as creative. She was careful to get a full account of the context in which the creative act occurred. Almost invariably, these factors were present in the contexts: (1) a patient in distress; (2) a failure of the usual procedures to do any good; (3) a deeply felt intrinsic motivation on the part of the nurse to help the patient; (4) improvisation, including the unusual use of common objects; (5) clever ways of distracting attention from painful procedures for just the few moments needed to get them over with; (6) having an ally among the other nurses; and (7) occasionally, having the courage to proceed counter to protocol (which meant risking censure, especially from the M.D. in charge).

I liked this thesis because it emphasized rather unpretentious creativity as lived in a professional situation. Dear old Einstein may have done more harm than anyone else to the cause of fostering simple, day-to-day creativeness, without in the least intending to—haven't you heard the phrase "He (she) is no Einstein," or even "I'm no Einstein"? The idea that the secret of our defiantly complex and mysterious cosmos can be expressed in a single equation of such surpassing originality and awesome elegance as his could well be discouraging to poor you and me. So it is awfully important to remember that the power to create is potential in all of us, and that we should express it in small ways if great and grand ways are beyond our means.

Measured individual intelligence plays a part, then, but not necessarily a big part, in creativity. And remember that intelligence is not a single substance, not by any means. An important consideration arises from the fact that intelligence is a many-sided thing, or, as the intelligence testers say, the structure of intellect is multifactorial. This means simply that it is composed of many different abilities, in a variety of media, and in chunks of meaning and feeling that range in size from the very small to the very large. It's not all words and numbers and visualization and spatial reasoning.

Creativity, too, is multifactorial, and not restricted to words, numbers, images, and spatial dimensions. A quick smile is gestural; so is a hesitant step. Both may be creative acts, not only for the persons involved but, should they occur in a play or movie, perhaps for many, many people. Great actresses and actors convey feeling creatively in many modes. A sob or a song may be the most intense expressions of feeling, using breath and voice, mouth and lungs; the entire meaning of human life may be in them. A painting is kinesthetic and visual and spatial; it may be as small and simple as a choice of color slashed or splashed on a canvas, or a dot in an empty space. But slashes and splashes may be complex as well as simple; it is not physical size but the universe of meaning, the gestalt if you will, that they signify.

So let's remember that not only is intelligence multifaceted, so too is creativity. Research has identified clusters of the many aspects of creativity: originality, fluency and volume of ideas, adaptive flexibility, spontaneous flexibility, expressional fluency, sensitivity to problems. All these can be expressed in a variety of sensory modalities, and in units large or small.

Just what is an IQ, anyway? It is a number, the quotient given by the ratio of presumed mental age to chronological age (multiplied by 100). Mental age is estimated by scores on a variety of mental tasks. The IQ test basically is a compendium of abilities: verbal comprehension and acquisition; facility in simple tasks of reasoning and problem-solving; ability to recognize and manipulate simple geometrical forms in space; memory for numbers, and alertness to principles of classification (i.e., in what ways are things similar or different?). Can we expect that these abilities, valuable though they are, will prove also to predict originality? Most intelligence test items call for a single answer, already decided on by the tester; but creativity in the world is open-ended, the solutions are not known, surprises big or little may be in store for us.

We should not be surprised to find that creativity as measured by tests proves to be only slightly related to measured IQ (Barron 1969; see the chapter on creativity and intelligence). And after an IQ of 115 or 120, there appears to be hardly any relationship at all; other factors of personality and motivation take over. These include the ability and motivation to work independently and autonomously rather than in a mindlessly conforming manner, a high level of general energy but particularly psychic energy, a drive to make sense of contradictory or divergent facts in a single theory or perception, and flexibility of thought and action.

2. Are there some motives, as well as personality traits, found more often in people known for their creativity?

Yes, there is a characteristic motivational pattern to be found in the creative. One such motive is simply the desire to create! Sometimes a person recognizes creativity as valuable yet does not make it a personal guiding force or chief motive in life. "Let others create; there's a lot else that must be done, and I can do it." Certainly no one can find fault with such a laissez-faire attitude. All we can say is, creative people are not that way. They want to create, above all. Even when they are stymied by life circumstances—by lack of opportunity in their job, for example—they are self-scheduled for finding a way to create in the future. It is a primary, and intrinsic, motive.

I have myself posited what I call "the cosmological motive" in creative people. This means that they seek to construct a cosmos in their own experience, even if it is only to study the insects in their back yard, or the people in their town, or, for that matter, their own personalities. Each of us is a potential cosmos. The drive to find order, to make sense of everything, is the mark of the cosmological motive at work.

As for personality, several traits stand out. One is independence of judgment, or the insistence on thinking for oneself. It often shows itself in resistance to conformity, or even rebelliousness against authority or the status quo. Without our creative dissidents, where would we be?

Another important trait, found consistently in the creative, is intuition. This is the ability to see to the heart of things, or to see beyond appearances. It is not logical; it may not even seem to be rational. Those crazy hunches that we get are our intuitions—sometimes spectacularly right, sometimes embarrassingly wrong.

The willingness to take the risk of being wrong and perhaps subjected to ridicule, punishment, or loss is another outstanding trait of the creative person. Such action does not mean to behave on foolish impulse, but to calculate the risks and then to take a chance. What on earth was Columbus doing when he set sail for the New World? Columbus is a symbol, whatever may have been the reality. As Herman Melville put it, "Who shall be the Columbus of the mind?"

Finally, some stylistic differences do tend to show up. Introversion is one style of personality that is a bit more often associated with creativity than is extroversion. However, there is an extroverted style of creating as well as an introverted one, and the differences are not so striking as to make us all want to be introverts. Even the same person may be introverted at one time and extroverted at another.

Some researchers insist that mental imbalance is in fact an asset in creativity. We discuss some aspects of this later. Certain it is that mental and emotional problems can be capitalized on and not just capitulated to.

The ingredients of creativity naturally include originality—the ability to see things in a new way—and also a willingness to challenge assumptions (a facet of independence of judgment). The ability to make connections is also important. The traits of personality shade over into traits of cognition and motivation in giving us a picture of the functioning of the creative individual.

3. Is creativity inherited?

Everything is getting to be inherited these days. Advances in the science of genetics, with more promised, have big implications for both the understanding and the control of the human design. Not only are the causal genes of many diseases and of psychopathology being specified, but the day is getting closer when the human genome, the entire genetic complement of humanity, may be mapped. Designer-designed descendants of other species are already in the news. This is creation with a vengeance, arrogant and fraught with the possibility of the destruction of a now endangered species—us. For who are going to be the designers, and what traits might they wish to foster? Mary Shelley's dark dream of Frankenstein, the scientist-creator, and his creation was a remarkable act of intuition. Do you have dreams that come true? Don't you hope that Mary Shelley didn't?

Meanwhile there is the more mundane meaning of *inherited* to consider. It has two main and significantly different meanings. Webster's Dictionary gives one as "passed down from predecessors," mechanism not suggested. The other is: "transmitted genetically or biologically from generation to generation." In both these senses, is creativity inherited?

In the DNA sense of the term, there is very little evidence of a significant genetic factor in the inheritance of creativity, especially when quantitative test measures of creativity are used. In brief, the psychometric evidence suggests a qualified *no*. Identical twins do correlate highly with one another on virtually all measures of intelligence and creativity, but when it comes to creativity alone, so do fraternal twins to almost the same degree. Twins aside, when families are studied over several generations, it does seem that there are certain family lines in which creativity "runs." It appears likely that a mix of genes and environments indeed affects creativity. A family is an enveloping environment as well as an envelope of similar genes. And then there is the great world outside, where we are on our own. In creativity as in many other traits, genetic influences are very difficult to separate from environmental ones. My personal preference is to put aside genetic differences, if any, and to look to environments (or, more broadly speaking, ecologies—as I have argued in my 1995 book, *No Rootless Flower: An Ecology of Creativity*).

The history of culture reveals a stream of connected and evolving consciousness. Ideas evolve; cultures evolve; environments are the transmitters of values, insights, opportunities. Some families foster creativity more than others do.

4. Are creative people more unstable mentally?

"Great wits are sure to madness near allied." So said the Enlightenment poet Dryden, following the ancient Seneca. Modern empirical studies suggest that certain aberrations of mood and consciousness are found more in creative people than in people in general. And there is some evidence that the two major kinds of psychosis, manic depression and schizophrenia, occur somewhat more commonly among the creative. Still, the rule that a little is often better than a lot seems to apply. If you don't go quite as high in the manic phase, or quite as low in the depressive, then a touch of that syndrome may be helpful rather than harmful. Similarly, if you can turn thought disorder into originality and have the ability to correct yourself, or to right yourself when you go off balance, even a genetically inherited disposition toward the schizophrenic personality can be an asset.

Many, many historical instances tell us unambiguously that the perception of beauty and truth, and the making of something beautiful and true, are not the exclusive possessions of sanity. Plato said that unless a person has something of "the divine madness" in his soul, he cannot create poetry. But note the qualifier "divine." On the back wards of mental hospitals the madness is rarely divine; it is a serious loss of contact with consensual reality, and is most often accompanied by apathy, despair, loss of feeling, and loss of hope. The chemistry of one's body may well play a part in this, and so may one's heredity. In recent years there have been remarkable advances in the therapy of both manic-depressive psychosis and schizophrenia, and what seems to be involved is a complex relationship of chemicals such as dopamine and serotonin and lithium carbonate with major variables of mood as well as perceptual-cognitive relationships to consensual reality. So let's be both curious and sympathetic, but not sentimental, about madness. The Greeks may have had a word for it, but their "madness" is something added, a gift from the gods or possession by one's daemon (or genius), not something subtracted, as in psychosis.

Yet often enough the mentally disturbed person is indeed unusually sensitive, in the best sense of the term. This very sensitivity is one of the reasons for the inability to adjust. Most of us erect walls against extreme feelings, unusual thoughts, moments of desolation or horror; sometimes the mentally ill person is one who either cannot or will not erect those walls and as a result has difficulty functioning in the way we call normal. Another result, however, may be that an unusual truth or an extreme beauty is experienced vividly and then communicated through some form that touches others. If we could have some of the advantages of mental agitation without the disabling disadvantages that usually accompany it, we might be persons of greater fulfillment.

Creative geniuses sometimes seem to have just such an unusual combination of traits; they may be able to push sanity almost to the breaking point, but they can usually swing back again, correct and integrate their perceptions, and make out of their transitory distress a social communication that they can give to the world and that the world can receive. Along with the disorganization and even chaos that marks the manic, there may be a grandiosity that, when tempered by adamant reality-testing, contributes to a sense of destiny.

Still, while there is a wealth of anecdote about the aberrations of genius, we must discount much of it. Extremeness is more vivid, more noticeable, and more memorable than the average sensibilities and behaviors, and anecdotes are often exaggerated. To give a sensible answer to the question, the whole range of human possibility must be studied, not just the extremes. As yet there are no such studies; they're expensive to carry out. In the Berkeley researches we found only about 4 percent of creative people with histories of mental disturbance. The 4 percent figure is close to that estimated by Havelock Ellis in his studies of British men of genius a hundred years earlier. It is a bit higher than the incidence of florid psychosis in the general population (about 1 percent throughout the world, almost a biological constant); so let us say once again that there is some relationship to be found, but a fairly slight one. If you feel that you're going bonkers, it is perhaps best to go and get some help; you can still write poetry or paint pictures or solve problems on the way.

5. Are there gender differences in creativity?

The psychometric evidence shows clearly that the potential for creativity, in terms of the identified factors of ability, is equal for women and men. A very big question is how this potential will be recognized and realized.

Cross-sexual traits are often found in creative people, especially in the arts. Some degree of femininity in men, and some degree of masculinity in women, may very well be a good thing. "Masculine" or "feminine" behaviors are mostly taught—that is, they are differentially reinforced (approved, or discouraged). Rounded personalities include many instances of both kinds of behavior, whatever the biological-sexual orientation. Yet often enough crosssexual elements that are indeed given at conception are at first concealed out of shame of being different from the cultural norm. This makes for a closed and perhaps closeted personality. One of the most encouraging developments in our time has been the courage shown by gays and lesbians in "coming out of the closet."

This is a domain of research on creativity in which there are many puzzles yet to be solved.

6. Is creativity related to age?

Most, but perhaps not all, creative children grow up to become creative adults. And most creative adults were once creative children (but not all; creativity may be dormant until life awakens it). It does seem that most creative people are creative all through their lives, and the astonishing thing is the sheer volume of work done by persons who are especially known for this or that particular contribution. Follow-up studies of architects and of graduate students at the University of California at Berkeley (in fourteen different teaching departments) have shown that creativity continues to flourish into old age in many people. There are historically impressive examples of this; one could fill many pages by just listing their names.

Indeed, many a person puts aside a creative interest for a period of years when she or he is involved in the bread-and-butter tasks of setting up a home, having a family, or perhaps pursuing a mundane career; then, with retirement, the nest emptied, the work taken over by someone else, and suddenly increased leisure, it becomes possible to return to that early interest and to find a fuller self-realization.

Yet routine need not be deadening; in the Berkeley studies of creative women mathematicians there were some interesting tales told of mathematical problems solved in the midst of household chores. Vivid testimony to the creatogenic value of simply walking, or being calmly observent of a familiar landscape, may be found in these pages. Also, many creators recognize that diligent exercise of their talents prepares them to take full advantage of inspiration. Routine may in fact be freeing.

Children are creative in a spontaneous way, usually without thought of discipline or style. That doesn't mean the style isn't there, or the discipline either. But often a considerable amount of self-sought discipline and hard training is necessary for creative work, as in musical composition, problem-solving in mathematics or physics, ballet dancing, painting, architecture, and many other endeavors. Such work is generally directed toward an audience capable of understanding or appreciating it, while children's inventiveness usually is not. Thus a certain amount of maturation of the talent, and discipline in its exercise, must precede its full expression. Since this also takes time, the complex, highly creative act can be expected to occur only rarely in childhood or before maturation has taken place. Still, creativity does show itself through a very wide age range, and it is not age itself that is important, but rather the time necessary for the full development of a talent.

7. Why does creative potential sometimes seem to go to waste, or to go unused for many years?

If the society we live in puts too much emphasis on an established "right" way of doing things, it may cause a loss of adventuresomeness and willingness to experiment. The creative is often the unconventional. To be original means to be different in some important way, and often it takes courage and daring to be different from those around us.

There are fears that must be faced. These include not only fear or ridicule from others for being too outlandish at times, but also fear in ourselves of becoming personally unbalanced if we entertain those "crazy hunches" that are often enough the beginning of a new way of looking at things. To this might be added "fear of having fun with ideas," for there is a certain playfulness about the creative process, a willingness to make light of what is usually taken seriously.

In addition to inhibiting fears, there are other big causes for the loss of creative potential. I call these creopathic factors. We've mentioned being caught up in routine. That happens to almost everyone. Then, too, we may become too self-absorbed, too worried about ourselves, to have any energy left for doing something new. We may feel hopeless about ever being able to change anything. These are symptoms of a neurosis that constricts our vision of new possibilities. Sometimes psychotherapy can help us get loose from the crippling aspects of neurosis, freeing our energy for new uses. Sometimes just seeing someone else do it is a big help. We all help one another when we act creatively.

8. Is an unhappy environment more likely to produce a creative individual than a happy one?

Let's hope not. But remember, it is not always easy to tell whether an environment is happy or unhappy. Your unhappiness may be my happiness, and vice versa. Who can say how many people are happy, and who they are? Unhappy circumstances, if they are not crippling, may be just the challenge we need to pull ourselves together and change things.

Whether the environment is happy or unhappy, as long as it is lively and complex and provides varied opportunity for self-expression and personal involvement, it seems to stimulate flexibility and spontaneity in the people who are part of it. Think of ancient Athens, with all those geniuses hanging out on the Acropolis or going on walks with one another. And think of the city of Florence during the Renaissance. All those churches to build and paint in, and the Piazza della Signoria to make open-air sculptures in! Not to mention the first creative banks and bankers! These were vitally interesting environments in which creativity flourished. Yet Greek tragedy and Florentine intrigue and violence testify to the fact that happiness, in the sense of bland contentment, did not characterize the people of those times. The ideal of the golden mean was something like church on Sunday, leaving the rest of the week free for human extremes and a bit of immoderate sinning—or sainting!

Perhaps an important condition of a creative environment is that unhappiness should not be the smothering or crippling sort, but of a kind that can be met, grappled with, transcended, or even capitalized on. Of course, there are many people who are both happy and creative—one certainly need not be unhappy to be interesting and to create.

THE FREEDOM TO CREATE

Taking it all in all—the "conversations" in the assessment setting, the consensus of research findings, the personal accounts by highly creative people selected for this book—one overriding theme seems to us to stand out in the midst of the complexity of questions and considerations. That theme is freedom.

Are we, as individuals and as a society, free to create? "Free to create" is a phrase that condenses several meanings. First, it suggests a balance of inner constraint and abandon, an openness to movement and action of mind, spirit, and emotion. Second, one needs space to create—a personal space. You must be free to go, free to stay; free to speak, free to be silent. Spinoza says somewhere that "freedom of thought is an indefeasible natural right," and that leaves lots of room for silence. Perhaps we should all make a slight bow in the direction of the hermit meditating amid the icy peaks of Mount Meru.

Third, "free to create" implies living within a society that does not seek to control the outcome of the creative process. What might European painters in the Middle Ages have painted were they not officially restricted to religious themes? What problems in our society might be easier to solve (e.g., drug addiction and unwanted pregnancy) if there were no moral censors disallowing free discussion? Because all creativity is collaborative, we need to communicate freely to be most effective. In a closed, judgmental society, persons with unpopular ideas may be risking their lives just to be heard.

Fourth, we may take the phrase to have an existential meaning: that in fact we are, right now, by reason of our very existence, free to create. We were made that way. "We human beings, free to create." This is the meaning of free will: that we are free and responsible creatures. It is a metaphysical, perhaps mystical, perhaps theological concept. If God is not free, what are we? And if we are not free, where does that leave God? Diminished, by far.

So freedom is most fundamental in creativity.

One needn't be metaphysical about it, of course. Think of freedom in a commonsense way. The Bill of Rights and the Four Freedoms cover a lot of ground. It was FDR who came up with the inspirational phrase in his 1941 proclamation, directed in the name of the "free world" against the oppression of fascism: freedom of speech, freedom of religion, freedom from want, freedom from fear. Everyone in the democratic countries agrees on the first and second freedoms. The third and fourth express an ideal. We propose, in conclusion, a fifth freedom: the freedom to create. We are created free; we must create to be free. We *should* be free to create.

There are people, individually and collectively, who have been creative in spite of a lack of the important extrinsic freedoms, but often enough they had to be creative first in a practical way to obtain and guard those freedoms. External freedoms are a form of insurance for the inner meaning and reality of the freedom to create.

READ ON, AND THINK FOR YOURSELF!

All these questions are food for thought. Much is still to be learned. The joy of discovery may be yours as you read the selections in this book and put things together for yourself. What we have here is an opportunity to communicate, even if only in our imagination, with people who have created. How did they do it? There are certainly many clues here. You are invited to work out for yourself your own ideas about creativity, especially in relation to your own life situation and your own goals.

i

THE UNCOVERED

HEART

What really counts is to strip
the soul naked. Painting or
poetry is made as we make
love; a total embrace,
prudence thrown to the
wind, nothing held back.

JOAN MIRÓ

In order to create there must be a dynamic force,
and what force is greater than love?

IGOR STRAVINSKY

The best work is done with the heart
breaking, or overflowing.

MIGNON MCLAUGHLIN

uncovering the heart means uncovering the vital center of the self. This is a move toward the unknown, even though it is a part of our own selves that we are uncovering. The heart, symbolically, is the organ of feeling and intuition. The death of the heart is a real danger.

Our self is placed in space and time, and sometimes our hearts remember, better than our analytical minds, the times and places of our deepest experiences. During times of personal breakdown the heart insists on revealing itself to us; we are forced to pay attention. These are the times of deep personal pain that most of us would instinctively like to escape, because we fear it may be possible to feel too much. And just as it is possible to close our eyes and not see the world around us, we can also close our hearts. We may choose to live in a world of surfaces, a flat, dry, and angular world that seems clean until we look under the carpet.

Uncovering the heart reveals a history within us, one we may have hidden or forgotten. We may be paying a price for feelings we are hiding from ourselves. One of the aims of the depth psychotherapies is to help us rediscover our lost selves gradually and integrate them again into our whole personalities.

When the heart speaks, it may seem unreasonable. But if we listen to it without losing our heads, we may find hope in it that what lies ahead is a new and better way of living. In that lies the strength of living with an uncovered heart. But there is that fearsome vulnerability too. We take a chance when we open ourselves to others. We can be hurt. Are we risking too much?

Some of the most timeless examples of creativity are those moments when hearts have been uncovered, when an individual has emerged who addresses those unique yet universal experiences that bind us together in the human condition. The uncovered heart reveals both vulnerability and strength. Its strength lies perhaps precisely in that ability to open itself to itself, with an elegance and grace that invites the hearts of others to do so too.

I.

why don't you try to write?

HENRY MILLER

Novelist Henry Miller contemplates the fate of genius, the ubiquitous nature of dreams, and the need to believe in oneself and be singleminded in the pursuit of one's vision. Particularly telling here are Miller's comments about not wanting to be a freak, standing outside the everyday world; as his prose shows so well, he was always in the midst of vital exchanges, always in dialogue with the world.

The little phrase—*Why don't you try to write?*—involved me, as it had from the very beginning, in a hopeless bog of confusion. I wanted to enchant but not to enslave; I wanted a greater, richer life, but not at the expense of others; I wanted to free the imagination of all men at once because without the support of the whole world, without a world imaginatively unified, the freedom of the imagination becomes a vice. I had no respect for writing *per se* any more than I had for God *per se*. Nobody, no principle, no idea has validity in itself. What is valid is only that much—of anything, God included—which is realized by all men in common. People are always worried about the fate of the genius. I never worried about the genius: genius takes care of the genius in a man. My concern was always for the nobody, the man who is lost in the shuffle, the man who is so common, so ordinary, that his presence is not even noticed. One genius does not inspire another. All geniuses are leeches, so to speak. They feed from the same source—the blood of life. The most important thing for the genius is to make himself useless, to be absorbed in the common stream, to become a fish again and not a freak of nature. The only benefit, I reflected, which the act of writing could offer me was to remove the differences which separated me from my fellow-man. I definitely did not want to become the artist, in the sense of becoming something strange, something apart and out of the current of life.

The best thing about writing is not the actual labor of putting word against word, brick upon brick, but the preliminaries, the spade work, which is done in silence, under any circumstances, in dream as well as in the waking state. In short, the period of gestation. No man ever puts down what he intended to say: the original creation, which is taking place all the time, whether one writes or doesn't write, belongs to the primal flux: it has no dimensions, no form, no time element. In this preliminary state, which is creation and not birth, what disappears suffers no destruction; something which was already there, something imperishable, like memory, or matter, or God, is summoned and in it one flings himself like a twig into a torrent. Words, sentences, ideas, no matter how subtle or ingenious, the maddest flights of poetry, the most profound dreams, the most hallucinating visions, are but crude hieroglyphs chiseled in pain and sorrow to commemorate an event which is untransmissible. In an intelligently ordered world there would be no need to make the unreasonable attempt of putting such miraculous happenings down. Indeed, it would make no sense, for if men only stopped to realize it, who would be content with the counterfeit when the real is at everyone's beck and call? Who would want to switch in and listen to Beethoven, for example, when he might himself experience the ecstatic harmonies which Beethoven so desperately strove to register? A great work of art, if it accomplishes anything, serves to remind us, or let us say to set us dreaming, of all that is fluid and intangible. Which is to say, *the universe*. It cannot be understood; it can only be accepted or rejected. If accepted we are revitalized; if rejected we are diminished. Whatever it purports to be it is not: it is always something more for which the last word will never be said. It is all that we put into it out of hunger for that which we deny every day of our lives. If we accepted *ourselves* as completely, the work of art, in fact *the whole world of art*, would die of malnutrition. Every man Jack of us moves without feet at least a few hours a day, when his eyes are closed and his body prone. The art of dreaming when wide awake will be in the power of every man one day. Long before that books will cease to exist, for when men are wide awake *and* dreaming their powers of communication (with one another and with the spirit that moves all men) will be so enhanced as to make writing seem like the harsh and raucous squawks of an idiot.

I think and know all this, lying in the dark memory of a summer's day, without having mastered, or even half-heartedly attempted to master, the art of the crude hieroglyph. Before ever I begin I am disgusted with the efforts of the acknowledged masters. Without the ability or the knowledge to make so much as a portal in the façade of the grand edifice, I criticize and lament the architecture itself. If I were only a tiny brick in the vast cathedral of this anti-quated façade I would be infinitely happier; I would have life, the life of the whole structure, even as an infinitesimal part of it. But I am outside, a barbarian who cannot make even a crude sketch, let alone a plan, of the edifice he dreams of inhabiting. I dream a new blazingly magnificent world which collapses as soon as the light is turned on. A world that vanishes but does not die, for I have only to become still again and stare wide-eyed into the darkness and it reappears. . . . There is then a world in me which is utterly unlike any world I know of. I do not think it is my exclusive property—it is only the angle of my vision which is exclusive in that it is unique. If I talk the language of my unique vision nobody understands; the most colossal edifice may be reared and yet remain invisible. The thought of that haunts me. What good will it do to make an invisible temple?

It was in Ulric's studio not so many months ago that I had finished my first book—the book about the twelve messengers. I used to work in his brother's room where some short time previously a magazine editor, after reading a few pages of an unfinished story, informed me cold-bloodedly that I hadn't an ounce of talent, that I didn't know the first thing about writing—in short that I was a complete flop and the best thing to do, my lad, is to forget it, try to make an honest living. Another nincompoop who had written a highly successful book about Jesus-the-carpenter had told me the same thing. And if rejection slips mean anything there was simple corroboration to support the criticism of these discerning minds. "Who *are* these shits?" I used to say to Ulric. "Where do they get off to tell me these things? What have they done, except to prove that they know how to make money?"

Well, I was talking about Joey and Tony, my little friends. I was lying in the dark, a little twig floating in the Japanese current. I was getting back to simple abracadabra, the straw that makes bricks, the crude sketch, the temple which must take on flesh and blood and make itself manifest to all the world. I got up and put on a soft light. I felt calm and lucid, like a lotus opening up. No violent pacing back and forth, no tearing the hair out by the roots. I sank slowly into a chair by the table and with a pencil I began to write. I described in simple words how it felt to take my mother's hand and walk across the sun-lit fields, how it felt to see Joey and Tony rushing towards me with arms open, their faces beaming with joy. I put one brick upon another like an honest brick-layer. Something of a vertical nature was happening—not blades of grass shooting up but something structural, something planned. I didn't strain myself to finish it; I stopped when I had said all I could. I read it over quietly, what I had written. I was so moved that the tears came to my eyes. It wasn't something to show an editor: it was something to put away in a drawer, to keep as a reminder of natural processes, as a promise of fulfillment.

Every day we slaughter our finest impulses. That is why we get a heartache when we read those lines written by the hand of a master and recognize them as our own, as the tender shoots which we stifled because we lacked the faith to believe in our own powers, our own criterion of truth and beauty. Every man, when he gets quiet, when he becomes desperately honest with himself, is capable of uttering profound truths. We all derive from the same source. There is no mystery about the origin of things. We are all part of creation, all kings, all poets, all musicians; we have only to open up, only to discover what is already there.

What happened to me in writing about Joey and Tony was tantamount to revelation. It was revealed to me that I could say what I wanted to say—if I thought of nothing else, if I concentrated upon that exclusively—*and* if I were willing to bear the consequences which a pure act always involves.

miscellany

FEDERICO FELLINI

In a fascinating series of reflections, legendary filmmaker Federico Fellini uncovers his heart as he describes his feelings about such subjects as the passion required for creativity, the exact moment he became a director, the sadness of laughter, and the joy of despair. Fellini was a man known for his enormously fertile, mythical imagination, and these brief statements provide us with a glimpse of his unique world view.

1. ONE DAY I NOTICED THAT I WAS A DIRECTOR. I think I can remember the exact moment. It was the first day of shooting *Lo sceicco bianco*. It is a true story but every time I tell it everyone looks at me as though I'm dishing up a piece of pure fiction. In fact it was like this: one morning I found myself on a boat taking me from Fiumicino to a motor-cutter which was out at sea with the cast and crew of *Lo sceicco bianco* on board. At what was still almost crack of dawn I had said good-bye to Giulietta with that same accelerated heartbeat and that same anxiety with which one goes in to an exam. I had even gone into a church and had tried to pray. I was driving my little Fiat and, on the way to Ostia, one of the tyres burst. The cast and crew, as I said, were already on the ship, and out there in the middle of the ocean I could see my fate awaiting me. I had to shoot a particularly complicated scene between Sordi and Brunella Bovo. As I approached the motor-cutter I could see the faces of the film-crew, the lights and the props. I couldn't stop asking myself: What am I going to do? I couldn't remember the film, I couldn't remember anything. I only had a strong desire to run away. But I had hardly set foot on the ship than I was giving instructions, demanding this that and the other, looking through the camera. Without knowing anything, without being aware of any objective. In the few minutes' voyage from the harbour to the ship I had become an exacting, pedantic, self-willed director with all the faults and all the merits which I had always loathed and admired in real directors. . . .

2. I LOVE BEING ALONE WITH MYSELF, and thinking. But I can be alone only among people. I can think only if I'm pushed and shoved, surrounded by difficulties, with questions to answer, problems to solve, wild beasts to tame. That warms me, sets me up.

I haven't always been like that. Before I started directing, the very idea of having to create in the middle of uproar seemed alarming. I felt like a writer who decided to write in the street, in the middle of a crowd: someone peers over your shoulder to see what you've written, someone else profits from a moment when you've decided to concentrate to get away with your pencil or paper, a third keeps yelling obsessively into your ear. That's the kind of thing that scared me at the start. And that's the stage I've reached today—I can't do anything unless I've got uproar all around me. . . .

3. I NEVER MAKE MORAL JUDGEMENTS, I'm not qualified to do so. I am not a censor, a priest or a politician. I dislike analysing, I am not an orator, a philosopher or a theorist. I am merely a story-teller and the cinema is my work.

I have invented myself entirely: a childhood, a personality, longings, dreams and memories, all in order to enable me to tell them.

I love movement around me. That is certainly the main reason why I make films. To me the cinema is an excuse to make things move. Some years ago I set up a production unit to make films by people who were young and unknown. A year later it went bust, but I'd had a lot of fun during that year. I loved the place, the atmosphere of it all: half like an English club, half like a convent. . . .

4. FOR AN ARTIST, EVEN THE LIFE OF THE FEELINGS IS ON THE SUR-FACE: I don't think I am capable of deep feelings, except in order to make films. I have an easy-going nature, but in order to get an artistic result I am capable of being harsh and cruel.

5. I DON'T WANT TO DEMONSTRATE ANYTHING; I WANT TO SHOW IT. I don't think I could live without making films. If you want to say that it's a good thing to have regrets (which, incidentally, I don't think it is), then I regret not having made more films. I should like to have made every kind: documentaries, advertising films, children's films, melodramas to show in public parks. . . .

I can watch things in a detached way, through the camera, for instance. I never put my eye to the camera. To hell with the objective. I've got to be in the middle of things. I must know everything about everyone, make love to everything around me. I don't like being just a tourist; I don't know how to be one. Rather, I'm a vagabond, curious about everything, entering everywhere, and all the time running the risk of being thrown out by the police. . . .

6. I HATE LOGICAL PLANS. I have a horror of set phrases that instead of explaining reality tame it in order to use it in a way that claims to be for the general good but in fact is no use to anyone.

I don't approve of definitions or labels. Labels should go on suitcases, nowhere else.

Myself, I should find it false and dangerous to start from some clear, well defined, complete idea and then put it into practice. I must be ignorant of what I shall be doing and I can find the resources I need only when I am plunged into obscurity and ignorance. The child is in darkness at the moment he is formed in his mother's womb. . . .

7. NOTHING IS SADDER THAN LAUGHTER; nothing more beautiful, more magnificent, more uplifting and enriching than the terror of deep despair. I believe that every man as long as he lives is a prisoner of this terrible fear within which all prosperity is condemned to founder, but which preserves even in its deepest abyss that hopeful freedom which makes it possible for him to smile in seemingly hopeless situations. That's why the intention of the real—that is, the deepest and most honest—writers of comedy is by no means only to amuse us, but wantonly to tear open our most painful scars so that we feel them all the more strongly. This applies to Shakespeare and Molière as well as to Terence and Aristophanes. On the other hand there is no true tragic poet—I'm thinking of Euripides, Goethe, Dante—who does not understand how to keep a certain ironic distance from even his most terrible sufferings.

That is why it is absurd to want to classify great creative men, to differentiate between comedians and philosophers, actors and authors, clowns and poets, painters and film-makers.

I have always taken Toulouse-Lautrec as a friend and brother, because, even before the invention of cinema by the brothers Lumière, he anticipated the attitudes and images of the film; also perhaps because he felt himself constantly drawn to the disinherited and the despised, to those who are designated as depraved by "respectable" people. It's rather difficult to be certain whom one has been influenced by during one's career. But I do know for sure that as long as I've been alive I've been thrilled by those Toulouse-Lautrec paintings, posters and lithographs. This aristocrat abhorred the "World of

Beauty"; he was convinced that the purest and loveliest flowers thrive on waste land and rubbish heaps. He loved men and women, people who were hardened, battered, unaffected by social constraints. He despised painted ladies, because he abhorred hypocrisy and artifice more than any other vice. He was simple and open, a magnificent man in spite of his ugliness. That is why he is not dead—he lives on in all our hearts through his pictures. . . .

8. YOU ALWAYS NEED AN EXCUSE TO SET OFF ON A JOURNEY. In the same way you need an excuse to start a film. A creator always needs excuses. Creators should almost be forced to create. It would be a good idea to have a state organisation that would make artists work without respite from morning till night. . . .

9. AS I DON'T CONSIDER MYSELF EXCEPTIONAL, BUT SIMPLY A STORY-TELLER, each of my stories is really a period of my life. Deep down I feel that criticism of my work—which is the most sincere and authentic vision of my-self—is unsuitable and immodest, whether it is favourable or unfavourable. Because, since I am identified totally with my work, it is as if someone were judging me as a man. I feel that my work is being judged by intruders who have no right to . . . yes, but they do have the right. But for myself, I always have the feeling that they're lacking in respect, in consideration. In the same way, I would never allow myself to criticise the human being before me: on the contrary, I try to understand him. I have a feeling that I never criticise anyone. . . .

10. I AM NOT YET HUMBLE ENOUGH TO MAKE MYSELF AN ABSTRACTION IN MY FILMS. I try in them to throw light on what I don't understand in my-self, but as I am a man, other men can no doubt see themselves in the same mirror too. What is autobiographical is the story of a kind of call that pierces the torpor of the soul and wakes me. I should very much like to stay in that state, in those moments when the call reaches me. I feel, then, that someone is knocking at the door and I don't go and open it. Of course I shall have to make up my mind to open it, some day or other. Basically, I must be a spiritual *vitellone*. . . .

11. AS A MAN I AM INTERESTED IN EVERYTHING, and as far as what you call problems are concerned I go in search of them, because I am curious, and anxious to learn. But as a film director, I am quite indifferent to abstract problems, those which are now called ideological. For an idea or a situation or an

atmosphere to kindle my mind or my imagination, to amuse me or to move me, it must come to me as a concrete fact. This may be a certain person or character that comes out to meet me; it may be the memory of a particular adventure or of a particular coincidence of human beings in a landscape or a situation. Then my imagination is kindled. If I were a composer I would then start writing down notes, if I were a painter I would scribble on the canvas. As a film director, I find my means of expression in the film image. I am a story-teller in the cinema and I can't honestly see what other qualification can be attributed to me apart from this—which may seem modest but, to me, is terribly demanding.

12. I BELIEVE—PLEASE NOTE, I AM ONLY SUPPOSING—THAT WHAT I CARE ABOUT MOST IS THE FREEDOM OF MAN, the liberation of the individual man from the network of moral and social convention in which he believes, or rather in which he thinks he believes, and which encloses him and limits him and makes him seem narrower, smaller, sometimes even worse than he really is. If you really want me to turn teacher, then condense it with these words: be what you are, that is, discover yourself, in order to love life. To me, life is beautiful, for all its tragedy and suffering, I like it, I enjoy it, I am moved by it. And I do my best to share this way of feeling with others.

3.

The Interviewer

PAMELA TRAVERS

In this moving short essay Pamela Travers, best known as the creator of Mary Poppins, is confronted with an interviewer's questions regarding the origin of one of her characters. The questioner, demanding an answer, leads Travers to reminisce about her childhood, and ultimately about not being able to answer questions with facts, but being able simply to answer with more questions. Nothing in life is ever finished, or, for that matter, answered, unless perhaps we are willing to lull ourselves into a false sense of security. Travers concludes with a brief meditation on the unknown, and the fundamental mystery of creativity, without forgetting "our essential place in the process." The creator creates, and is created by the creating.

He had written from a distant country asking if he might come and see me to talk about a series of books known to us both for an article in his newspaper. He would not take much of my time, he assured me, just an hour or so between plane journeys.

Yes, I replied, knowing that the compliant word, written down, would not reveal the reluctance it might contain, if spoken. I am shy of interviewers. They try to ferret out from one's heart things that even the stethoscope can not be privy to. But, to come all that way! I could not refuse.

So he arrived, hurrying out of the sky, as it were, clearly eager for the fray, a blue silk handkerchief peeping out of his breast pocket and his arms full of blue flowers.

My favorite color—a good omen, I thought. Perhaps he was one of those journalists, rarely, admittedly, to be found, who have themselves something to contribute, perception, a streak of understanding.

And he had! Taking me warmly by both hands, "These books," he declared, "are not invented. That is why they are so interesting." Here was another good omen.

"How could they be?" I asked, laughing. "You invent motorcycles and atom bombs."

"So tell me," he said eagerly, settling himself into a chair and taking out his notebook. "Where did you get the idea?"

The good omens took to their heels. How many times had I heard that question from people of all ages. Must I face it again?

"Where does anyone get an idea?"

"But it must—it can't help it—come from somewhere."

"Why not from nowhere?" I suggested.

He waved this aside as frivolous.

"Well, did you ever know, at some point in your life, anybody like her?" He named the book's chief character.

"What? Someone who slides up bannisters? No, never, Did you?"

"Of course not! How could you ask that? I am being serious."

"So am I," I assured him. "Never more so."

"But you have to face the facts, you know." He was gentle but determined.

"I don't see why. And there *are* no facts. Or none that I am aware of."

"Oh, yes, there are!" he insisted. And with something of a flourish, a gesture of triumph, he took from his notebook a newspaper cutting. "I have here an interview with your sister in Australia. In it she says that you told her about this character when she was a very small child."

"Well, if she was so very small, I myself could hardly have been much larger. But it's not true, I'm afraid."

"It must be. It's here in black and white."

"And black and white makes things true? Printer's ink on a scrap of paper?"

"Then what *did* you tell her? If you could recall that it might give us a clue to what came later."

"I have no idea. Stories are like birds flying, here and gone in a moment."

"But this one must have stayed with her. How else could she remember?"

"A matter of hindsight, I suppose. A linking—or mislinking—of one thing with another."

"Well, *what* thing? Think back, think back, think back!" he urged me. "The time, the place, the season, the weather."

The weather!

Suddenly he was no longer there. Oh, he was substantial in his chair, but in essence he did not exist for me. I was hearing a cataract of rain stabbing a corrugated iron roof with sharp resonant sword-thrusts. And beneath it the silence that had fallen as the three children ceased their playing.

For *she* was standing by the door, her blue robe hanging from her shoulders, hair in a walnut braid down her back, her face white and distraught.

"I have had enough. I can stand no more. I am going down to the creek," she said. And she went out, closing the door behind her.

If I had run after her, she would have certainly turned back. Mother in her very essence, she would never have allowed the barrage from Heaven to be unleashed on her child.

But at the age of ten—or almost—I was as green and tightly folded as a bud on a winter branch, not knowing what would later ripen; what woman-stuff, now in embryo, would comprehend the inner ferment that tonight had clearly reached its climax and urged her out into the storm—the husband dead at forty-three, she herself eleven years younger, left to be sole resource, the one loved object, of three ebullient children; the commodious house full of helping hands exchanged for what, by comparison, was about as capacious as a wren's nest; no stables, there were no more horses; sugar and flour, once bought by the bushel, tea in mahogany boxes embossed with Chinese ideograms, were now bought in packets from the grocer; bread from a baker's basket instead of out of the oven; a whole spacious bushland way of existence suddenly expunged and a new life laboriously to be made.

Such a making did not trouble the children. For them it was all adventure as long as she was there, the playmate, the comforter, the constant pillar round whom their lives revolved.

And, indeed, would have been adventure for her, with all her lively zest for life, had she not had to do it alone.

The sound that the door made in closing was as if a bell had tolled. It made the silence in the room seem louder than the rain.

Large-eyed, the little ones looked at me—she and I called them the little ones, both of us aware that an eldest child, no matter how young, can never experience the heart's ease that little ones enjoy.

And I knew that what they needed from me was what we all needed from her—security, reassurance.

I put a log on the failing fire, brought an eiderdown from a bedroom and we lay together on the hearth rug, the warm downy quilt around us like a bird's wing shielding a hatch of nestlings.

There was no need for me to think of a story for suddenly he was there before us, the little horse—a colt, rather, finely made with narrow withers—I can see him now—mane and tail neatly trimmed, hurrying off on some pilgrimage.

"He's white!" said one of them.

"Grey!" said the other.

"No," I told them. "Spickled and speckled like a guinea fowl."

And there we were, all gathered behind him, watching him moving over the ocean, sparks of light flashing from his hooves as he trod the smooth dark waters, head thrown up, scenting the way.

"Perhaps he is going to his home!"

"No, he's coming from it," I said, "to a place that has no name. He can see it far away in the distance, a great big cloud of light."

"Will he get there safe and sound?"

"Of course! He is a magic horse."

(The creek is not deep. There are crayfish in it. Surely no one could drown in it, unless, like Ophelia in the picture, they lay down and let it cover them.)

"If he is magic, can he do everything? Fizzle up the world in a frying pan?"

"Yes!"

(But the creek flows into a wide pool. Nobody knows how deep it is. We are not allowed there without a grown-up. A thrown stone has many rings around it.)

"Can he fly into the air without wings?"

"Yes!"

"And dive to the bottom of the sea?"

"Yes!"

(What happens to children who have lost both parents? Do they go into Children's Homes and wear embroidered dressing-gowns, embroidery that is really darning?)

"Perhaps he will never get to the light!"

"Oh, he will. Remember, he is magic."

(Will rich relations come and get us and turn us into poor relations?)

"Is there corn in that land for him to eat?"

"Yes, and a bundle of hay."

(Perhaps they will send us to different places, one here, another there. No one will be a little one.)

"And a pail of water, all lit with light?"

"Yes!"

(Maybe she has gone from the creek to the pool. How long does it take a person to drown? Oh, I will be good, I promise!)

"Could he carry us to the shiny land, all three on his back?"

"Yes!"

I had to say Yes to comfort them and also to comfort myself. But the horse was so small, not yet ready for burdens. I knew that he had to go alone. And, somehow, they must have known it, too, for the three of us moved more closely together, drawing the eiderdown tightly, tightly around us, watching him toss up his speckled head as his hooves, dainty and precise, struck ever brighter sparks from the dark, with never a splash from the water.

I tried to think only of the horse and what would happen when he arrived. I was afraid of my other thoughts.

The logs slipped sideways with a falling sound as they reddened in the grate. And at that moment she came in, rain streaming from her clothes and hair, looking young, forlorn, and lonely but somehow with her mind made up.

The little ones leapt and ran to her, crying, laughing, embracing her, drawing her into the warm room, squeezing the water out of her gown, kissing her in every possible place.

And she gave herself to their ministrations, accepting the welcome gratefully, leaning on their joy.

As they ran to find towels and dry clothes, she looked at me expectantly, waiting for me to go to her.

But I turned away without a word and went to light the primus stove — a thing I was not supposed to do, it was only for grown-ups. When the kettle came to the boil, I filled a rubber hot-water bottle and took it to her room.

They were in the big bed, all of them, the little ones huddled on either side, holding her tightly, safely, between them as they told her excitedly the story of the horse. She looked at me across their heads and lovingly held out her arms.

But I stood silent in the doorway and with all the strength I could find in myself, flung the hot-water bottle at her and went to my own room.

"Oh, you cold-hearted child," she cried. "The others are so pleased to see me. What has happened to you?"

I could not answer. It was true, however, that I was cold, not only in my heart but throughout the whole of my body. I lay in my bed still as a stone, feeling and knowing nothing. . . .

All that was Now. It was still Now when I roused myself and found I had been thinking aloud, and also that I was weeping.

I looked across at the Interviewer who, when I had last been aware of him, had been madly scribbling in his notebook.

But his chair was empty. And in my lap lay the blue silk handkerchief and a note on a strip of paper. He must have quietly slipped away and left me to my tears, the tears that had stayed unshed within me, forgotten, concealed, biding their time till something they needed called them forth. And as the blue handkerchief absorbed them—that had been a delicate gesture—I knew they were not for myself only.

The tight green bud had long unfolded and now I could go with her through the storm, silently sharing what then had moved in her mind—the bed, once proportionate to conjugal life with its whispered, sleepy confabulations; Yin breath and Yang breath flowing together; naked foot over naked foot; the day dissolved, absolved by the night—was now as wide as a desert. What had once been borne by two had now to be carried by one. Fullness had become emptiness.

I wept for her and at the same time could not allow myself to rejoice that she had come back through the door to be still the pillar, the sharer of all joys and sorrows, loving and loved for the rest of her life.

I put the handkerchief away and took up the strip of paper.

"I have my answer," it said. "The horse! The horse that can do everything! It is wonderful that from so much sorrow such happiness could come."

His answer indeed! I flew to the door, hoping that I could catch him. But the little street, like his chair, was empty—only, at the end of it, a young man leaping into a taxi. I would like to have shouted wildly, "Stop!" But what would the neighbors think? A citizen held to be, relatively, sane shouting "Stop!" to nothing!

Besides, I knew he would hurry home to tap out on his typewriter his gleanings from the morning. Tomorrow they would be in "black and white" on a host of breakfast tables, a fallacious account of a book's begetting transmogrified into fact. Nothing could stop that happening.

But if I could have brought him back I would have told him that there are no answers, there are only questions.

Fallible creatures that we are and being ourselves in question, we inevitably demand answers to ease the lack within us. All things must be capable of explanation, every effect must have a cause, each problem a solution. It is thus that we arrive at conclusion, for conclusion brings about the ending that we mistake for an answer. "That's finished," we say, mendaciously. "We can go on to something else."

But nothing in life—nor, perhaps, in death—is ever really finished. A book, for instance, is no book at all, unless, when we come to the last page, it goes on and on within us.

You, I would say to the Interviewer, took the magic horse for an answer, the clue, the code to be cracked. It did not occur to you to enquire from whence the idea came to the child. Or whether at some point in her life she had encountered such a creature. Nor, indeed, what lay beneath the horse, the cause of which he was the effect. And the cause beneath that cause. Doubtless, had you pursued this course, you would have had to fall back on that too much bandied about Unconscious, which people with little knowledge of psychology, and even those with much, make use of as a sort of psychic Rag Bag in which to throw any old concept.

I have pondered long upon that phrase—is the Unconscious unconscious of itself?—and never felt quite at home with it. There seemed to be something lacking.

Then I read in a book by Sri Mahada Ashish of Mirtola that in his view it should properly be translated as The *Unconscioussed*. But would such a large ungainly word take root in common parlance? I tried it on several scholarly minds, but while its accuracy was accepted it was not received with enthusiasm. They would stick to their old-fashioned fallacies.

Later, however, one of our leading analytical psychologists, being quoted in the magazine *Resurgence*, set all my unease at ease. "It means," he said—and I verified this with one of his *confrères*—"it means, simply, the Unknown."

The Unknown—our beautiful Anglo-Saxon word, intimate, reverberant, profound, not so much to be understood but stood under while it rains upon us—that is something I could well live with and, indeed, have revered, cherished, and tried to serve for many a year and day.

Call it the Unknown and one can conceive of the creative process as being a next door neighbor to it. Though, with the general decline of language this phrase, too, is too often used without discrimination and applied to the scribblings of every passing rhymester.

C. S. Lewis, in a letter to a friend, says, "There is only one Creator and we merely mix the elements he gives us"—a statement less simple than it seems. For that "mere mixing," while making it impossible for us to say "I myself am the maker," also shows us our essential place in the process. Elements among elements we are there to shape, order, define, and in doing this we, reciprocally, are defined and shaped and ordered. The potter, molding the receptive clay, is himself being molded.

But let us admit it. With that word "creative," when applied to any human endeavor, we stand under a mystery. And from time to time that mystery, as if it were a sun, sends down upon one head or another, a sudden shaft of light—by grace one feels, rather than deserving—for it always comes as something given, free, unsought, unexpected. It is useless, possibly even profane, to ask for explanations. Somehow, somewhere, the Unknown is known, perhaps—who can say?—to the wild bee!

4.

The process is
the purpose

ANNA HALPRIN

In this interview with Vera Maletic, dancer Anna Halprin tells us that the key to her method of teaching dance is her conviction that personal growth is part and parcel of artistic growth. We are all dancers, she says. The process of growth as a dancer is identical with the purpose of learning and teaching. To find one's center, and one's own rhythm (of breathing, of moving, of being alone, and of being together with others) is the purpose, and the purpose is found in the process. This means the dropping of defenses, of body armor, of character armor, to become soft and pliant in one's own inner being.

Maletic: It seems to me that your personal approach to movement has evolved from some specific needs of our contemporary life, particularly in the U.S.A. and [on] the West Coast. What do you aim for with your educational and performance activities in relation to the trainees and in relation to the audience?

HALPRIN: Of course, this is not the easiest question to answer. It's like asking what your whole life is about. But I think I can start with the first notion that comes into my head, and that is I have developed an enormous concern and interest in movement as it relates to a more natural outgrowth of expression. In other words, I am disinterested in movement so highly stylized that we must say this is a Dancer. Anybody's a dancer to me at any time when I am involved in communicating with that person through his movement. This has led me to a way of working with students that does not rely so much on traditional or conventional means, which tend to make the kind of dancer image that I'm really interested in for myself.

More and more I have begun to stress breathing as a base, because I find that the deeper the student can get into the breathing center, the more open he becomes to releasing areas in his body which become alive and accessible to him for his work. So this is a very important base of our work. You know, my training has been with Margaret H'Doubler from Wisconsin University. Of course she was always interested in movement as an expressive medium for communication and was never interested in style and patterns of movement. In a very convincing way she grounded me in a more biological approach to movement—movement that is more natural to the nervous system, to the bone structure, to the muscle action. I found that in my training with her, the stress in movement was on understanding your body as action and, at the same time, being able to appreciate feedback, so that the relationship of the feeling to the movement was complete. Now when you learn patterned movement, you're so involved in learning the pattern that the tendency is simply to cut off the feeling aspect. And by feeling, I'm not referring to a kind of free-style self-expression. I mean just the feeling that's inherent when you clench your fist in anger, or stamp your feet, or jump in exhilaration. These are all natural and the most expressive movements we do. And when you become aware of the movement and the feeling it's evoking, you begin to have the freedom to use it consciously and excitingly, and that's when you begin to become an artist in your material.

It's that approach to movement that I'm talking about. I've never taught classes in which I teach a style, or a pattern, or set progression. First of all, I keep changing from year to year. I keep finding new things that I keep incorporating. Recently I've gotten very involved in developing a new use of body training through principles that have to do with getting the body into positions of stress. And then—it's almost like isometric exercises—from the stress position it goes into a trembling that gets you into a kind of forced breathing. It must change the chemistry in the body, because it's as if your whole circulatory system just comes alive. This is something very new to me, because I've never been able to get at the circulatory system before. I'll show you some of the movements afterwards, if you'd like to see them. The efficiency is just incredible. By placing your body in a position, you get all the strength and a fantastic sense of your body as a totality. So we've been experimenting, as we constantly do, with new methods to get deeper and deeper into the body itself.

Maletic: I think you have answered my second question already. It was: how would you define your approach to education, art, and theatre, apart from traditional concepts?

HALPRIN: Well, I think this goes back to the way I have always related myself to dance and life. That is, I try not to separate the experiences of life, because we are in confrontation with our experiences, constantly, in art. And this brings me to an appreciation of, or an emphasis on, the relationship between personal growth and artistic growth. For the two must go hand in hand; otherwise there is no maturity that ever takes place. Since I've been working simultaneously in education and theatre all my life, it's hard for me to know the source for an idea. But I do know that in the theatre experiences, I want very much to deal with people on that stage who are identifying with very real experiences in life, in such a way that the audiences can identify themselves with the so-called performers. Rather than just looking at somebody doing something very unusual, I want the audience to be able to identify and realize that this is a person more than he is a dancer, a person who identifies with very real things.

We don't even accept the theatre as a conventional place where the audience is here and you're there, but it *is* a place, and whatever you do in that place is valid because it's the place. You don't have to be on the stage separating here from there. This desire to merge a very life-like situation into the concept of the dance is very true also in my training. Everything we do in dance somehow or other usually relates to who you are as a person, and this affects how you see things and feel things and relate to people. Again, it's this nonseparation of life and art, so that somehow or other it becomes a heightening process.

Maletic: Do you feel there is a difference between self-exploration or self-expression as individual therapeutic experience and as an artistic expression?

HALPRIN: This is a hard question to answer right now, because the word therapy is being used by so many different people in so many different ways. So is the word creativity. At one time, you could use the word creativity and feel fairly safe, but now there's creative merchandise. Everything's creative—you can get a creative ice cream cone. The word therapy is beginning to become like a tea party. You know, let's get together and have a little therapy session. So it gets a little difficult. But I would say that if you use the word therapy in terms of personal growth, any art experience that is valid to a person and that is based on personal experience certainly, automatically, must have therapeutic value. But if your attention as an artist is only on what you are getting therapeutically, you are not paying attention to the fact that essentially you're a craftsman, that essentially your job is to be a vehicle for other people.

To me, a performer is simply a vehicle, a submergence of the ego. Otherwise, you may as well stay in your studio. But when you take the responsibility for performing for an audience, you are then accepting the fact that you must go through some sort of distilling process in which the personal experience has become so zeroed and so heightened by a clarity that you know exactly what you're dealing with, in terms of an element. You have so much skill that you can get right down to the essence of that element. Then you find the movement—spatial, dynamic—essence of that idea inherent not only in how your body moves, but in an awareness of where you are in space, an awareness of the total thing. That has therapeutic value—that's OK—but that shouldn't be your concern.

Maletic: What is your criterion for determining whether a performance is true or genuine in involvement and feeling, or whether it is a phony? Also, what is your criterion for determining the choice of events for a public theatre performance?

HALPRIN: This is very difficult to answer, because we're in such a violent, explosive period of experimentation. At least I am, and certainly all the young artists I work with are. Yet I know that before I ever present a work in public, I've gone through two years' research, two years of going through many, many sketches. And I work very hard to have a score which externalizes the elements so I can get further and further detached from the source, so I can be detached from it and still be very much involved. Other than that, I don't know how to make any judgment about other people's work. First of all, being here on the West Coast, I don't see an awful lot, and what I have seen coming on tour is working in such a different direction from mine. It's hard to know. But because I've spent so many years in movement, I can, just intuitively, tell when a performance is lacking in what I call the audience dimension. And I usually can tell on the basis that the experience just hasn't been structured at all, that the individual is behaving, not moving. There's a difference.

Maletic: What are the concepts of your kinetic theatre?

HALPRIN: The theatre is based on the human expression which comes primarily from movement, from motion. But it goes into the other areas of human expression, which include the visual and the speaking and all of the things that represent a total kind of experience. And this is what I am most interested in developing, a theatre which uses the total resources of the human being. So, rather than call it dance, which seems always to be limited, I'd rather find a new word right now. Although it's basically what dance was in its more primitive time.

Maletic: Of the main streams in psychology, Jungian, Gestalt, Existential, etc., which do you feel the closest affinity with?

HALPRIN: I feel most closely aligned with the Gestalt therapy, but that may be because of my contact with Fritz Perls. When I read his book, *Gestalt Therapy*, or when I work with him, I'm continually reminded of similarities. It's the coming together of all the parts. That is important to me, and it seems this is what is stressed in the Gestalt. I feel very identified with it.

Maletic: Have you had any psychedelic experiences and, if so, have they influenced your creativity?

HALPRIN: Yes, I have had a psychedelic experience, only once, and it did get me in touch with a very deep breathing experience in which I was able to sense what the Chinese call the red spot. I was able to start the radiation all through my body, and this relaxation that set in was so profound, it completely changed my body structure. This happened at the University of California. Somebody was filming it.* Afterwards, I felt very different in posture and alignment, and when I started to move I felt very different. But when I saw the film, I didn't even recognize myself. My body went into a very effortless type of alignment, and my movements had no effort. Without getting out of breath I was able to move with so much more strength and richness. I felt so much more alive. Because I was able to direct it towards the discovery of relaxation through breathing, the experience had very illuminating effects.

Maletic: Could you tell me something about your professional background and the persons who influenced you?

HALPRIN: I have been dancing ever since I was a little girl, in a very free and natural way. When I went to college, I studied with Margaret H'Doubler. I would say that she was my great teacher. The more I work on my own, the more I keep coming back and saying oh, this is what she meant, of course. Even though I have gone into a slightly different emphasis, I still feel I'm her student and I'm still learning. She's such a wealth of ideas, it's taken me years to accumulate the information that substantiates what she was saying. My husband has been very much a teacher for me because of his work in landscape architecture. He's made me enormously aware of the choreography of

---

*This happened in the course of research at the University of California at Berkeley—in fact, it was our senior editor, unremembered by name, who conducted the psychedelic session, and the "somebody" who filmed it was the San Francisco poet Michael McClure. (Eds.)

space. A very important teacher in my life was Rabbi Kadushin, who made me very aware of philosophical concepts in Judaism which reinforced my belief in creativity as a means of strengthening a sense of self-affirmation, not only to oneself, but to the many layers penetrating from oneself to others. This certainly developed a desire for, and a belief in, human encounter on a creative level.

Maletic: Since I come from Europe, I wonder if you can tell me if there are particular needs in this part of America which create your kind of work. Is this kind of activity specific to the West Coast?

HALPRIN: I suppose I again may sound a little biological, but I think that the word is ecology and I think that there is something so vital about our natural surroundings that we have become, perhaps unconsciously. . . . How can you live in this kind of landscape, with the ocean, with the cliffs, with the vital forces of nature at your feet all the time, and not be affected by the so-called nature-oriented point of view? You become vitally concerned with the materials, the sensual materials of our lives, and with the almost primitive naiveness of being an extension of your environment. This begins to free you to appreciate the very characteristics of what a human being is, and from there you start coming out again. And when you start coming out and relaxing, you are working in a sort of nonintellectual way.

I'll speak for myself. I have a tremendous faith in the process of a human mechanism, and in creativity as an essential attribute of all human beings. This creativity is stimulated only when the sense organs are brought to life. This faith in the process is the only goal or purpose I need. What happens as a result creates and generates its own purpose. So I don't question the purpose beforehand; I've already accepted the process as the purpose. In this sense it's nonintellectual. I don't get all sorts of intellectual theories that this dance work or this new piece in this blah blah blah, but this is where we are in our growth, this is where we are in our educational commitment. The process is the purpose; let it be, let it keep growing, and something will happen. And what happens generates its own purpose. I'm being very repetitive, but in this sense it's nonintellectual and very nature-oriented.

5.

The Name and
Nature of poetry

A. E. HOUSMAN

*In "The Name and Nature of Poetry," poet A. E. Housman relates the creation of
poems to physical sensations, and gives us an insight into the way a sensitivity to
changes in consciousness, whether through drinking a pint of beer or taking a walk,
can assist the creative process.*

Nymphs and shepherds, dance no more—what is it that can draw tears, as I
know it can, to the eyes of more readers than one? What in the world is there
to cry about? Why have the mere words the physical effect of pathos when the
sense of the passage is blithe and gay? I can only say, because they are poetry,
and find their way to something in man which is obscure and latent, something older than the present organisation of his nature, like the patches of fen
which still linger here and there in the drained lands of Cambridgeshire.

Poetry indeed seems to me more physical than intellectual. A year or two
ago, in common with others, I received from America a request that I would
define poetry. I replied that I could no more define poetry than a terrier can
define a rat, but that I thought we both recognised the object by the symptoms which it provokes in us. One of these symptoms was described in con-
nexion with another object by Eliphaz the Temanite: "A spirit passed before
my face: the hair of my flesh stood up." Experience has taught me, when I am
shaving of a morning, to keep watch over my thoughts, because, if a line of
poetry strays into my memory, my skin bristles so that the razor ceases to act.
This particular symptom is accompanied by a shiver down the spine; there is
another which consists in a constriction of the throat and a precipitation of
water to the eyes; and there is a third which I can only describe by borrowing
a phrase from one of Keats's last letters, where he says, speaking of Fanny

Brawne, "everything that reminds me of her goes through me like a spear." The seat of this sensation is the pit of the stomach.

My opinions on poetry are necessarily tinged, perhaps I should say tainted, by the circumstance that I have come into contact with it on two sides. We were saying a while ago that poetry is a very wide term, and inconveniently comprehensive: so comprehensive is it that it embraces two books, fortunately not large ones, of my own. I know how this stuff came into existence; and though I have no right to assume that any other poetry came into existence in the same way, yet I find reason to believe that some poetry, and quite good poetry, did. Wordsworth for instance says that poetry is the spontaneous overflow of powerful feelings, and Burns has left us this confession, "I have two or three times in my life composed from the wish rather than the impulse, but I never succeeded to any purpose." In short I think that the production of poetry, in its first stage, is less an active than a passive and involuntary process; and if I were obliged, not to define poetry, but to name the class of things to which it belongs, I should call it a secretion; whether a natural secretion, like turpentine in the fir, or a morbid secretion, like the pearl in the oyster. I think that my own case, though I may not deal with the material so cleverly as the oyster does, is the latter; because I have seldom written poetry unless I was rather out of health, and the experience, though pleasurable, was generally agitating and exhausting. If only that you may know what to avoid, I will give some account of the process.

Having drunk a pint of beer at luncheon—beer is a sedative to the brain, and my afternoons are the least intellectual portion of my life—I would go out for a walk of two or three hours. As I went along, thinking of nothing in particular, only looking at things around me and following the progress of the seasons, there would flow into my mind, with sudden and unaccountable emotion, sometimes a line or two of verse, sometimes a whole stanza at once, accompanied, not preceded, by a vague notion of the poem which they were destined to form part of. Then there would usually be a lull of an hour or so, then perhaps the spring would bubble up again. I say bubble up, because, so far as I could make out, the source of the suggestions thus proffered to the brain was an abyss which I have already had occasion to mention, the pit of the stomach. When I got home I wrote them down, leaving gaps, and hoping that further inspiration might be forthcoming another day. Sometimes it was, if I took my walks in a receptive and expectant frame of mind; but sometimes the poem had to be taken in hand and completed by the brain, which was apt to be a matter of trouble and anxiety, involving trial and disappointment, and sometimes ending in failure. I happen to remember distinctly the genesis of the piece which stands last in my first volume. Two of the stanzas, I do not say which, came into my head, just as they are printed, while I was crossing the corner of Hampstead Heath between the Spaniard's Inn and the footpath to Temple Fortune. A third stanza came with a little coaxing after tea. One more was needed, but it did not come: I had to turn to and compose it myself, and that was a laborious business. I wrote it thirteen times, and it was more than a twelvemonth before I got it right.

6.

Letters to Merline

RAINER MARIA RILKE

The Austrian poet Rainer Maria Rilke discusses the need to keep silent about his work, his "inner labor," and explains how, when starting a new work, he always seeks a return to "primal innocence." A beginner's mind, both wise and foolish, perhaps is what Rilke seeks to invite the angel of inspiration.

Since this solitude closed in around me (and it was absolute from the very first day), I am experiencing yet again the awful, inconceivable polarity between life and all-encompassing work. How far from me is the work, how far the angels!

I will shuffle slowly ahead, each day moving forward but a half-step, and often losing ground. And with each step will I seem to leave you farther behind, for where I am going no name has any value, no memory can remain; one must reach it as one reaches the dead, in consigning all one's forces to the hands of the Angel who leads you. I am leaving you behind — but as I will be making full circle, I will again draw nearer with each step. The bow is strung to let the arrow fly at the heavenly bird; but if it falls to earth, it will have passed harmlessly through the bird, and it will fall from on high into your heart.

Please do not expect me to speak to you of my inner labor — I must keep it silent; it would be tiresome to keep track, even for myself, of all the reversals of fortune I will have to undergo in my struggle for concentration. This sudden shifting of all one's forces, these about-faces of the soul, never occur without many a crisis; the majority of artists avoid them by means of distraction, but that is why they never manage to return to the center of their productivity, whence they started out at the moment of their purest impulse. At the onset of every work, you must recreate that primal innocence, you must return to that ingenuous place where the Angel found you, when he brought

53

you that first message of commitment; you must seek through the brambles for the bed in which you then slept; this time you won't sleep: you will pray, wail—anything; if the Angel condescends to come, it will be because you have persuaded him, not with your tears, but by your humble decision always to start afresh: *Anfänger zu sein!**

---

*To be a beginner!

ii

THE OPENED
MIND

Convictions make convicts.

ROBERT ANTON WILSON

If I ever feel I am
getting to the point
where I'm playing
it safe, I'll stop.
That's all I can tell
you about how I
plan for the future.

MILES DAVIS

Dare to be naive.

R. BUCKMINSTER FULLER

when we think of the creative mind, we think of the generative mind, full of ideas and brilliant new insights. But the creative mind is both full and empty. It is able to create within itself a space for the new to arise. It is a mind that is constantly opening itself to the internal and external world.

The opened mind can be relaxed and playful. It is filled with curiosity and wonder. There is something childlike about it. It loves to get off the beaten track, to explore paths that are not the ones taken by social convention. Playfulness is sometimes important. The opened mind likes to play with an idea or object, and enjoys looking at it as if for the first time. It remains open to the possibility that we may not know everything there is to know—and what we do know may be wrong. It challenges assumptions, makes new connections, finds new ways of viewing the world. The opened mind can wander playfully into areas others do not take seriously, and return with creations that must be approached in all seriousness.

Some of the most creative minds of all time have allowed themselves to drift into reveries and dream states, into extended meditations during which they courted the irrational, the symbolic, the metaphorical, and the mysterious. Often enough they bring back images that they translate into theories, compositions, and actions.

This journey into the unfamiliar can be scary. Some discoveries may be so strange we want to cover them back up and run. Whether exploring the depths of the human soul or the depths of matter, artists, mystics, and scientists have come face-to-face with chaos and disorder. But the opened mind thrives on difference and remains open to the contradictory.

7.

LOST in the woods

CATHY JOHNSON

In this lovely short essay, naturalist author Cathy Johnson uses the metaphor of getting lost in the woods to illuminate the opportunity for discovery and serendipity of journeys into the unknown — whether planned or not.

We humans are a curious enough lot. If we admit it — if we drop for a moment the guise of sophistication and give up our pretense of "cool," we are as curious as cats. "What's that?" we ask ourselves. And, "Why?"

"What's new?" is more than just a greeting to a friend. The discovery of what is new, what can be done that we've only just imagined, what we haven't seen, what is not us, is a basic human need. When I am at my best, my most alive, the question is never far from mind. It doesn't take much to resurrect it: blowing on the embers of curiosity builds a blazing flame in seconds. Only answers can quench it.

Wandering is the best way I know to feed that flame, to answer those questions. Wandering — but with a conscious step, an openness to experience. "Wandering" may *sound* aimless, a flotsam and jetsam drift, but it is as purposeful in its way as the migration of monarchs each fall. Like their erratic, drifting flight, it only looks aimless taken a step at a time. In the larger picture a good wander is a search for questions, for the answers that lead inevitably — and happily — to more questions. I may not see the pattern if I look only at individual shards with their cryptic, broken makings, turning them over in my mind, but from the perspective of time my wandering is as intentional as the butterfly's, and as necessary. It is taking me where I most need to go, allowing room for growth and time for learning.

When, instead, I become too single-minded and goal-oriented, straight ahead, one foot in front of the other, I might as well be a robot or a computer. Humanity fades: the joy is gone.

How will I know what lies over the next ridge, beyond the next trail's

turning, along a creek, in the corners of my mind, if I don't give myself permission to wander? It is in a sense permission. I seem to think I need a plan,
an itinerary, a map. And that's all well and good when the destination is
Cleveland. If it is discovery instead, I need to let the experience direct me,
one find leading to the next. I unravel a thread left by nature, follow it
through labyrinths and long, slow loops, and bring home treasures I never
could have planned: the pale, coral tubers of a wildflower uncovered by a
night's hard rain; the memory of a bird's uncharacteristic pugnaciousness; the
mineralized nodules beneath a limestone ledge; a piece of crinoid's fossilized
flower in a place unexpected—and unlikely—telling me the great inland
sea once licked at all the corners of my territory. Wandering gives me a new
set of eyes—or removes adulthood's blinders from the ones I have. It is
permission to *see* as well as to wander, to be an archaeologist of my own life.
The treasure *is* there; wandering is the itinerary, discovery itself the map. My
archaeologist's tools are my eyes and mind—and a willingness to go beyond
my safe, homey environment, my comfortable and comforting preconcep-
tions.

Serendipity. It is a word meaning "coming upon an unexpected good, a
treasure." If I give myself permission to wander, these small serendipities are
as good as mine already. I may never make a discovery worthy of the scientific
journals; I don't suppose I'd recognize one if I did. I know so little and forget
so much; I am often frustrated by the well of my ignorance. But as I line the
walls of the shaft with the tangible stones of discovery, at least my well holds
water.

My father had an unshakable need to wander. Thank God, it was a
legacy passed on from father to child. When I was young and only beginning
to learn the ways of wandering, I was afraid of the unknown. My security consisted of four walls and enough food to fill a small belly at more or less regular intervals. The long, convoluted rides into new territory made me uneasy.

"But Daddy, we're lost. I don't know where we *are*. I want to go home!"
And still he was drawn to the far side of the next hill, the next curve in a wind-
ing country road, taking me along for the ride. Our old car was a party of one
in a safari of back-country discovery. "We're not lost," he'd tell me—"as long
as we have gas in the car and a dime in our pockets for the phone."

Though today it costs more by far to use the phone—if I should chance
to find one on my rambles—and my wandering is more often on foot than behind the wheel of a car, the love of the far side of the hill is still an antidote
against the fear of being lost. As long as my feet will agree to carry me, as long
as I am not starving or hypothermic or injured, as long as I am in possession

of a good unanswered question or two, I'm not lost. No matter that I don't, in fact, know just where I am. If I keep going, I'll be somewhere—and the sights and sounds and smells of the unknown are my souvenirs. . . .

There is an art to wandering. If I have a destination, a plan—an objective— I've lost the ability to find serendipity. I've become too focused, too single-minded. I am on a quest, not a ramble. I search for the Holy Grail of particularity and miss the chalice freely offered, filled full and overflowing.

There are times when I go to the woods to find specific wildflowers or plants or animals, to illustrate an article or book, armed with sketchpad and pencils. At those times I set my inner viewfinder for plants, or animals, or whatever—and my larger vision is as limited as if I were looking through the wrong end of the telescope. I've preconceived a notion and closed my mind and my eyes to whatever else may be offered free, gratis.

When I go unprogrammed, "eyes only" and open to experience, the world expands as if taking a deep breath. There is more to see—or perhaps I am able now to see it. It is a Zen-like openness, a meditative awareness. I can accept everything—or very nearly—because I am willing to. I can see what is just beyond my peripheral vision.

It's hard to maintain that free-form openness in morel season. That rich de-lectability focuses me without my willing it—*against* my will, zeroing me in like the "X" on a pirate's treasure map.

Last week my husband, Harris, and I walked the mill path down the long hill through April woods tender with wildflowers. A jack-in-the-pulpit thrust its exotic orchid form up through the leaf mold; it was the first of the season and normally would cause me some excitement. But there, just next to its cool, striped elegance, was the gnarled, stunted, squatting shape of a pale beige morel. The jack was instantly invisible—the chase was on. I had lost my wide-angle vision and was strapped with a macro: I could see nothing else.

The mushroom's shape was everywhere, imagined in the curl of last year's oak leaf, the insect-gnawed holes in a dead branch, the ancient marine pockmarks in a limestone rock. It was a leprechaun, leading me by the nose—or by the tastebuds—through the woods. The short time we had snatched to enjoy the ephemeral perfection of the spring day was suddenly concentrated in one squat form and the finding of it.

Eyes that might have seen the wood thrush in the trees overhead or the red-necked grebe on the water were instead nailed tight to the ground like a bloodhound's informed nose. The phantom taste of a remembered morel concentrates the attention wonderfully: the one I cupped in my hand had an aroma that recalled a lifetime's all-too-infrequent feasts.

And when our short time was spent, frittered away like lottery winnings, we had found only that one, the one seen just as we entered the wood. The rest were wraiths and wishful thinking, imagined mushrooms winking slyly beneath the disregarded beauty of April. Chopped and sauteed, it made a tea-spoon each to sprinkle on a burger.

8.

The Dignified professor

RICHARD FEYNMAN

Nobel Prize–winning physicist Richard Feynman recounts how playfulness and unbridled curiosity led him to a great discovery. Indeed, playfulness and humor are great antidotes to stultifying habit, a way of stepping outside established categories of thought. There are significant parallels between the Ha-ha! and the Aha! experience. Feynman was no stranger to insight and humor, and he even called one of his books "Surely You're Joking, Mr. Feynman!"

I *don't* believe I can really do without teaching. The reason is, I have to have something so that when I don't have any ideas and I'm not getting anywhere I can say to myself, "At least I'm living; at least I'm *doing* something; I'm making *some* contribution"—it's just psychological.

When I was at Princeton in the 1940s I could see what happened to those great minds at the Institute for Advanced Study, who had been specially selected for their tremendous brains and were now given this opportunity to sit in this lovely house by the woods there, with no classes to teach, with no obligations whatsoever. These poor bastards could now sit and think clearly all by themselves, OK? So they don't get any ideas for a while: They have every opportunity to do something, and they're not getting any ideas. I believe that in a situation like this a kind of guilt or depression worms inside of you, and you begin to *worry* about not getting any ideas. And nothing happens. Still no ideas come.

Nothing happens because there's not enough *real* activity and challenge: You're not in contact with the experimental guys. You don't have to think how to answer questions from the students. Nothing!

In any thinking process there are moments when everything is going good and you've got wonderful ideas. Teaching is an interruption, and so it's the greatest pain in the neck in the world. And then there are the *longer* periods of time when not much is coming to you. You're not getting any ideas, and if you're doing nothing at all, it drives you nuts! You can't even say, "I'm teaching my class."

If you're teaching a class, you can think about the elementary things that you know very well. These things are kind of fun and delightful. It doesn't do any harm to think them over again. Is there a better way to present them? Are there any new problems associated with them? Are there any new thoughts you can make about them? The elementary things are *easy* to think about; if you can't think of a new thought, no harm done; what you thought about it before is good enough for the class. If you *do* think of something new, you're rather pleased that you have a new way of looking at it.

The questions of the students are often the source of new research. They often ask profound questions that I've thought about at times and then given up on, so to speak, for a while. It wouldn't do me any harm to think about them again to see if I can go any further now. The students may not be able to see the thing I want to answer, or the subtleties I want to think about, but they *remind* me of a problem by asking questions in the neighborhood of that problem. It's not so easy to remind *yourself* of these things.

So I find that teaching and the students keep life going, and I would *never* accept any position in which somebody has invented a happy situation for me where I don't have to teach. Never.

But once I was offered such a position.

During the war, when I was still in Los Alamos, Hans Bethe got me this job at Cornell, for $3700 a year. I got an offer from some other place for more, but I like Bethe, and I had decided to go to Cornell and wasn't worried about the money. But Bethe was always watching out for me, and when he found out that others were offering more, he got Cornell to give me a raise to $4000 even before I started.

Cornell told me that I would be teaching a course in mathematical methods of physics, and they told me what day I should come — November 6, I think, but it sounds funny that it could be so late in the year. I took the train from Los Alamos to Ithaca, and spent most of my time writing final reports for the Manhattan Project. I still remember that it was on the night train from Buffalo to Ithaca that I began to work on my course.

You have to understand the pressures at Los Alamos. You did everything as fast as you could; everybody worked very, very hard; and everything was finished at the last minute. So, working out my course on the train a day or two before the first lecture seemed natural to me.

Mathematical methods of physics was an ideal course for me to teach. It was what I had done during the war—apply mathematics to physics. I knew which methods were *really* useful, and which were not. I had lots of experience by that time, working so hard for four years using mathematical tricks. So I laid out the different subjects in mathematics and how to deal with them, and I still have the papers—the notes I made on the train. . . .

Anyway, I began to teach the course in mathematical methods in physics, and I think I also taught another course—electricity and magnetism, perhaps. I also intended to do research. Before the war, while I was getting my degree, I had many ideas: I had invented new methods of doing quantum mechanics with path integrals, and I had a lot of stuff I wanted to do.

At Cornell, I'd work on preparing my courses, and I'd go over to the library a lot and read through the *Arabian Nights* and ogle the girls that would go by. But when it came time to do some research, I couldn't get to work. I was a little tired; I was not interested; I couldn't do research! This went on for what I felt was a few years, but when I go back and calculate the timing, it couldn't have been that long. Perhaps nowadays I wouldn't think it was such a long time, but then, it seemed to go on for a *very* long time. I simply couldn't get started on any problem: I remember writing one or two sentences about some problem in gamma rays and then I couldn't go any further. I was convinced that from the war and everything else (the death of my wife) I had simply burned myself out.

I now understand it much better. First of all, a young man doesn't realize how much time it takes to prepare good lectures, for the first time, especially—and to give the lectures, and to make up exam problems, and to check that they're sensible ones. I was giving good courses, the kind of courses where I put a lot of thought into each lecture. But I didn't realize that that's a *lot* of work! So here I was, "burned out," reading the *Arabian Nights* and feeling depressed about myself.

During this period I would get offers from different places—universities and industry—with salaries higher than my own. And each time I got something like that I would get a little more depressed. I would say to myself, "Look, they're giving me these wonderful offers, but they don't realize that I'm burned out! Of course I can't accept them. They expect me to accomplish something, and I can't accomplish anything! I have no ideas. . . ."

Finally there came in the mail an invitation from the Institute for Advanced Study: Einstein . . . von Neumann . . . Wyl . . . all these great minds! *They* write to me, and invite me to be a professor *there*! And not just a regular professor. Somehow they knew my feelings about the Institute: how it's too theoretical; how there's not enough *real* activity and challenge. So they write, "We appreciate that you have a considerable interest in experiments and in teaching, so we have made arrangements to create a special type of professorship, if you wish: half professor at Princeton University, and half at the Institute."

Institute for Advanced Study! Special exception! A position better than Einstein, even! It was ideal; it was perfect; it was absurd!

It *was* absurd. The other offers had made me feel worse, up to a point. They were expecting me to accomplish something. But this offer was so ridiculous, so impossible for me ever to live up to, so ridiculously out of proportion. The other ones were just mistakes; this was an absurdity! I laughed at it while I was shaving, thinking about it.

And then I thought to myself, "You know, what they think of you is so fantastic, it's impossible to live up to it. You have no responsibility to live up to it!"

It was a brilliant idea: You have no responsibility to live up to what other people think you ought to accomplish. I have no responsibility to be like they expect me to be. It's their mistake, not my failing.

It wasn't a failure on my part that the Institute for Advanced Study expected me to be that good; it was impossible. It was clearly a mistake—and the moment I appreciated the possibility that they might be wrong, I realized that it was also true of all the other places, including my own university. I am what I am, and if they expected me to be good and they're offering me some money for it, it's their hard luck.

Then, within the day, by some strange miracle—perhaps he overheard me talking about it, or maybe he just understood me—Bob Wilson, who was head of the laboratory there at Cornell, called me in to see him. He said, in a serious tone, "Feynman, you're teaching your classes well; you're doing a good job, and we're very satisfied. Any other expectations we might have are a matter of luck. When we hire a professor, we're taking all the risks. If it comes out good, all right. If it doesn't, too bad. But you shouldn't worry about what you're doing or not doing." He said it much better than that, and it released me from the feeling of guilt.

Then I had another thought: Physics disgusts me a little bit now, but I used to *enjoy* doing physics. Why did I enjoy it? I used to *play* with it. I used to do whatever I felt like doing—it didn't have to do with whether it was important for the development of nuclear physics, but whether it was interesting and amusing for me to play with. When I was in high school, I'd see water running out of a faucet growing narrower, and wonder if I could figure out what determines that curve. I found it was rather easy to do. I didn't *have* to do it; it wasn't important for the future of science; somebody else had already done it. That didn't make any difference: I'd invent things and play with things for my own entertainment.

So I got this new attitude. Now that I *am* burned out and I'll never accomplish anything, I've got this nice position at the university teaching classes which I rather enjoy, and just like I read the *Arabian Nights* for pleasure, I'm going to *play* with physics, whenever I want to, without worrying about any importance whatsoever.

Within a week I was in the cafeteria and some guy, fooling around, throws a plate in the air. As the plate went up in the air I saw it wobble, and I noticed the red medallion of Cornell on the plate going around. It was pretty obvious to me that the medallion went around faster than the wobbling.

I had nothing to do, so I start to figure out the motion of the rotating plate. I discover that when the angle is very slight, the medallion rotates twice as fast as the wobble rate—two to one. It came out of a complicated equation! Then I thought, "Is there some way I can see in a more fundamental way, by looking at the forces or the dynamics, why it's two to one?"

I don't remember how I did it, but I ultimately worked out what the motion of the mass particles is, and how all the accelerations balance to make it come out two to one.

I still remember going to Hans Bethe and saying, "Hey, Hans! I noticed something interesting. Here the plate goes around so, and the reason it's two to one is . . ." and I showed him the accelerations.

He says, "Feynman, that's pretty interesting, but what's the importance of it? Why are you doing it?"

"Hah!" I say. "There's no importance whatsoever. I'm just doing it for the fun of it." His reaction didn't discourage me; I had made up my mind I was going to enjoy physics and do whatever I liked.

I went on to work out equations of wobbles. Then I thought about how electron orbits start to move in relativity. Then there's the Dirac Equation in electrodynamics. And then quantum electrodynamics. And before I knew it (it was a very short time) I was "playing"—working, really—with the same old problem that I loved so much, that I had stopped working on when I went to Los Alamos: my thesis-type problems; all those old-fashioned, wonderful things.

It was effortless. It was easy to play with these things. It was like uncorking a bottle: Everything flowed out effortlessly. I almost tried to resist it! There was no importance to what I was doing, but ultimately there was. The diagrams and the whole business that I got the Nobel Prize for came from that piddling around with the wobbling plate.

9.

The screwdriver

KARY MULLIS

In this freewheeling interview with molecular biologist Kary Mullis, we get a feeling for his iconoclastic creativity, the devotion he has for his work, his controversial use of psychedelic drugs, and his relationship to the corporate world. Mullis shows what it means to have an open mind — and how large, bureaucratic organizations can have very closed minds.

Omni: What inspired PCR*?

Mullis: I wasn't developing a way to amplify DNA at all. It was like I was randomly putting Tinkertoys together and finally made a structure and said, "You know what? If I turn this toy wheel over there, that damn thing would wind string." Driving up to Mendocino and thinking about an experiment to look at one particular letter of the genetic code, I designed a system in my mind. As I repaired the things I thought could go wrong with it, suddenly I generated something that if I did it over and over again would be PCR. It would go 2, 4, 8, 16, 32 . . . in 30 cycles make as many base pairs from one little region as I had in the whole genome! That was the eureka point. I said holy shit! By putting the triphosphates [DNA building blocks] in there myself, I could do this process over and over and amplify the DNA.

I slammed on the brakes and stopped by the side of the road to calculate it out. Then I drove on, because my lab assistant was pissed. I said, "I have just come up with something incredible." She'd been sleeping in the car. She was the only person in Mendocino that night who knew anything about biochemistry, but she didn't think it was any good.

A couple of miles down the road I stopped again. I realized I could use

---

*Polymerase chain reaction. (Eds.)

these bastards, the oligonucleotides [short pieces of DNA], and get the enzymes to reproduce as big a piece as I wanted to. They didn't have to be aimed at just one base pair. Hell, I could do a whole sequence. I realized you can cut the sequence out from a great big molecule. Pretty cool! Just cut, paste, and amplify. This is going to be a tool that's spread around the world!

I said, "If you get up and listen and help me with this, I'll put you on the invention." But she was just like the others at Cetus. She did not believe I could possibly have invented anything interesting because she knew me. She is not on the invention!

Omni: How does PCR work, starting with one oligonucleotide?

MULLIS: I have suggested dropping that clumsy word from the dictionary. An oligonucleotide is a short piece of several nucleotides, of single-stranded DNA. In PCR it acts as a primer, anchoring itself onto a long, single strand of DNA and getting elongated by the polymerase, the enzyme molecule. The polymerase copies the DNA by snatching these little monomers [DNA constituents] out of the solution and stuffing them in at the right place on the oligonucleotide. The polymerase copies down the information from the long strand. With PCR, the first copy you make has one end defined, so it can't get elongated. During the next cycle, the other end is closed off, too, so the polymerase just copies the target section of DNA you want. Then in cycles after that, only the defined DNA piece will be copied. It can be copied forever.

Omni: So you end up with a pure sample of the DNA you're after?

MULLIS: PCR detects a very, very small amount of some sequence interspersed in a whole bunch of similar sequences. Then PCR makes so much of the sequence, you end up with something that is almost all what you're interested in. It purifies as it amplifies because it only amplifies one thing. It's like a radio amplifying only one wavelength amid all that are coming in.

Omni: You made history at Cetus. Why aren't you still its superstar?

MULLIS: If Cetus had been more attentive to the needs of its inventors, I would have stayed and invented more things. At first it was a good environment. I used the Cetus computer to set up a lab to make oligonucleotides and then had nothing to do. My boss said, "Don't tell them you've got it beat. Just play." I started thinking of what we could do with all the oligonucleotides. I'd no real responsibilities for about two years, and just played. By the end, I had PCR.

Omni: What went wrong?

MULLIS: When they finally realized that someone among them had discovered something royally good, every sonofabitch administrator who wanted to make a name for himself suddenly decided he wanted to be my boss. There were wolves all around me. They all started proposing experiments for me to do, treating me like a grad student. By then I was working on what I thought would be the future direction of PCR. Nobody quite understood. They demanded I write down what I did and present it to a committee who'd decide if it was okay. I said, "I don't think that's necessary. I should be able to drift, okay?" They said no.

They put me over the flames—"You haven't done this control, that control." I said, "I've done it before and can probably do it again, but I am not a technician. If I have to do things your way I'll end up doing things just like you and that's all."

They should've said, "Okay, you just produced something that might make us a hundred million bucks, maybe a billion. What can we do to make life easier?" But they took the golden goose and cut its head off.

I was screaming for a year and a half about how important PCR was and no one was listening. They didn't expect an important breakthrough in genetics to come from an oligonucleotides lab. They didn't understand that important inventions almost always cross the lines of disciplines. You don't develop an invention by having one hundred guys working for five years to produce an invention. You have one guy who may even be flaky in his field and who jumps around and puts shit together in unlikely ways and sees something it's hard to imagine even a good administrator having a sense of how it works. If he did, he'd be an inventor himself because it's more fun.

Most administrators work in sleazy ways, conferring in back rooms and coming in and acting as if the decision hasn't been made, and suddenly you think, What happened here? And they're off again to have another big meeting.

There's nothing on the agenda of the board meeting on "What We Have Done This Week for People Who Have No Legal Right to It"!

Omni: You didn't even get a promotion as a result of your discovery?

MULLIS: I didn't ever hang out in situations that lead to that. How do you do it—put a sign up in the bathroom? I used to hang out with the younger people in the company. A mistake. But I don't generally like people my age. Most of my good male friends are former boyfriends of my daughters.

Omni: In other words, you're not interested in power?

MULLIS: Over my own life, yes, but not over anybody else's. I had power, I ran the oligo lab and went up and said, "Let me out of this, I want to work by myself in the lab."

Omni: What is the direction PCR's going in right now?

MULLIS: It's so widely used by molecular biologists that its future direction is the future of molecular biology itself. It's like asking what is the future direction of the screwdriver—it's whatever people use screws for. PCR is to DNA what the screwdriver is to screws. For now PCR's future is wherever anything is being done with DNA. There is a PCR machine in every DNA lab already.

Omni: What neat things are PCR machines making possible?

MULLIS: A rather complex one is a way of re-creating evolution. This will have major significance in designing pharmaceuticals. PCR enables you to re-create molecular evolution fast in the lab. You start with a mass of molecules and select the property you want. Then PCR pulls the molecules with that property away from the rest—one part in a trillion—[and] amplifies that. In the process, you introduce new mutations and select for those with the properties you want. Craig Turek at the University of Colorado has already used it to select for RNA molecules and is now using it to select for protein molecules.

Omni: Why did you decide to call your cabin up in Mendocino the Institute for Further Study?

MULLIS: A lot of papers end with the phrase "This result deserves further study," trying to get a grant. The IFS is a place where this can be done, where no study can be considered complete, where all results will be held pending further study, where no publications will be forthcoming, and all appointments are tentative. I am the provisional director awaiting study of the committee studying the provisional status of the director!

Omni: Do you think that you will be able to come up with a second PCR–type breakthrough?

MULLIS: My blood sampler may benefit some of their physics expertise and might be more valuable to the world than PCR. To identify the hundreds of compounds in a blood sample, I'll use a scanning probe microscope that can see atoms one at a time. The aspect I'm working on now is cluster coding molecules—like putting bar codes in a grocery store. The checker never has to look at the article you're buying but just has to pull it over the bar-code reader. I'm trying to do that for clinical chemistry to find a way to recognize the molecules in a blood sample without having to observe them directly. If you can put a bar code on each kind of molecule and find some way to read it, the problem is over.

Omni: You'll put a blood sample in your machine and out will come a list of its constituents?

MULLIS: All the things in it, and much more efficiently than before. A machine in hospitals gives the levels of some 12 chemicals in blood—sodium, calcium, potassium, and so on. But there's no such thing that will work for hundreds of proteins, really complex molecules. I'm going to try for 32 compounds at first. Then it should be no problem to do it for 64, or 128. That's as many things as anybody gives a darn about in blood. If it works, there's no reason it can't be done in a doctor's office. Commercially it would be enormous; you could take over all of clinical diagnostics, a $5-billion-a-year market. I have to figure out how to make it work or get someone else to. The concept is biologically valid, though technical problems need to be solved, just like with PCR.

This time I'm not going to hand it over to some company like Cetus without something saying it's mine. If anyone makes $300 million off it, I'm going to be part of that. Cetus has sold the rest of PCR they had not already sold for $300 million. This is the most money ever paid in history for a patent. You couldn't tell that from looking at my carpet in here that's not even clean. And it's not ermine, either!

Omni: Couldn't they have given you a million dollars?

MULLIS: I said, "Hey, why don't you make it $301 million? Send it in the mail; it will be good publicity for you?" But I'm going to do all right. You don't expect the world to take care of you. [There is] absolutely no reason to think businessmen are going to behave like philosophers. Fair is not business, and business will grow, despite nasties and crummies in your tummy, as Dr. Seuss said. I don't have any resentment. You'd have to be neurotic to expect that business will be fair.

Omni: How did you come to write your 1968 paper for *Nature* on the cosmological reversal of time?

MULLIS: Courses in astrophysics gave me two competing descriptions of the universe: big-bang and steady-state theory. I thought both were sophomoric approaches, because each is based on the premise that you could actually step outside the universe and look at it. That's stupid. Relativity makes it clear you can't talk about the universe from outside. If you look at it from inside and assume relativity is part of what's going on—which neither theory did then—it makes sense.

I was at Berkeley and taking acid every week. That's what people did for entertainment: drink beer or go out into Tilden Park and take 500 micrograms of LSD and sit all day thinking about the universe, time going backwards and forward. Some mornings I'd wake up and think I ought to write that out. So I did.

Moving between fields is the way to be creative. Keep your fingers in a lot of pies. I do it because I'm curious. I'm the only person I know who goes into a poster session [at a scientific meeting] and stops at the first poster I have no idea what it's about. Find the poster you don't know anything about and look at it for a long time, and you might learn something totally different.

IO.

Living in
the medium

J .   G .   B E N N E T T

Mystic and philosopher J. G. Bennett gives us here a lucid discussion of the process known as incubation. We have all had the experience of forgetting somebody's name, trying desperately to remember it and failing miserably, only to find that the name pops up at the oddest time after we've given up, or "let go," of the search. In a similar way, it has been argued that the creative process involves a period of "letting go" that follows the initial immersion in one's subject. The argument is that we need time to "digest" the issue, perhaps let the unconscious mull it over without conscious interference. The potential reward is that our idea will then pop up when we least expect it—say in the shower. "For something to enter," Bennett writes, "a place must be made for it."

I hope to convey to you something of what I have been able to recognize over many years' experience of the factors important to creative thinking. What are the conditions for creativity? First of all, one must be living in the medium. People are not creative in some medium with which they have no real contact. In that sense, if we wish to think creatively we have to be in the process of thinking. Then we have somehow to bring into it additional factors which will give that process the quality of creativity for which we are looking.

There is the saying that creativity is ninety-nine parts perspiration and one part inspiration—in other words, that it is mostly very hard work. But there is no doubt of the importance of some second element in creativity that we ourselves cannot control. I am going to call that element spontaneity. If you read accounts of creative activity by scientists, artists or others, you see in these accounts that the spontaneous element is really out of the person's control. Yet, though it comes unexpectedly, spontaneity does not come without certain conditions being satisfied; we will come to these conditions later.

Let us take one classical example of creativity which has often been reported. Lawrence Bragg gives an account of the way in which he made a particular step in understanding crystallography when he was working with his father, William Bragg. They came across some experimental work which did not fit into the accepted theory of the crystal lattice. They verified their experiments and they verified what other people had done, and then they were stuck. No combination or adjustment of the existing theories would make it all fit together. Then one day, as Lawrence Bragg describes it, when he had almost given up hope of finding the answer without new experimental evidence turning up to give a clue, he was walking down the Backs of Cambridge and *in a flash* the whole thing came clearly in front of him. He was able to go back immediately and do the necessary mathematical analysis with his father, and the new theory became clearer even though it required several months' work before it was ready for publication.

The actual creative step, as he describes it and as hundreds of other people have described it on other occasions, came "in a flash," unexpectedly. One of the questions that we shall have to talk about is whether anything can be done about this or whether it is entirely out of our power and wholly dependent upon good luck, as it is sometimes supposed to be.

There is a third element that enters into all this which I shall call *technique*. Let us take the example of an artist. Without technique, the moment of creative insight can hardly be made fruitful. The same is true for the scientist. This means that one must know the form that will enable one to clothe the moment of insight in some expression. First, one must know the form of thought for oneself, so that the insight may become clear, and afterwards one must know the form of expression so that it may be communicated to others. Let us take these three factors for the moment and look at them. First, one needs to be grounded in the subject matter one wishes to develop creatively, where one feels that a creative step has to be made. Second, one must have this spontaneous arising of the new vision, or understanding, or insight into the situation. Third, one needs the ability to translate that into something which can be thought about and expressed.

So far, all of these factors are concerned with creative activity in general. All of this is equally true for the artist, the scientist, or the man of action who has to take a creative decision. An example is the general who is in front of a strategical or tactical problem, or the doctor who is in front of sickness — whenever there is something that cannot be dealt with by routine steps alone and therefore some kind of creative step is needed.

I said that the first factor is being well grounded in the subject with which one is dealing. But this grounding is itself a special process: one must know what has to be known about the subject and then one must put out of one's attention all that is unnecessary to it—that is to say, this grounding is itself a selective activity. One must know just what it is that one is going to work at. In this work of grounding, the artist, a painter for instance, must select, reject and also assemble his material—that is, he has to decide how he will treat it. In all the work of preparing the ground he is not called upon to make a creative step; if by chance this should happen at this point there is a great risk that he will not complete his grounding, and his final construction will be lacking despite the flash of genius.

When we are concerned with the need for creative thought, this grounding has to be made in our heads. There is no doubt that this part of the work is hard in the field of thinking. Sometimes when people set themselves to understand something or to make creative investigations of a subject, they proceed to get all the relevant information down in front of them. They write it down on a sheet of paper or make a card index. But this is not at all sufficient. It is necessary that one should do that work of selection, elimination and assembly (as far as possible) *inwardly.* I know from my own experience that this is a hard discipline and that there is always an inclination to get thoughts down on paper or to read up on the subject. But if one wants to bring thinking into the sphere of creativity, this preparatory work has to be done in a special way; it has to go through the mill of one's own past experience and one has to come to terms with the subject. If I have to do such work as this I just do a preliminary collecting together of what I happen to know about the subject. Then I sit down and try to *put it together in my mind* in order to see what it is that I really know about the subject and what I intend to do with that knowledge. In the course of doing that I may find that there is something clearly missing and that I have to go out and study the topic or perhaps make some investigations or experiments. But in doing this I am still only preparing the ground; I must not be looking, at this point, for a solution to the problem, and even if I seem to see the situation more clearly and am ready to make progress with it, it is essential to exercise self-restraint so as not to allow myself to make a premature step forward in understanding. Thus there is a special discipline which one has to learn and impose on oneself, and I shall certainly be saying more about it in the course of these lectures. This preliminary stage goes through the whole process and does not remain static. One does not, as is said, "bone up" on the subject and decide what one knows about it and then leave it to go on to the other stages. This ground work *must be kept fluid* so that there can be a process of transformation. One must constantly remind oneself that the solution has not yet taken shape; we must remember that even though we assemble data and try to give the problem a coherent form so that we can at least hold it in our minds, this is not the goal, not what we are aiming for.

This work of grounding oneself in the subject makes this process different from other sorts of learning where it is sufficient to learn what one has to know about a subject and then fix it in the mind by memorization or by making the necessary notes so that, when information is needed, one can find the necessary sources or bring it to mind. We are not concerned with learning but with something else. And for this something else, any kind of fixing is the one factor which can *spoil the whole process*. One caution I must make here is that that which is necessary for creative thinking may be quite harmful or even destructive for other kinds of activity where it is necessary, for example, to settle upon what one knows and act upon it and stick to the decision that has been made. This sort of thing is very necessary for other purposes, but this is the very thing which must be thrown aside when one is trying to make a new creative step.

I find for myself that the process becomes like a kaleidoscope: patterns of ideas pass in front of my attention and I do not allow myself to dwell on anything in particular so that other patterns arise. Out of all of this I expect nothing of any value to come. In fact, it very seldom, if ever, does come.

When you are ready to bring in the next factor you have to see to it that you provide the necessary conditions. That is, *you must ask yourself a clear question.* In the example I gave you about Lawrence Bragg, he has a very clear question: how is he to fit these measurements of lattice energies in with the present theories of crystal structure? The question was clear enough to know *whether or not it was answered.*

Now, what is to be done about the element of spontaneity? Here I think that I really can offer you something which is not generally understood, something I have gained from my own experience and which I have learned from others. I am sure that there is a practical means whereby one can bring about the conditions for this spontaneous step to be made. Some of you may remember how we used to speak about thinking at Coombe Springs. I always answered this question of "how to think" with "The way to think is not to think." If you grasp this, then you will be able to follow what I mean.

If I have some question which I cannot answer by the ordinary processes, by calling upon what I know about a subject, and I have satisfied myself that I do not already have the answer, then it is no use in going on looking for it. I have become habituated, by doing this for many years, to quite quickly stop looking for an answer and to go to this other, opposite, condition of putting the whole thing away except for *the question*. I stop all thinking "about" the subject, even to the extent of chasing away any thoughts that seem interesting or suggestive. Even the question ceases to be present in the form of words, or an image which I can hold. All that remains is *the need to find an answer*.

This has to be practiced. You must not think that because I have explained this to you that you can do it at once. I am going to help you with this over a series of lectures, and therefore you will not have to pick it up all in one go. But the process, as far as I can describe it, is this: Having brought the question in front of me, I then empty my mind of all that I know about the subject. I also have to prevent my mind from wandering off on to other subjects, which of course it will want to do because it abhors a vacuum. And I suppose that it is really this abhorrence of a vacuum that draws to the mind some new thought or new insight, and makes for this spontaneous or creative step I am looking for.

Several of you have probably quite often done something similar to this when you have had a lapse of memory. You have known, or have heard, that the best way of dealing with a lapse of memory is to keep from trying to remember what one has forgotten. And then, somehow, by emptying the mind this forgotten or lost memory is drawn back into one's consciousness. This simple procedure is not difficult when it comes to a memory that is actually latent in our minds but is outside the sphere of our conscious experience at the moment. The point here is that the same method can carry us much further into attracting, into our conscious experience, ideas which we have not had before — even ideas which no one has ever had before — that is, truly original thoughts. This will depend entirely upon the strength of one's mind and the power that one has to reject anything which is incomplete, anything which is not evidently the required step forward. There is a tremendously strong temptation to follow up on whatever comes into the mind which sheds some light on the subject or is very interesting. But this means that the step which is made is only half, or less than half. Though there is an enrichment of our thinking, it is not a truly creative step.

Those who have the real creative power always have this strength of mind that enables them to deny or to reject anything but the truth, the insight or moment of understanding that is required. But all of us can strengthen our minds quite simply by this practice. All that is required is, having found the theme with which to practice, we resolutely refuse to think about it.

You all know the famous kind of mental trick which consists in asking someone how long they cannot think about a white elephant, and as soon as they try to do this, they find it is impossible. They can think about nothing else than white elephants, and the more they want not to think about it, the more white elephants march up and down in front of them. If you refuse resolutely to think about white elephants, then who knows, a white elephant may come marching in the window—a real one! So if your power of thought is strong enough to refuse anything but what you are actually determined to have, it will come; that is in the nature of this power.

This has to be practiced in simple things to start with, but you must understand that there is nothing that I can do for you in this particular respect. If you are not sufficiently interested, all that these lectures can do for you is to give you an interesting theory *about* creativity thinking. I am sure of this: there is no substitute for this particular discipline.

The same effect can be produced unintentionally by fatiguing the mind—for example, as in the case of Lawrence Bragg. He told me about this himself. Lawrence Bragg so occupied his mind with the problem that his mind finally got tired of it and would not think about it any more. Then, when by sheer fatigue he had succeeded in not thinking about the question any more, the answer came. But in reality, this is an extremely clumsy way of doing the job. Strangely enough, it is almost the only way that is known to even the best scientists and therefore things very often take much longer than they need to take. It is true that the mind is fatigued by the process of rejection, but it is not nearly so hazardous, uncertain and chancy to do it this way as to try to understand the subject and go on thinking about it until at last your mind refuses to think about it. There are, as you know, exercises that are taught by masters of Zen Buddhism—like the *koan*—where the mind is to be held resolutely upon some absurdity which is impossible to think about. By holding the attention on something which cannot be thought about because of its inherent absurdity, a vacuum is finally created. In this case, the exercise is to allow for the entry of a complete insight into the nature of man; this is called *Satori*. But it is connected with the one essential technique: *for something to enter, a place must be made for it*. Gurdjieff used to refer to this by simply saying "Must make vacuum," and he used this technique for other things besides thinking; for example, he used it as a technique for making money.

But first, if you want to practice this, you have to practice it for a relatively short time without expecting to arrive at anything spectacular, because this refusal to think about what you wish to understand is an unusual thing for most people. And I know from my own experience what kind of inner resistance there is to it, in the peculiar way something in us revolts and is ready to take any excuse for stopping this and doing something else instead. But I have no doubt at all that practicing this technique has an extraordinary, liberating effect upon the hidden powers of the mind.

II.

The symbolism
of poetry

WILLIAM BUTLER YEATS

In "The Symbolism of Poetry," Nobel Prize–winning poet and Irish patriot William Butler Yeats (1865–1939) equates mind to will, and will is the enemy of creation. The mind must be free to wander and wonder, to sink into contemplation, to meditate. The rhythm of poetry (and of music) is prolonged by trance, and in the entranced moment the symbols of poetry are liberated. The trance may last only a second, yet in that second a whole world of symbols comes into consciousness. Is this the "flash" of insight, the sudden reorganization of the perceptual field, of which the gestalt psychologist speaks? The use of consciously induced hypnotic trance, combined with gestalt analysis of the elements of the dreamlike state that results, is a modern fruit of this poetic theory. Yeats and Jung were alike in many ways, especially in their recourse to dream and symbol as the key to open what Jung called the collective unconscious and Yeats called the great memory.

The purpose of rhythm, it has always seemed to me, is to prolong the moment of contemplation, the moment when we are both asleep and awake, which is the one moment of creation, by hushing us with an alluring monotony, while it holds us waking by variety, to keep us in that state of perhaps real trance, in which the mind liberated from the pressure of the will is unfolded in symbols. If certain sensitive persons listen persistently to the ticking of a watch, or gaze persistently on the monotonous flashing of a light, they fall into the hypnotic trance; and rhythm is but the ticking of a watch made softer, that one must needs listen, and various, that one may not be swept beyond memory or grow weary of listening; while the patterns of the artist are but the monotonous flash woven to take the eyes in a subtler enchantment. I have heard in meditation voices that were forgotten the moment they had spoken; and I have been swept, when in more profound meditation, beyond all memory but of those things that came from beyond the threshold of waking life. I was writing once at a very symbolical and abstract poem, when my pen fell on the ground; and as I stooped to pick it up, I remembered some fantastic adventure that yet did not seem fantastic, and then another like adventure, and when I asked myself when these things had happened, I found that I was remembering my dreams for many nights. I tried to remember what I had done the day before, and then what I had done that morning; but all my waking life had perished from me, and it was only after a struggle that I came to remember it again, and as I did so that more powerful and startling life perished in its turn. Had my pen not fallen on the ground and so made me turn from the images that I was weaving into verse, I would never have known that meditation had become trance, for I would have been like one who does not know that he is passing through a wood because his eyes are on the pathway. So I think that in the making and in the understanding of a work of art, and the more easily if it is full of patterns and symbols and music, we are lured to the threshold of sleep, and it may be far beyond it, without knowing that we have ever set our feet upon the steps of horn or of ivory.

12.

Heaven and
Earth in Jest

ANNIE DILLARD

Novelist Annie Dillard questions the Creator's motives, and the motives of creation. Was this all made in jest, or in earnest? And is the Creator still around? What of the creation of evil—and of beauty? Dillard says she is an explorer—no scientist, mind you, but an explorer nevertheless, of nature and of neighborhoods, finding wonderment in the world around her.

A couple of summers ago I was walking along the edge of the island to see what I could see in the water, and mainly to scare frogs. Frogs have an inelegant way of taking off from invisible positions on the bank just ahead of your feet, in dire panic, emitting a froggy "Yike!" and splashing into the water. Incredibly, this amused me, and, incredibly, it amuses me still. As I walked along the grassy edge of the island, I got better and better at seeing frogs both in and out of the water. I learned to recognize, slowing down, the difference in texture of the light reflected from mudbank, water, grass, or frog. Frogs were flying all around me. At the end of the island I noticed a small green frog. He was exactly half in and half out of the water, looking like a schematic diagram of an amphibian, and he didn't jump.

He didn't jump; I crept closer. At last I knelt on the island's winterkilled grass, lost, dumbstruck, staring at the frog in the creek just four feet away. He was a very small frog with wide, dull eyes. And just as I looked at him, he slowly crumpled and began to sag. The spirit vanished from his eyes as if snuffed. His skin emptied and drooped; his very skull seemed to collapse and settle like a kicked tent. He was shrinking before my eyes like a deflating football. I watched the taut, glistening skin on his shoulders ruck, and rumple, and fall. Soon, part of his skin, formless as a pricked balloon, lay in floating folds like bright scum on top of the water: it was a monstrous and terrifying thing. I gaped bewildered, appalled. An oval shadow hung in the water behind the drained frog; then the shadow glided away. The frog skin bag started to sink.

I had read about the giant water bug, but never seen one. "Giant water bug" is really the name of the creature, which is an enormous, heavy-bodied brown bug. It eats insects, tadpoles, fish, and frogs. Its grasping forelegs are mighty and hooked inward. It seizes a victim with these legs, hugs it tight, and paralyzes it with enzymes injected during a vicious bite. That one bite is the only bite it ever takes. Through the puncture shoot the poisons that dissolve the victim's muscles and bones and organs—all but the skin—and through it the giant water bug sucks out the victim's body, reduced to a juice. This event is quite common in warm fresh water. The frog I saw was being sucked by a giant water bug. I had been kneeling on the island grass; when the unrecognizable flap of frog skin settled on the creek bottom, swaying, I stood up and brushed the knees of my pants. I couldn't catch my breath.

Of course, many carnivorous animals devour their prey alive. The usual method seems to be to subdue the victim by downing or grasping it so it can't flee, then eating it whole or in a series of bloody bites. Frogs eat everything whole, stuffing prey into their mouths with their thumbs. People have seen frogs with their wide jaws so full of live dragonflies they couldn't close them. Ants don't even have to catch their prey: in the spring they swarm over newly hatched, featherless birds in the nest and eat them tiny bite by bite.

That it's rough out there and chancy is no surprise. Every live thing is a survivor on a kind of extended emergency bivouac. But at the same time we are also created. In the Koran, Allah asks, "The heaven and the earth and all in between, thinkest thou I made them *in jest?*" It's a good question. What do we think of the created universe, spanning an unthinkable void with an unthinkable profusion of forms? Or what do we think of nothingness, those sickening reaches of time in either direction? If the giant water bug was not made in jest, was it then made in earnest? Pascal uses a nice term to describe the notion of the creator's, once having called forth the universe, turning his back to it: *Deus Absconditus.* Is this what we think happened? Was the sense of it there, and God absconded with it, ate it, like a wolf who disappears round the edge of the house with the Thanksgiving turkey? "God is subtle," Einstein said, "but not malicious." Again, Einstein said that "nature conceals her mystery by means of her essential grandeur, not by her cunning." It could be that God has not absconded but spread, as our vision and understanding of the universe have spread, to a fabric of spirit and sense so grand and subtle, so powerful in a new way, that we can only feel blindly of its hem. In making the thick darkness a swaddling band for the sea, God "set bars and doors" and said, "Hitherto shalt thou come, but no further." But have we come even that far? Have we rowed out to the thick darkness, or are we all playing pinochle in the bottom of the boat?

Cruelty is a mystery, and the waste of pain. But if we describe a world to compass these things, a world that is a long, brute game, then we bump against another mystery: the inrush of power and light, the canary that sings on the skull. Unless all ages and races of men have been deluded by the same mass hypnotist (who?), there seems to be such a thing as beauty, a grace wholly gratuitous. About five years ago I saw a mockingbird make a straight vertical descent from the roof gutter of a four-story building. It was an act as careless and spontaneous as the curl of a stem or the kindling of a star.

The mockingbird took a single step into the air and dropped. His wings were still folded against his sides as though he were singing from a limb and not falling, accelerating thirty-two feet per second per second, through empty air. Just a breath before he would have been dashed to the ground, he unfurled his wings with exact, deliberate care, revealing the broad bars of white, spread his elegant, white-banded tail, and so floated onto the grass. I had just rounded a corner when his insouciant step caught my eye; there was no one else in sight. The fact of his free fall was like the old philosophical conundrum about the tree that falls in the forest. The answer must be, I think, that beauty and grace are performed whether or not we will or sense them. The least we can do is try to be there.

Another time I saw another wonder: sharks off the Atlantic coast of Florida. There is a way a wave rises above the ocean horizon, a triangular wedge against the sky. If you stand where the ocean breaks on a shallow beach, you see the raised water in a wave is translucent, shot with lights. One late afternoon at low tide a hundred big sharks passed the beach near the mouth of a tidal river in a feeding frenzy. As each green wave rose from the churning water, it illuminated within itself the six- or eight-foot-long bodies of twisting sharks. The sharks disappeared as each wave rolled toward me; then a new wave would swell above the horizon, containing in it, like scorpions in amber, sharks that roiled and heaved. The sight held awesome wonders: power and beauty, grace tangled in a rapture with violence.

We don't know what's going on here. If these tremendous events are random combinations of matter run amok, the yield of millions of monkeys at millions of typewriters, then what is it in us, hammered out of those same typewriters, that they ignite? We don't know. Our life is a faint tracing on the surface of mystery, like the idle, curved tunnels of leaf miners on the face of a leaf. We must somehow take a wider view, look at the whole landscape, really see it, and describe what's going on here. Then we can at least wail the right question into the swaddling band of darkness, or, if it comes to that, choir the proper praise.

At the time of Lewis and Clark, setting the prairies on fire was a well-known signal that meant, "Come down to the water." It was an extravagant gesture, but we can't do less. If the landscape reveals one certainty, it is that the extravagant gesture is the very stuff of creation. After the one extravagant gesture of creation in the first place, the universe has continued to deal exclusively in extravagances, flinging intricacies and colossi down aeons of emptiness, heaping profusions on profligacies with ever-fresh vigor. The whole show has been on fire from the word go. I come down to the water to cool my eyes. But everywhere I look I see fire; that which isn't flint is tinder, and the whole world sparks and flames. . . .

Like the bear who went over the mountain, I went out to see what I could see. And, I might as well warn you, like the bear, all that I could see was the other side of the mountain: more of same. On a good day I might catch a glimpse of another wooded ridge rolling under the sun like water, another bivouac. I propose to keep here what Thoreau called "a meteorological journal of the mind," telling some tales and describing some of the sights of this rather tamed valley, and exploring, in fear and trembling, some of the unmapped dim reaches and unholy fastnesses to which those tales and sights so dizzyingly lead.

I am no scientist. I explore the neighborhood. An infant who has just learned to hold his head up has a frank and forthright way of gazing about him in bewilderment. He hasn't the faintest clue where he is, and he aims to learn. In a couple of years, what he will have learned instead is how to fake it: he'll have the cocksure air of a squatter who has come to feel he owns the place. Some unwonted, taught pride diverts us from our original intent, which is to explore the neighborhood, view the landscape, to discover at least *where* it is that we have been so startlingly set down, if we can't learn why.

So I think about the valley. It is my leisure as well as my work, a game. It is a fierce game I have joined because it is being played anyway, a game of both skill and chance, played against an unseen adversary—the conditions of time—in which the playoffs, which may suddenly arrive in a blast of light at any moment, might as well come to me as anyone else. I stake the time I'm grateful to have, the energies I'm glad to direct. I risk getting stuck on the board, so to speak, unable to move in any direction, which happens enough,

God knows; and I risk the searing, exhausting nightmares that plunder rest and force me face down all night long in some muddy ditch seething with hatching insects and crustaceans.

But if I can bear the nights, the days are a pleasure. I walk out; I see something, some event that would otherwise have been utterly missed and lost; or something sees me, some enormous power brushes me with its clean wing, and I resound like a beaten bell.

I am an explorer, then, and I am also a stalker, or the instrument of the hunt itself. Certain Indians used to carve long grooves along the wooded shafts of their arrows. They called the grooves "lightning marks," because they resembled the curved fissure lightning slices down the trunks of trees. The function of lightning marks is this: if the arrow fails to kill the game, blood from a deep wound will channel along the lightning mark, streak down the arrow shaft, and spatter to the ground, laying a trail dripped on broadleaves, on stones, that the barefoot and trembling archer can follow into whatever deep or rare wilderness it leads. I am the arrow shaft, carved along my length by unexpected lights and gashes from the very sky, and this book is the straying trail of blood.

Something pummels us, something barely sheathed. Power broods and lights. We're played on like a pipe; our breath is not our own. James Houston describes two young Eskimo girls sitting cross-legged on the ground, mouth on mouth, blowing by turns each other's throat cords, making a low, unearthly music. When I cross again the bridge that is really the steers' fence, the wind has thinned to the delicate air of twilight; it crumples the water's skin. I watch the running sheets of light raised on the creek's surface. The sight has the appeal of the purely passive, like the racing of light under clouds on a field, the beautiful dream at the moment of being dreamed. The breeze is the merest puff, but you yourself sail headlong and breathless under the gale force of the spirit.

III

THE WEB OF
IMAGINATION

Do I contradict myself?
Very well then I contradict myself,
(I am large, I contain multitudes.)

WALT WHITMAN

One must have chaos in one, to give birth to a dancing star.

FRIEDRICH NIETZSCHE

ɪmaɡination maʏ weave unusual webs. The web of imagination can be the novelist's tale, the composer's music, or the scientist's theory, where fragments of experience, ideas, and impressions are united into a whole. The value of the imagining lies in the originality and strength of the pattern created.

Myriad connections, though perhaps unseen, exist between all things. While I may jump in the air, I fall down again; and the sun energizes plants and they energize us; molecule after molecule is stacked up to make a tree, which is pulverized to make the paper for this book in your hand; ideas float on the air between mouths, between cultures, and the world is changed; a painter's palette expresses emotion, as well as a photochemical reaction in his eye; zeroes and ones in particular sequence solve differential equations that describe complicated natural systems; a long-lost friend telephones just after she is remembered; slate under pressure over eons becomes diamond; musicians get in tune by feeling for beats; water and oxygen flow continually through our bodies; DNA connects grandmothers to mothers to daughters; electrical sparks across synapses connect neurons together in thought, and axons to muscle in limbs, so we are mobile; shadowy imprints of dinosaurs and asteroid dust, ancient cities, are layered underneath earth's lively crust; ancient plant bogs formed carboniferous pools of oil, which now power industries and automobiles; an atom metamorphosed becomes light; wishes become dreams become realities; and black holes suck in plasma to where? Another universe?

Universal patterns inform creative symbols and the symbolizing mind of the creator. The ancient Greeks called such patterns archetypes. Archetypes or not, history is always there, but ahead of it there is a future not determined by anyone or anything, but contingent on the products of our own creation. It is we who make the future, and our imagination of the future affects who we are and what we do now.

An important premise in Gestalt psychology is the notion that the whole contains within it a tendency toward unity. It moves toward an elegant simplicity. The creative act seeks unity in variety. Finding simplicity in complexity is another way of putting it. Diffusion may lead to integration, leading to more diffusion, then more integration—this succession of states makes up the cycle of life and generation. The sense of the whole may be one of inner satisfaction, primarily, or it may be an unfolding of potentialities.

Are we weaving a web that weaves us? The web of life and the web of imagination are intertwined as we create.

13.

The genesis of frankenstein

MARY SHELLEY

Mary Wollstonecraft Shelley describes the birth of her famous novel Frankenstein *in an account that speaks to us of her dreams and of humanity's dream to conquer nature and death. Conversation, with Shelley and Byron, about ghost stories and Darwin's revelations, led to a dream, to inspiration. In our dreams we often reassemble the events and impressions of the day—as Shelley herself said, "Invention, it must be humbly admitted, does not consist in creating out of the void, but out of chaos; the materials must, in the first place, be afforded."*

The publishers of the standard novels, in selecting *Frankenstein* for one of their series, expressed a wish that I should furnish them with some account of the origin of the story. I am the more willing to comply because I shall thus give a general answer to the question so very frequently asked me—how I, then a young girl, came to think of and to dilate upon so very hideous an idea. It is true that I am very averse to bringing myself forward in print, but as my account will only appear as an appendage to a former production, and as it will be confined to such topics as have connection with my authorship alone, I can scarcely accuse myself of a personal intrusion.

It is not singular that, as the daughter of two persons of distinguished literary celebrity, I should very early in life have thought of writing. As a child I scribbled, and my favourite pastime during the hours given me for recreation was to "write stories." Still, I had a dearer pleasure than this, which was the formation of castles in the air—the indulging in waking dreams—the following up trains of thought, which had for their subject the formation of a succession of imaginary incidents. My dreams were at once more fantastic and agreeable than my writings. In the latter I was a close imitator—rather doing as others had done than putting down the suggestions of my own mind. What

I wrote was intended at least for one other eye—my childhood's companion and friend; but my dreams were all my own; I accounted for them to nobody; they were my refuge when annoyed—my dearest pleasure when free.

I lived principally in the country as a girl and passed a considerable time in Scotland. I made occasional visits to the more picturesque parts, but my habitual residence was on the blank and dreary northern shores of the Tay, near Dundee. Blank and dreary on retrospection I call them; they were not so to me then. They were the aerie of freedom and the pleasant region where unheeded I could commune with the creatures of my fancy. I wrote then, but in a most common-place style. It was beneath the trees of the grounds belonging to our house, or on the bleak sides of the woodless mountains near, that my true compositions, the airy flights of my imagination, were born and fostered. I did not make myself the heroine of my tales. Life appeared to me too common-place an affair as regarded myself. I could not figure to myself that romantic woes or wonderful events would ever be my lot; but I was not confined to my own identity, and I could people the hours with creations far more interesting to me at that age than my own sensations.

After this my life became busier, and reality stood in place of fiction. My husband, however, was from the first very anxious that I should prove myself worthy of my parentage and enrol myself on the page of fame. He was forever inciting me to obtain literary reputation, which even on my own part I cared for then, though since I have become infinitely indifferent to it. At this time he desired that I should write, not so much with the idea that I could produce anything worthy of notice, but that he might himself judge how far I possessed the promise of better things hereafter. Still I did nothing. Travelling, and the cares of a family, occupied my time; and study, in the way of reading or improving my ideas in communication with his far more cultivated mind was all of literary employment that engaged my attention.

In the summer of 1816 we visited Switzerland and became the neighbours of Lord Byron. At first we spent our pleasant hours on the lake or wandering on its shores; and Lord Byron, who was writing the third canto of *Childe Harold*, was the only one among us who put his thoughts upon paper. These, as he brought them successively to us, clothed in all the light and harmony of poetry, seemed to stamp as divine the glories of heaven and earth, whose influences we partook with him.

But it proved a wet, ungenial summer, and incessant rain often confined us for days to the house. Some volumes of ghost stories translated from the German into French fell into our hands. There was the *History of the Inconstant Lover*, who, when he thought to clasp the bride to whom he had pledged his vows, found himself in the arms of the pale ghost of her whom he had deserted. There was the tale of the sinful founder of his race whose miserable doom it was to bestow the kiss of death on all the younger sons of his fated house, just when they reached the age of promise. His gigantic, shadowy form, clothed like the ghost in *Hamlet*, in complete armour, but with the beaver up, was seen at midnight, by the moon's fitful beams, to advance slowly along the gloomy avenue. The shape was lost beneath the shadow of the castle walls; but soon a gate swung back, a step was heard, the door of the chamber opened, and he advanced to the couch of the blooming youths, cradled in healthy sleep. Eternal sorrow sat upon his face as he bent down and kissed the forehead of the boys, who from that hour withered like flowers snapped upon the stalk. I have not seen these stories since then, but their incidents are as fresh in my mind as if I had read them yesterday.

"We will each write a ghost story," said Lord Byron, and his proposition was acceded to. There were four of us. The noble author began a tale, a fragment of which he printed at the end of his poem of Mazeppa. Shelley, more apt to embody ideas and sentiments in the radiance of brilliant imagery and in the music of the most melodious verse that adorns our language than to invent the machinery of a story, commenced one founded on the experiences of his early life. Poor Polidori had some terrible idea about a skull-headed lady who was so punished for peeping through a key-hole—what to see I forget: something very shocking and wrong of course; but when she was reduced to a worse condition than the renowned Tom of Coventry, he did not know what to do with her and was obliged to dispatch her to the tomb of the Capulets, the only place for which she was fitted. The illustrious poets also, annoyed by the platitude of prose, speedily relinquished their uncongenial task.

I busied myself *to think of a story*—a story to rival those which had excited us to this task. One which would speak to the mysterious fears of our nature and awaken thrilling horror—one to make the reader dread to look round, to curdle the blood, and quicken the beatings of the heart. If I did not accomplish these things, my ghost story would be unworthy of its name. I thought and pondered—vainly. I felt that blank incapability of invention which is the greatest misery of authorship, when dull Nothing replies to our anxious invocations. "Have you thought of a story?" I was asked each morning, and each morning I was forced to reply with a mortifying negative.

Everything must have a beginning, to speak in Sanchean phrase; and that beginning must be linked to something that went before. The Hindus give the world an elephant to support it, but they make the elephant stand upon a tortoise. Invention, it must be humbly admitted, does not consist in creating

out of void, but out of chaos; the materials must, in the first place, be afforded: it can give form to dark, shapeless substances but cannot bring into
being the substance itself. In all matters of discovery and invention, even of
those that appertain to the imagination, we are continually reminded of the
story of Columbus and his egg. Invention consists in the capacity of seizing
on the capabilities of a subject and in the power of moulding and fashioning
ideas suggested to it.

Many and long were the conversations between Lord Byron and Shelley
to which I was a devout but nearly silent listener. During one of these, various philosophical doctrines were discussed, and among others the nature of
the principle of life, and whether there was any probability of its ever being
discovered and communicated. They talked of the experiments of Dr. Darwin (I speak not of what the doctor really did or said that he did, but, as more
to my purpose, of what was then spoken of as having been done by him), who
preserved a piece of vermicelli in a glass case till by some extraordinary
means it began to move with voluntary motion. Not thus, after all, would life
be given. Perhaps a corpse would be reanimated; galvanism had given token
of such things: perhaps the component parts of a creature might be manu-
factured, brought together, and endued with vital warmth.

Night waned upon this talk, and even the witching hour had gone by before we retired to rest. When I placed my head on my pillow I did not sleep,
nor could I be said to think. My imagination, unbidden, possessed and guided
me, gifting the successive images that arose in my mind with a vividness far
beyond the usual bounds of reverie. I saw—with shut eyes, but acute mental
vision—I saw the pale student of unhallowed arts kneeling beside the thing
he had put together. I saw the hideous phantasm of a man stretched out, and
then, on the working of some powerful engine, show signs of life and stir with
an uneasy, half-vital motion. Frightful must it be, for supremely frightful
would be the effect of any human endeavour to mock the stupendous mechanism of the Creator of the world. His success would terrify the artist; he
would rush away from his odious handiwork, horror-stricken. He would hope
that, left to itself, the slight spark of life which he had communicated would
fade, that this thing which had received such imperfect animation would sub-
side into dead matter, and he might sleep in the belief that the silence of the
grave would quench forever the transient existence of the hideous corpse
which he had looked upon as the cradle of life. He sleeps; but he is awakened; he opens his eyes; behold, the horrid thing stands at his bedside, opening his curtains and looking on him with yellow, watery, but speculative eyes.

I opened mine in terror. The idea so possessed my mind that a thrill of fear ran through me, and I wished to exchange the ghastly image of my fancy for the realities around. I see them still: the very room, the dark parquet, the closed shutters with the moonlight struggling through, and the sense I had that the glassy lake and white high Alps were beyond. I could not so easily get rid of my hideous phantom; still it haunted me. I must try to think of something else. I recurred to my ghost story—my tiresome, unlucky ghost story! Oh! If I could only contrive one which would frighten my reader as I myself had been frightened that night!

Swift as light and as cheering was the idea that broke in upon me. "I have found it! What terrified me will terrify others; and I need only describe the spectre which had haunted my midnight pillow." On the morrow I announced that I had *thought of a story*. I began that day with the words "It was on a dreary night of November," making only a transcript of the grim terrors of my waking dream.

At first I thought but of a few pages, of a short tale, but Shelley urged me to develop the idea at greater length. I certainly did not owe the suggestion of one incident, nor scarcely of one train of feeling, to my husband, and yet but for his incitement it would never have taken the form in which it was presented to the world. From this declaration I must except the preface. As far as I can recollect, it was entirely written by him.

And now, once again, I bid my hideous progeny go forth and prosper. I have an affection for it, for it was the offspring of happy days, when death and grief were but words which found no true echo in my heart. Its several pages speak of many a walk, many a drive, and many a conversation, when I was not alone; and my companion was one who, in this world, I shall never see more. But this is for myself; my readers have nothing to do with these associations.

I will add but one word as to the alterations I have made. They are principally those of style. I have changed no portion of the story nor introduced any new ideas or circumstances. I have mended the language where it was so bald as to interfere with the interest of the narrative; and these changes occur almost exclusively in the beginning of the first volume. Throughout they are entirely confined to such parts as are mere adjuncts to the story, leaving the core and substance of it untouched.

London, October 15, 1831

14.

first years

CARL G. JUNG

Psychologist Carl Gustav Jung describes one of those epiphanies in which suddenly the meaning of things becomes startlingly clear, and the mind is opened in a trice. The illumination occurred in Jung's early childhood, and it was his "first conscious trauma." Young Carl was engrossed in playing in the sand when, looking up, he saw a figure. . . . It is a story of fear, growing to terror, and indicative of the fact the opening of the mind is sometimes frightening. It was a "big dream," as Jung was later to call those dreams in which, to use his terminology, the archetypes acting in one's life come together and the collective unconscious presses into consciousness. Such archetypal manifestations are often the stimulus to creative development in the self, as this one was for the great Swiss psychiatrist. The theme of this dream was to occupy him for the rest of his life.

One hot summer day I was sitting alone, as usual, on the road in front of the house, playing in the sand. The road led past the house up a hill, then disappeared in the wood on the hilltop. So from the house you could see a stretch of the road. Looking up, I saw a figure in a strangely broad hat and a long black garment coming down from the wood. It looked like a man wearing women's clothes. Slowly the figure drew nearer, and I could now see that it really was a man wearing a kind of black robe that reached to his feet. At the sight of him I was overcome with fear, which rapidly grew into deadly terror as the frightful recognition shot through my mind: "That is a Jesuit." Shortly before, I had overheard a conversation between my father and a visiting colleague concerning the nefarious activities of the Jesuits. From the half-irritated, half-fearful tone of my father's remarks I gathered that "Jesuits" meant something specially dangerous, even for my father. Actually I had no idea what Jesuits were, but I was familiar with the word "Jesus" from my little prayer.

The man coming down the road must be in disguise, I thought; that was why he wore women's clothes. Probably he had evil intentions. Terrified, I ran helter-skelter into the house, rushed up the stairs, and hid under a beam in the darkest corner of the attic. I don't know how long I remained there, but it must have been a fairly long time, because, when I ventured down again to the first floor and cautiously stuck my head out of the window, far and wide there was not a trace of the black figure to be seen. For days afterward the hellish fright clung to my limbs and kept me in the house. And even when I began to play in the road again, the wooded hilltop was still the object of my uneasy vigilance. Later I realized, of course, that the black figure was a harmless Catholic priest.

At about the same time—I could not say with absolute certainty whether it preceded this experience or not—I had the earliest dream I can remember, a dream which was to preoccupy me all my life. I was then between three and four years old.

The vicarage stood quite alone near Laufen castle, and there was a big meadow stretching back from the sexton's farm. In the dream I was in this meadow. Suddenly I discovered a dark, rectangular, stone-lined hole in the ground. I had never seen it before. I ran forward curiously and peered down into it. Then I saw a stone stairway leading down. Hesitantly and fearfully, I descended. At the bottom was a doorway with a round arch, closed off by a green curtain. It was a big, heavy curtain of worked stuff like brocade, and it looked very sumptuous. Curious to see what might be hidden behind, I pushed it aside. I saw before me in the dim light a rectangular chamber about thirty feet long. The ceiling was arched and of hewn stone. The floor was laid with flagstones, and in the center a red carpet ran from the entrance to a low platform. On this platform stood a wonderfully rich golden throne. I am not certain, but perhaps a red cushion lay on the seat. It was a magnificent throne, a real king's throne in a fairy tale. Something was standing on it which I thought at first was a tree trunk twelve to fifteen feet high and about one and a half to two feet thick. It was a huge thing, reaching almost to the ceiling. But it was of a curious composition: it was made of skin and naked flesh, and on top there was something like a rounded head with no face and no hair. On the very top of the head was a single eye, gazing motionlessly upward.

It was fairly light in the room, although there were no windows and no apparent source of light. Above the head, however, was an aura of brightness. The thing did not move, yet I had the feeling that it might at any moment crawl off the throne like a worm and creep toward me. I was paralyzed with terror. At that moment I heard from outside and above me my mother's voice. She called out, "Yes, just look at him. That is the man-eater!" That intensified my terror still more, and I awoke sweating and scared to death. For many nights afterward I was afraid to go to sleep, because I feared I might have another dream like that.

This dream haunted me for years. Only much later did I realize that what I had seen was a phallus, and it was decades before I understood that it was a ritual phallus. I could never make out whether my mother meant, "*That* is the man-eater," or, "That is the *man-eater*." In the first case she would have meant that not Lord Jesus or the Jesuit was the devourer of little children, but the phallus; in the second case that the "man-eater" in general was symbolized by the phallus, so that the dark Lord Jesus, the Jesuit, and the phallus were identical.

The abstract significance of the phallus is shown by the fact that it was enthroned by itself, "ithyphallically" (ἰθύς, upright). The hole in the meadow probably represented a grave. The grave itself was an underground temple whose green curtain symbolized the *meadow*, in other words the mystery of Earth with her covering of green vegetation. The carpet was *blood-red*. What about the vault? Perhaps I had already been to the Munôt, the citadel of Schaffhausen? This is not likely, since no one would take a three-year-old child up there. So it cannot be a memory-trace. Equally, I do not know where the anatomically correct phallus can have come from. The interpretation of the *orificium urethrae* as an eye, the source of light apparently above it, points to the etymology of the word phallus (φαλός, shining, bright).

At all events, the phallus of this dream seems to be a subterranean God "not to be named," and such it remained throughout my youth, reappearing whenever anyone spoke too emphatically about Lord Jesus. Lord Jesus never became quite real for me, never quite acceptable, never quite lovable, for again and again I would think of his underground counterpart, a frightful revelation which had been accorded me without my seeking it. The Jesuit's "disguise" cast its shadow over the Christian doctrine I had been taught. Often it seemed to me a solemn masquerade, a kind of funeral at which the mourners put on serious or mournful faces but the next moment were secretly laughing and not really sad at all. Lord Jesus seemed to me in some ways a god of death, helpful, it is true, in that he scared away the terrors of the night, but himself uncanny, a crucified and bloody corpse. Secretly, his love and kindness, which I always heard praised, appeared doubtful to me, chiefly because the people who talked most about "dear Lord Jesus" wore black frock coats and shiny black boots which reminded me of burials. They were my father's colleagues as well as eight of my uncles—all parsons. For many years they inspired fear in me—not to speak of occasional Catholic priests who reminded me of the terrifying Jesuit who had irritated and even alarmed my father. In later years and until my confirmation, I made every effort to force myself to take the required positive attitude to Christ. But I could never succeed in overcoming my secret distrust.

The fear of the "black man," which is felt by every child, was not the essential thing in that experience; it was, rather, the recognition that stabbed through my childish brain: "That is a Jesuit." So the important thing in the dream was its remarkable symbolic setting and the astounding interpretation: "That is the man-eater." Not the child's ogre of a man-eater, but the fact that *this* was the man-eater, and that *it* was sitting on a golden throne beneath the earth. For my childish imagination it was first of all the king who sat on a golden throne; then, on a much more beautiful and much higher and much more golden throne far, far away in the blue sky, sat God and Lord Jesus, with golden crowns and white robes. Yet from this same Lord Jesus came the "Jesuit," in black women's garb, with a broad black hat, down from the wooded hill. I had to glance up there every so often to see whether another danger might not be approaching. In the dream I went down into the hole in the earth and found something very different on a golden throne, something non-human and underworldly, which gazed fixedly upward and fed on human flesh. It was only fifty years later that a passage in a study of religious ritual burned into my eyes, concerning the motif of cannibalism that underlies the symbolism of the Mass. Only then did it become clear to me how exceedingly unchildlike, how sophisticated and oversophisticated was the thought that had begun to break through into consciousness in those two experiences. Who was it speaking in me? Whose mind had devised them? What kind of superior intelligence was at work? I know every numbskull will babble on about "black man," "man-eater," "chance," and "retrospective interpretation," in order to banish something terribly inconvenient that might sully the familiar picture of childhood innocence. Ah, these good, efficient, healthy-minded people, they always remind me of those optimistic tadpoles who bask in a puddle in the sun, in the shallowest of waters, crowding together and amiably wriggling their tails, totally unaware that the next morning the puddle will have dried up and left them stranded.

Who spoke to me then? Who talked of problems far beyond my knowledge? Who brought the Above and Below together, and laid the foundation for everything that was to fill the second half of my life with stormiest passion? Who but that alien guest who came both from above and from below?

Through this childhood dream I was initiated into the secrets of the earth. What happened then was a kind of burial in the earth, and many years were to pass before I came out again. Today I know that it happened in order to bring the greatest possible amount of light into the darkness. It was an initiation into the realm of darkness. My intellectual life had its unconscious beginnings at that time.

15.

visibility

ITALO CALVINO

The Italian novelist Italo Calvino discusses the value of visibility, and outlines two sources of imaginative inspiration. Reminiscing about his own childhood, when he looked at the comics he was not yet able to read, Calvino ponders the fate of imagination in a postmodern "civilization of images" and describes the transformation of images into words, and words into images.

Where do they come from, these images that rain down into the fantasy? Dante, justifiably, had a high opinion of himself, to the point of having no scruples about proclaiming the direct divine inspiration of his visions. Writers closer to us in time (with the exception of those few cases of prophetic vocation) establish their contacts through earthly transmitters, such as the individual or the collective unconscious; the time regained in feelings that reemerges from time lost; or "epiphanies," concentrations of being in a single spot or point of time. In short, it is a question of processes that, even if they do not originate in the heavens, certainly go beyond our intentions and our control, acquiring—with respect to the individual—a kind of transcendence.

Nor is it only poets and novelists who deal with this problem. A specialist on the nature of intelligence, Douglas Hofstadter, does a similar thing in his famous book *Gödel, Escher, Bach,* in which the real problem is the choice between various images that have rained down into the fantasy:

> Think, for instance, of a writer who is trying to convey certain ideas which to him are contained in mental images. He isn't quite sure how those images fit together in his mind, and he experiments around, expressing things first one way and then another, and finally settles on some version. But does he know where it all came from? Only in a vague sense. Much of the source, like an iceberg, is deep underwater, unseen—and he knows that. (Vintage edition, 1980, p. 713)

But perhaps we should first take a look at how this problem has been posed in the past. The most exhaustive, comprehensive, and clear history of the idea of imagination I have found is an essay by Jean Starobinski, "The Empire of the Imaginary" (included in the volume *La relation critique*, 1970). From the Renaissance magic of the neo-Platonists originates the idea of the imagination as a communication with the world soul, an idea that was to re-cur in romanticism and surrealism. This notion contrasts with that of the imagination as an instrument of knowledge, according to which the imagi-nation, while following channels other than those of scientific knowledge, can coexist with the latter and even assist it, indeed be a phase the scientist needs in order to formulate his hypotheses. On the other hand, theories of the imagination as a depository of the truths of the universe can agree with a *Naturphilosophie* or with a kind of theosophical knowledge, but are incom-patible with scientific knowledge—unless we divide what can be known into two parts, leaving the external world to science and isolating imaginative knowledge in the inner self of the individual. It is this second attitude that Starobinski recognizes as the method of Freudian analysis, while Jung's method, which bestows universal validity on archetypes and the collective unconscious, is linked to the idea of imagination as participation in the truth of the world.

At this point, there is a question I cannot evade: in which of the two ten-dencies outlined by Starobinski would I place my own idea of the imagina-tion? To answer that question I am forced to look back at my own experience as a writer, and especially at the part that has to do with "fantastic" narrative writing. When I began to write fantastic stories, I did not yet consider theo-retical questions; the only thing I knew was that there was a visual image at the source of all my stories. One of these images was a man cut in two halves, each of which went on living independently. Another example was a boy who climbs a tree and then makes his way from tree to tree without ever coming down to earth. Yet another was an empty suit of armor that moves and speaks as if someone were inside.

In devising a story, therefore, the first thing that comes to my mind is an image that for some reason strikes me as charged with meaning, even if I can-not formulate this meaning in discursive or conceptual terms. As soon as the image has become sufficiently clear in my mind, I set about developing it into a story; or better yet, it is the images themselves that develop their own implicit potentialities, the story they carry within them. Around each image others come into being, forming a field of analogies, symmetries, confronta-tions. Into the organization of this material, which is no longer purely visual but also conceptual, there now enters my deliberate intent to give order and sense to the development of the story; or rather, what I do is try to establish which meanings might be compatible with the overall design I wish to give the story and which meanings are not compatible, always leaving a certain margin of possible alternatives. At the same time, the writing, the verbal product, acquires increasing importance. I would say that from the moment I start putting black on white, what really matters is the written word, first as a search for an equivalent of the visual image, then as a coherent development of the initial stylistic direction. Finally, the written word little by little comes to dominate the field. From now on it will be the writing that guides the story toward the most felicitous verbal expression, and the visual imagination has no choice but to tag along.

In *Cosmicomics* (1965) the procedure was a little different, since the point of departure was a statement taken from the language of science; the independent play of the visual images had to arise from this conceptual statement. My aim was to show that writing using images typical of myth can grow from any soil, even from language farthest away from any visual image, as the language of science is today. Even in reading the most technical scientific book or the most abstract book of philosophy, one can come across a phrase that unexpectedly stimulates the visual imagination. We are therefore in one of those situations where the image is determined by a preexistent written text (a page or a single sentence that I come across in my reading), and from this may spring an imaginative process that might either be in the spirit of the text or go off in a direction all its own.

The first cosmicomic I wrote, "The Distance of the Moon," is possibly the most "surrealistic," in the sense that the impulse, derived from gravitational physics, leaves the door open to a dreamlike fantasy. In other cosmicomics the plot is guided by an idea more in keeping with the scientific point of departure, but always clad in a shell of imagination and feeling, and spoken by either one voice or two. In short, my procedure aims at uniting the spontaneous generation of images and the intentionality of discursive thought. Even when the opening gambit is played by the visual imagination, putting its own intrinsic logic to work, it finds itself sooner or later caught in a web where reasoning and verbal expression also impose their logic. Yet the visual solutions continue to be determining factors and sometimes unexpectedly come to decide situations that neither the conjectures of thought nor the resources of language would be capable of resolving.

One point to be cleared up about anthropomorphism in *Cosmicomics*: although science interests me just because of its efforts to escape from anthropomorphic knowledge, I am nonetheless convinced that our imagination cannot be anything *but* anthropomorphic. This is the reason for my anthropomorphic treatment of a universe in which man has never existed, and I would add that it seems extremely unlikely that man could ever exist in such a universe.

The time has come for me to answer the question I put to myself regarding Starobinski's two modes of thought: imagination as an instrument of knowledge or as identification with the world soul. Which do I choose? From what I have said, I ought to be a determined supporter of the first tendency, since for me the story is the union of a spontaneous logic of images and a plan carried out on the basis of a rational intention. But, at the same time, I have always sought out in the imagination a means to attain a knowledge that is outside the individual, outside the subjective. It is right, then, for me to declare myself closer to the second position, that of identification with the world soul.

Still there is another definition in which I recognize myself fully, and that is the imagination as a repertory of what is potential, what is hypothetical, of what does not exist and has never existed, and perhaps will never exist but might have existed. In Starobinski's treatment of the subject, this comes up when he mentions Giordano Bruno. According to Bruno, the *spiritus phantasticus* is "mundus quidem et sinus inexplebilis formarum et specierum," that is, a world or a gulf, never saturable, of forms and images. So, then, I believe that to draw on this gulf of potential multiplicity is indispensable to any form of knowledge. The poet's mind, and at a few decisive moments the mind of the scientist, works according to a process of association of images that is the quickest way to link and to choose between the infinite forms of the possible and the impossible. The imagination is a kind of electronic machine that takes account of all possible combinations and chooses the ones that are appropriate to a particular purpose, or are simply the most interesting, pleasing, or amusing.

I have yet to explain what part the *indirect* imaginary has in this gulf of the fantastic, by which I mean the images supplied by culture, whether this be mass culture or any other kind of tradition. This leads to another question: What will be the future of the individual imagination in what is usually called the "civilization of the image"? Will the power of evoking images of things that are *not there* continue to develop in a human race increasingly inundated by a flood of prefabricated images? At one time the visual memory of an individual was limited to the heritage of his direct experiences and to a restricted repertory of images reflected in culture. The possibility of giving form to personal myths arose from the way in which the fragments of this memory came together in unexpected and evocative combinations. We are bombarded today by such a quantity of images that we can no longer distinguish direct experience from what we have seen for a few seconds on television. The memory is littered with bits and pieces of images, like a rubbish dump, and it is more and more unlikely that any one form among so many will succeed in standing out.

If I have included visibility in my list of values to be saved, it is to give warning of the danger we run in losing a basic human faculty: the power of bringing visions into focus with our eyes shut, of bringing forth forms and colors from the lines of black letters on a white page, and in fact of *thinking* in terms of images. I have in mind some possible pedagogy of the imagination that would accustom us to control our own inner vision without suffocating it or letting it fall, on the other hand, into confused, ephemeral daydreams, but would enable the images to crystallize into a well-defined, memorable, and self-sufficient form, the *icastic* form.

This is of course a kind of pedagogy that we can only exercise upon ourselves, according to methods invented for the occasion and with unpredictable results. In my own early development, I was already a child of the "civilization of images," even if this was still in its infancy and a far cry from the inflations of today. Let us say that I am a product of an intermediate period, when the colored illustrations that were our childhood companions, in books, weekly magazines, and toys, were very important to us. I think that being born during that period made a profound mark on my development. My imaginary world was first influenced by the illustrations in the *Corriere dei piccoli*, the most widely circulated weekly for children. I am speaking of my life between three and thirteen years of age, before a passion for the cinema became an absolute obsession, one that lasted all through my adolescence. In fact I believe that the really vital time was between three and six, before I learned to read.

In Italy in the twenties the *Corriere dei piccoli* used to publish the best-known American comic strips of the time: Happy Hooligan, the Katzenjammer Kids, Felix the Cat, Maggie and Jiggs, all of them rebaptized with Italian names. And there were also Italian comic strips, some of them of excellent quality, according to the graphic taste and style of the period. In Italy they had not yet started to use balloons for dialogue (these began in the thirties with the importation of Mickey Mouse). The *Corriere dei piccoli* redrew the American cartoons without balloons, replacing them with two or four rhymed lines under each cartoon. However, being unable to read, I could easily dispense with the words—the pictures were enough. I used to live with this little magazine, which my mother had begun buying and collecting even before I was born and had bound into volumes year by year. I would spend hours following the cartoons of each series from one issue to another, while in my mind I told myself the stories, interpreting the scenes in different ways—I produced variants, put together the single episodes into a story of broader scope, thought out and isolated and then connected the recurring elements in each series, mixing up one series with another, and invented new series in which the secondary characters became protagonists.

When I learned to read, the advantage I gained was minimal. Those simple-minded rhyming couplets provided no illuminating information; often they were stabs in the dark like my own, and it was evident that the rhymster had no idea of what might have been in the balloons of the original, either because he did not understand English or because he was working from cartoons that had already been redrawn and rendered wordless. In any case, I preferred to ignore the written lines and to continue with my favorite occupation of daydreaming *within* the pictures and their sequence.

This habit undeniably caused a delay in my ability to concentrate on the written word, and I acquired the attention needed for reading only at a later stage and with effort. But reading the pictures without words was certainly a schooling in fable-making, in stylization, in the composition of the image. For example, the elegant way in which Pat O'Sullivan could draw the background in a little, square cartoon showing the black silhouette of Felix the Cat on a road that lost itself in a landscape beneath a full moon in a black sky: I think that has remained an ideal for me.

The work I did later in life, extracting stories from the mysterious figures of the tarot and interpreting the same figure in a different way each time, certainly had its roots in my obsessive porings over pages and page of cartoons when I was a child. What I was trying to do in *The Castle of Crossed Destinies* (*Il castello dei destini incrociati*) is a kind of "fantastic iconology," not only with the tarot but also with great paintings. In fact I attempted to interpret the paintings of Carpaccio in San Giorgio degli Schiavoni in Venice, following the cycles of St. George and St. Jerome as if they were one story, the life of a single person, and to identify my own life with that of this George-Jerome. This fantastic iconology has become my habitual way of expressing my love of painting. I have adopted the method of telling my own stories, starting from pictures famous in the history of art or at any rate pictures that have made an impact on me.

Let us say that various elements concur in forming the visual part of the literary imagination: direct observation of the real world, phantasmic and oneiric transfiguration, the figurative world as it is transmitted by culture at its various levels, and a process of abstraction, condensation, and interiorization of sense experience, a matter of prime importance to both the visualization and the verbalization of thought. All these features are to some extent to be found in the authors I acknowledge as models, above all at those times particularly favorable to the visual imagination—that is, in the literatures of the Renaissance, the Baroque, and the Romantic age. In an anthology that I compiled of nineteenth-century fantastic tales, I followed the visionary and spectacular vein that pulses in the stories of Hoffmann, Chamisso, Arnim, Eichendorff, Potocki, Gogol, Nerval, Gautier, Hawthorne, Poe, Dickens, Turgenev, Leskov, and continues down to Stevenson, Kipling, and Wells. And along with this I followed another, sometimes in the very same authors: the vein that makes fantastic events spring from the everyday—an inner, mental, invisible fantasy, culminating in Henry James.

Will the literature of the fantastic be possible in the twenty-first century, with the growing inflation of prefabricated images? Two paths seem to be open from now on. (1) We could recycle used images in a new context that changes their meaning. Postmodernism may be seen as the tendency to make ironic use of the stock images of the mass media, or to inject the taste for the marvelous inherited from literary tradition into narrative mechanisms that accentuate its alienation. (2) We could wipe the slate clean and start from scratch. Samuel Beckett has obtained the most extraordinary results by reducing visual and linguistic elements to a minimum, as if in a world after the end of the world.

16.

The order
of Things

MICHEL FOUCAULT

French philosopher Michel Foucault remembers bursting out with laughter at the impossible categorization of animals that Jorge Luis Borges claims to have found in a Chinese encyclopedia. "Impossible by whose standards?" asks Foucault, who then embarks on a long meditation about the way we in the West have structured and categorized our world, and given order to our things. Foucault is breaking out of mental categories as a way of taking a fresh look at the world, not only uncovering in the process cultural and mental habits, but also asking the question: "Says who?"

This book first arose out of a passage in Borges, out of the laughter that shattered, as I read the passage, all the familiar landmarks of my thought—*our* thought, the thought that bears the stamp of our age and our geography—breaking up all the ordered surfaces and all the planes with which we are accustomed to tame the wild profusion of existing things, and continuing long afterwards to disturb and threaten with collapse our age-old distinction between the Same and the Other. This passage quotes a "certain Chinese encyclopaedia" in which it is written that "animals are divided into: (a) belonging to the Emperor, (b) embalmed, (c) tame, (d) sucking pigs, (e) sirens, (f) fabulous, (g) stray dogs, (h) included in the present classification, (i) frenzied, (j) innumerable, (k) drawn with a very fine camelhair brush, (l) *et cetera*, (m) having just broken the water pitcher, (n) that from a long way off look like flies." In the wonderment of this taxonomy, the thing we apprehend in one great leap, the thing that, by means of the fable, is demonstrated as the exotic charm of another system of thought, is the limitation of our own, the stark impossibility of thinking *that*.

But what is it impossible to think, and what kind of impossibility are we faced with here? Each of these strange categories can be assigned a precise meaning and a demonstrable content; some of them do certainly involve fantastic entities—fabulous animals or sirens—but, precisely because it puts them into categories of their own, the Chinese encyclopaedia localizes their powers of contagion; it distinguishes carefully between the very real animals (those that are frenzied or have just broken the water pitcher) and those that reside solely in the realm of imagination. The possibility of dangerous mixtures has been exorcized, heraldry and fable have been relegated to their own exalted peaks: no inconceivable amphibious maidens, no clawed wings, no disgusting, squamous epidermis, none of those polymorphous and demoniacal faces, no creatures breathing fire. The quality of monstrosity here does not affect any real body, nor does it produce modifications of any kind in the bestiary of the imagination; it does not lurk in the depths of any strange power. It would not even be present at all in this classification had it not insinuated itself into the empty space, the interstitial blanks *separating* all these entities from one another. It is not the "fabulous" animals that are impossible, since they are designated as such, but the narrowness of the distance separating them from (and juxtaposing them to) the stray dogs, or the animals that from a long way off look like flies. What transgresses the boundaries of all imagination, of all possible thought, is simply that alphabetical series (a, b, c, d) which links each of those categories to all the others.

Moreover, it is not simply the oddity of unusual juxtapositions that we are faced with here. We are all familiar with the disconcerting effect of the proximity of extremes, or, quite simply, with the sudden vicinity of things that have no relation to each other; the mere act of enumeration that heaps them all together has a power of enchantment all its own: "I am no longer hungry," Eusthenes said. "Until the morrow, safe from my saliva all the following shall be: Aspics, Acalephs, Acanthocephalates, Amoebocytes, Ammonites, Axolotls, Amblystomas, Aphislions, Anacondas, Ascarids, Amphisbaenas, Angleworms, Amphipods, Anacrobes, Annelids, Anthozoans. . . ." But all these worms and snakes, all these creatures redolent of decay and slime are slithering, like the syllables which designate them, in Eusthenes' saliva: that is where they all have their *common locus*, like the umbrella and the sewing-machine on the operating table; startling though their propinquity may be, it is nevertheless warranted by that *and*, by that *in*, by that *on* whose solidity provides proof of the possibility of juxtaposition. It was certainly improbable that arachnids, ammonites, and annelids should one day mingle on Eusthenes' tongue, but, after all, that welcoming and voracious mouth certainly provided them with a feasible lodging, a roof under which to coexist.

The monstrous quality that runs through Borges's enumeration consists, on the contrary, in the fact that the common ground on which such meetings are possible has itself been destroyed. What is impossible is not the propinquity of the things listed, but the very site on which their propinquity would be possible. The animals "(i) frenzied, (j) innumerable, (k) drawn with a very fine camelhair brush"—where could they ever meet, except in the immaterial sound of the voice pronouncing their enumeration, or on the page transcribing it? Where else could they be juxtaposed except in the non-place of language? Yet, though language can spread them before us, it can do so only in an unthinkable space. The central category of animals "included in the present classification," with its explicit reference to paradoxes we are familiar with, is indication enough that we shall never succeed in defining a stable relation of contained to container between each of these categories and that which includes them all: if all the animals divided up here can be placed without exception in one of the divisions of this list, then aren't all the other divisions to be found in that one division too? And then again, in what space would that single, inclusive division have *its* existence? Absurdity destroys the *and* of the enumeration by making impossible the *in* where the things enumerated would be divided up. Borges adds no figure to the atlas of the impossible; nowhere does he strike the spark of poetic confrontation; he simply dispenses with the least obvious, but most compelling, of necessities; he does away with the *site*, the mute ground upon which it is possible for entities to be juxtaposed. A vanishing trick that is masked or, rather, laughably indicated by our alphabetical order, which is to be taken as the clue (the only visible one) to the enumerations of a Chinese encyclopaedia. . . . What has been removed, in short, is the famous "operating table"; and rendering to Roussel a small part of what is still his due, I use that world "table" in two superimposed senses: the nickel-plated, rubbery table swathed in white, glittering beneath a glass sun devouring all shadow—the table where, for an instant, perhaps forever, the umbrella encounters the sewing-machine; and also a table, a *tabula*, that enables thought to operate upon the entities of our world, to put them in order, to divide them into classes, to group them according to names that designate their similarities and their differences—the table upon which, since the beginning of time, language has intersected space.

That passage from Borges kept me laughing a long time, though not without a certain uneasiness that I found hard to shake off. Perhaps because there arose in its wake the suspicion that there is a worse kind of disorder than that of the *incongruous*, the linking together of things that are inappropriate; I mean the disorder in which fragments of a large number of possible orders glitter separately in the dimension, without law or geometry, of the *hetero-clite*; and that word should be taken in its most literal, etymological sense: in such a state, things are "laid," "placed," "arranged" in sites so very different from one another that it is impossible to find a place of residence for them, to define a *common locus* beneath them all. *Utopias* afford consolation: although they have no real locality there is nevertheless a fantastic, untroubled region in which they are able to unfold; they open up cities with vast avenues, superbly planted gardens, countries where life is easy, even though the road to them is chimerical. *Heterotopias* are disturbing, probably because they secretly undermine language, because they make it impossible to name this *and* that, because they shatter or tangle common names, because they destroy "syntax" in advance, and not only the syntax with which we construct sentences but also that less apparent syntax which causes words and things (next to and also opposite one another) to "hold together." This is why utopias permit fables and discourse: they run with the very grain of language and are part of the fundamental dimension of the *fabula*; heterotopias (such as those to be found so often in Borges) desiccate speech, stop words in their tracks, contest the very possibility of grammar at its source; they dissolve our myths and sterilize the lyricism of our sentences.

It appears that certain aphasiacs, when shown various differently coloured skeins of wool on a table top, are consistently unable to arrange them into any coherent pattern; as though that simple rectangle were unable to serve in their case as a homogeneous and neutral space in which things could be placed so as to display at the same time the continuous order of their identities or differences as well as the semantic field of their denomination. Within this simple space in which things are normally arranged and given names, the aphasiac will create a multiplicity of tiny, fragmented regions in which nameless resemblances agglutinate things into unconnected islets; in one corner, they will place the lightest-coloured skeins, in another the red ones, somewhere else those that are softest in texture, in yet another place the longest, or those that have a tinge of purple or those that have been wound up into a ball. But no sooner have they been adumbrated than all these groupings dissolve again, for the field of identity that sustains them, however limited it may be, is still too wide not to be unstable; and so the sick mind continues to infinity, creating groups then dispersing them again, heaping up diverse similarities, destroying those that seem clearest, splitting up things that are identical, superimposing different criteria, frenziedly beginning all over again, becoming more and more disturbed, and teetering finally on the brink of anxiety.

The uneasiness that makes us laugh when we read Borges is certainly related to the profound distress of those whose language has been destroyed: loss of what is "common" to place and name. Atopia, aphasia. Yet our text from Borges proceeds in another direction; the mythical homeland Borges assigns to that distortion of classification that prevents us from applying it, to that picture that lacks all spatial coherence, is a precise region whose name alone constitutes for the West a vast reservoir of utopias. In our dreamworld, is not China precisely this privileged *site* of *space?* In our traditional imagery, the Chinese culture is the most meticulous, the most rigidly ordered, the one most deaf to temporal events, most attached to the pure delineation of space; we think of it as a civilization of dikes and dams beneath the eternal face of the sky; we see it, spread and frozen, over the entire surface of a continent surrounded by walls. Even its writing does not reproduce the fugitive flight of the voice in horizontal lines; it erects the motionless and still recognizable images of things themselves in vertical columns. So much so that the Chinese encyclopaedia quoted by Borges, and the taxonomy it proposes, lead to a kind of thought without space, to words and categories that lack all life and place, but are rooted in a ceremonial space, overburdened with complex figures, with tangled paths, strange places, secret passages, and unexpected communications. There would appear to be, then, at the other extremity of the earth we inhabit, a culture entirely devoted to the ordering of space, but one that does not distribute the multiplicity of existing things into any of the categories that make it possible for us to name, speak, and think.

17.

The plunge
into colour

MARION MILNER

Learning to paint, or learning any art form, can be a journey into the self. Marion Milner, noted psychoanalyst and author, illustrates this point very clearly as she discusses the implications of her "plunge into colour," facing her apparent unwillingness to explore color. But encountering the nature of color, and the boundaries—or lack of them—between colors, leads Marion to question the very boundaries between self and not-self.

Colour in painting had been a subject which for years I had been quite unable to think about. It was as if it had been so important that to think about it, to know just what one was trying to do with one's paints, had been to risk losing something; it seemed at first glance as if an experience so intimate and vital must be kept remote and safe from the cold white light of consciousness which might destroy its glories. In fact it was as if colour and the light of knowing were differences which must be kept firmly separate, just as objects had to be kept separated and not seen in their mutual effect upon each other. So, up to now I had used paint blindly and the results had only on rare occasions been satisfactory.

When I did eventually arrive at trying to learn something about the deliberate use of colour it was again after attempting to follow instructions from the books. For instance, I read that in order to learn how to manage paint it was best to begin with a still-life; two objects were to be arranged against a simple background and to be drawn in a heavy line with brush and Indian ink. But when I had tried a still-life of this kind there was nothing in the result to suggest that it had been worth doing; and when, instead of trying to follow instructions, I set about observing what the eye liked, in the way of colour experiences, the result was a quite opposite conclusion about the way to use colour.

These observations about colour began when, on looking through some
earlier attempts at landscape, I noticed that the only glimmer of interest came
where there was a transition of colour; for instance, where the yellow lichen
on a barn roof had tempted me into letting the yellows and reds merge, un-
protected by any felt division, so that you could not say exactly where one
colour began and another ended. Also I noticed that a smear of paint left on
the palette after painting, where white merged into red, blue, brown, was interesting and alive; whereas the picture painted with the same colours but
carefully separated by felt lines was dead. And another hint had come from
looking at a roof painted with a tiny streak of blue in the shadow. There had
certainly been no blue in the colour of the actual roof; yet this touch of a
colour that was not there was the most vital thing in the picture. After noticing this fact I forgot it again; but some time later, having decided that the old
sketches were not worth preserving so they might as well be used for experiments, I had taken one of a church and had begun to repaint it, choosing the
colours without any thought of how the tower and trees and roof had looked
at that particular place on that particular day. When it was finished the light,
which in the original version had been an attempt to take into account the
actual position of the sun on an afternoon in August, now glowed up from the
ground at the foot of the church tower in a quite impossible manner, it spread
warm colours over the grey stone that had never been there at all. Then I had
tried freely painting over another sketch, one of a village with a haystack in
the foreground; and the result was that the original lamely copied yellow of
the haystack lit by pale September sun had become something on fire from
within with colour that spread up over the whole village.

In both these re-paintings the light seemed to come from the earth rather
than from the sky, and the colour also flooded up from the earth, once it was
let loose from bondage to natural appearance and outline.

Then I began to notice something else. Although finding it very difficult to
paint a whole picture I had for a long time been making mental notes of colour
impressions. One evening on a summer holiday, I had recalled the colour of
the grass-edge between stubble field and sea-shore, the mixed pale green and
creamy yellow of sunbleached August grass; and as I watched the memory of
the colour it had seemed to change and grow in vividness. After this, I had
tried to observe colour impressions more closely and make written notes.

How colours in nature alter when I shut my eyes; they seem to grow and
glow and develop. It looks as if colour ought to be very free to develop in
its own way from the first impression—and it needs time, willingness to

wait and see what it does. Yet in saying this I have a flicker of fear, fear of where it may go with no checks, no necessity to copy exactly the colour of the object as it seems at first sight. I think I have been trying to hold it down to a formula, painting a green tree green, with light and darker bits, yes, but essentially green—afraid to let other colours flow in—and yet the only exciting bits are when the colours are split, making a sort of chord so that they seem to move and live against each other—certainly the flat matching of colour to the object, saying "Is this green the same as that green of the tree?" produces a terribly dead effect.

This feeling of colour as something moving and alive in its own right, not fixed and flat and bound like the colouring of a map, grew gradually stronger. Again and again it happened that when I closed my eyes and tried to recall color combinations seen in nature, the memory did grow and glow and develop in the most surprising way. So here was a meeting of the conscious inner eye and the blind experience of colour which resulted from the willingness to watch and wait. And it was a meeting which neither destroyed the dark possibilities of colour nor dimmed the light of consciousness; in fact it produced a new and vital whole between them, and one which seemed to glow up from the depths of one's existence, like the light in my sketches which had flooded up from the earth. But in spite of this discovery I still found it very difficult to achieve this watching and waiting, part of my mind still wanted to keep colour firmly within boundaries and staying the same.

Here also were certainly two different ways of feeling about experience. One way had to do with a common sense world of objects separated by outline, keeping themselves to themselves and staying the same, the other had to do with a world of change, of continual development and process, one in which there was no sharp line between one state and the next, as there is no fixed boundary between twilight and darkness but only a gradual merging of the one into the other. But though I could know, in retrospect, that the changing world seemed nearer the true quality of experience, to give oneself to this knowledge seemed like taking some dangerous plunge; to part of my mind the changing world seemed near to a mad one and the fixed world the only sanity. And this idea of there being no fixed outline, no boundary between one state and another, also introduced the idea of no boundary between one self and another self, it brought in the idea of one personality merging with another. Here I could not help remembering what Cézanne is reported to have said about looking at a picture:

The part, the whole, the volumes, the values, the composition, the emotional quiver, everything, is there . . . Shut your eyes, wait, think of nothing. Now, open them . . . One sees nothing but a great coloured undulation. What then? An irradiation and glory of colour. That is what a picture should give us, a warm harmony, an abyss in which the eye is lost, a secret germination, a coloured state of grace. All these tones circulate in the blood, don't they? One is revivified, born into the real world, one finds oneself, one becomes the painting. To love a painting, one must first have drunk deeply of it in long draughts. Lose consciousness. Descend with the painter into the dim tangled roots of things, and rise again from them in colours, be steeped in the light of them.

(J. Gasquet, *Cézanne*)

This idea of the very eye which sees being lost, drowned in the flood of colour, sounded all right, as long as it was a coloured state of grace and one did rise again. But supposing one did not? And supposing that it was not a picture but a person that was loved like this? As yet I could not see very far along this way, but later it was to become clear that some of the foreboded dangers of this plunge into colour experience were to do with fears of embracing, becoming one with, something infinitely suffering, fears of plunging into a sea of pain in which both could become drowned. At present, however, I only knew that there was some unknown fear to be encountered in this matter of colour and the plunge into full imaginative experience of it.

Persistent following up of any clue to what the eye liked had then led to this: to having to face the fact of a warmth and a glow and a delight flooding up from within, dictated by no external copy but existing and developing and changing in its own right, as a result of one's own awareness of the developing relation between oneself and what one was looking at. But at the same time the dispensing with an external copy brought dangers of its own. Certainly it seemed that as long as one is content to live amongst the accepted realities of the common sense world, the fear of losing one's hold on the solid earth may remain unrecognized; but that as soon as one tries to use one's imagination, to see with the inner as well as with the outer eye, then it may have to be faced. I say "may" because obviously there are some people for whom ventures into the world of imagination are not beset with dangers, or, at least, not always. I remembered Bunyan's description of the valley of the Shadow of Death, how some saw in it:

. . . hobgoblins, satyrs, dragons of the pit.

While Faithful's report was that for him the sun had shone all the way.

18.

Evening over Sussex: Reflections in a Motor Car

VIRGINIA WOOLF

British novelist Virginia Woolf describes her experience of an evening in Sussex and relates it to her need as an artist to express and interpret experience. In a psychologically very sophisticated way, Woolf describes the splitting of many selves— observers, critics, and thinkers within herself, all attempting to get a handle on experience. As she finally orchestrates this plurality of selves, Woolf comes to rest in the simple experience of her own body.

Evening is kind to Sussex, for Sussex is no longer young, and she is grateful for the veil of evening as an elderly woman is glad when a shade is drawn over a lamp, and only the outline of her face remains. The outline of Sussex is still very fine. The cliffs stand out to sea, one behind another. All Eastbourne, all Bexhill, all St. Leonards, their parades and their lodging houses, their bead shops and their sweet shops and their placards and their invalids and *chars-à-bancs,** are all obliterated. What remains is what there was when William came over from France ten centuries ago: a line of cliffs running out to sea. Also the fields are redeemed. The freckle of red villas on the coast is washed over by a thin lucid lake of brown air, in which they and their redness are drowned. It was still too early for lamps; and too early for stars.

But, I thought, there is always some sediment of irritation when the moment is as beautiful as it is now. The psychologists must explain; one looks up, one is overcome by beauty extravagantly greater than one could expect— there are now pink clouds over Battle; the fields are mottled, marbled—one's

---

*Horse carriages.

perceptions blow out rapidly like air balls expanded by some rush of air, and then, when all seems blown to its fullest and tautest, with beauty and beauty and beauty, a pin pricks; it collapses. But what is the pin? So far as I could tell, the pin had something to do with one's own impotency. I cannot hold this— I cannot express this—I am overcome by it—I am mastered. Somewhere in that region one's discontent lay; and it was allied with the idea that one's nature demands mastery over all that is receives; and mastery here meant the power to convey what one saw now over Sussex so that another person could share it. And further, there was another prick of the pin: one was wasting one's chance; for beauty spread at one's right hand, at one's left; at one's back too; it was escaping all the time; one could only offer a thimble to a torrent that could fill baths, lakes.

But relinquish, I said (it is well known how in circumstances like these the self splits up and one self is eager and dissatisfied and the other stern and philosophical), relinquish these impossible aspirations; be content with the view in front of us, and believe me when I tell you that it is best to sit and soak; to be passive; to accept; and do not bother because nature has given you six little pocket knives with which to cut up the body of a whale.

While these two selves then held a colloquy about the wise course to adopt in the presence of beauty, I (a third party now declared itself) said to myself, how happy they were to enjoy so simple an occupation. There they sat as the car sped along, noticing everything: a hay stack; a rust red roof; a pond; an old man coming home with his sack on his back; there they sat, matching every colour in the sky and earth from their colour box, rigging up little models of Sussex barns and farmhouses in the red light that would serve in the January gloom. But I, being somewhat different, sat aloof and melancholy. While they are thus busied, I said to myself: Gone, gone; over, over; past and done with, past and done with. I feel life left behind even as the road is left behind. We have been over that stretch, and are already forgotten. There, windows were lit by our lamps for a second; the light is out now. Others come behind us.

Then suddenly a fourth self (a self which lies in ambush, apparently dormant, and jumps upon one unawares. Its remarks are often entirely disconnected with what has been happening, but must be attended to because of their very abruptness) said: "Look at that." It was a light; brilliant, freakish; inexplicable. For a second I was unable to name it. "A star"; and for that second it held its odd flicker of unexpectedness and danced and beamed. "I take your meaning," I said. "You, erratic and impulsive self that you are, feel that the light over the downs there emerging, dangles from the future. Let us try to understand this. Let us reason it out. I feel suddenly attached not to the past but to the future. I think of Sussex in five hundred years to come. I think much grossness will have evaporated. Things will have been scorched up, eliminated. There will be magic gates. Draughts fan-blown by electric power will cleanse houses. Lights intense and firmly directed will go over the earth, doing the work. Look at the moving light in that hill; it is the headlight of a car. By day and by night Sussex in five centuries will be full of charming thoughts, quick, effective beams."

The sun was now low beneath the horizon. Darkness spread rapidly. None of my selves could see anything beyond the tapering light of our headlamps on the hedge. I summoned them together. "Now," I said, "comes the season of making up our accounts. Now we have got to collect ourselves; we have got to be one self. Nothing is to be seen any more, except one wedge of road and bank which our lights repeat incessantly. We are perfectly provided for. We are warmly wrapped in a rug; we are protected from wind and rain. We are alone. Now is the time of reckoning. Now I, who preside over the company, am going to arrange in order the trophies which we have all brought in. Let me see; there was a great deal of beauty brought in to-day: farmhouses; cliffs standing out to sea; marbled fields; mottled fields; red feathered skies; all that. Also there was disappearance and the death of the individual. The vanishing road and the window lit for a second and then dark. And then there was the sudden dancing light, that was hung in the future. What we have made then to-day," I said, "is this: that beauty; death of the individual; and the future. Look, I will make a little figure for your satisfaction; here he comes. Does this little figure advancing through beauty, through death, to the economical, powerful and efficient future when houses will be cleansed by a puff of hot wind satisfy you? Look at him; there on my knee." We sat and looked at the figure we had made that day. Great sheer slabs of rock, tree tufted, surrounded him. He was for a second very, very solemn. Indeed it seemed as if the reality of things were displayed there on the rug. A violent thrill ran through us; as if a charge of electricity had entered in to us. We cried out together: "Yes, yes," as if affirming something, in a moment of recognition.

And then the body who had been silent up to now began its song, almost at first as low as the rush of the wheels: "Eggs and bacon; toast and tea; fire and a bath; fire and a bath; jugged hare," it went on, "and red currant jelly; a glass of wine; with coffee to follow, with coffee to follow—and then to bed; and then to bed."

"Off with you," I said to my assembled selves. "Your work is done. I dismiss you. Good-night."

And the rest of the journey was performed in the delicious society of my own body.

19.

Edge of
Taos Desert

MABEL DODGE LUHAN

At times we can literally see the web of imagination. Author and arts patron Mabel Dodge Luhan describes such a moment. Out in the desert, she experiences the interconnectedness of everything with everything else. Is this what all musicians, painters, in fact what all artists look for, she wonders? And if everything is really interconnected, is the web of imagination at all separate from reality?

"Coffee! Coffee ready!" an Indian sang, and I pushed the sheet aside and poked my head out. Juan Concha giggled tenderly. "All well now?" he asked.

"Weak," I told him, feeling happy.

"That's nothin'. Weak! Some weakness good."

"Come on!" Tony called to me from the fire. He stood with his back to it, with his hands stretched out to the blaze behind him. His head was thrown back and he looked down towards me with his beautiful eyelids like hoods over his deep eyes. He was smiling and natural again. His smile was sometimes mysterious as though he knew things I didn't, a knowing smile, and sometimes it was purely kind and affectionate and comforting and so it was this morning.

I got up and went over near him and the hot coffee was wonderful and restoring.

All day as we slowly wound our way up the Hondo road, back and forth, over nine bridges, crossing the cold, rough stream again and again, I felt weak, and I could hardly hold myself upright on my horse, but Tony was solicitous and tried to make me forget myself by calling my attention to the red-winged birds that flitted into the shadows, or the brightly singing invisible birds in the higher branches. Once he dismounted and gathered a few huge mauve columbines and brought them to me and they were like large butterflies.

When we finally reached Twining at four o'clock, it was raining again and all I wanted on earth was to lie down.

The old white abandoned hotel was there, empty, and Tony and Juan Concha helped me into it while the others unpacked. They spread blankets on the floor and I lay down gratefully. Tony went out to look for Jack Bidwell but he was away that day.

I don't know how long I lay there. The others came in to see me once in a while, but I told them I was really all right, only very tired, and they left me to myself. There were fires to be made and cabins to choose for themselves, empty and windowless but dry, and then supper had to be cooked. The quiet, persistent rain made a soft, soothing whisper on the roof and I was comfortable enough.

Finally Tony and Juan Concha appeared, carrying a lighted lantern. Juan Concha knelt down beside me and offered me a tin cup, saying, "Here. Drink this. Help you."

"What is it?" I asked them, raising up on my elbow.

"Medicine Juan fix for you. Better drink," Tony told me.

I would do anything he told me to do, and I obediently took the cup from the gentle, solicitous figure bending over me and drained it. It was very hot and bitter. "What *is* it?" I sputtered.

"The medicine," Tony said gravely.

Peyote! Well!!

Tony arranged the blanket so it covered me up and then they, too, left me to myself. Immediately the Indian singing commenced out beside the fire.

The medicine ran through me, penetratingly. It acted like an organizing medium co-ordinating one part with another, so all the elements that were combined in me shifted like the particles in a kaleidoscope and fell into an orderly pattern. Beginning with the inmost central point in my own organism, the whole universe fell into place; I in the room and the room I was in, the old building containing the room, the cool wet night space where the building stood, and all the mountains standing out like sentries in their everlasting attitudes. So on and on into wider spaces farther than I could divine, where all the heavenly bodies were contented with the order of the plan, and system within system interlocked in grace. I was not separate and isolated any more. The magical drink had revealed the irresistible delight of spiritual composition; the regulated relationship of one to all and all to one.

Was it this, I wondered, something like this, that *artists* are perpetually trying to find and project upon their canvases? Was this what musicians imagine and try to formulate? Significant Form!

I laughed there alone in the dark, remembering the favorite phrase that had seemed so hackneyed for a long time and that I had never really understood. Significant form, I whispered; why, that means that all things are *really* related to each other.

These words had an enormous vitality and importance when I said them, more than they ever had afterwards when from time to time I approximately understood and realized their secret meaning after I relapsed into the usual dream-like state of everyday life.

The singing filled the night and I perceived its design which was written upon the darkness in color that made an intricate pictured pattern, not static like one that is painted but organic and moving like blood currents, and composed of a myriad of bright living cells. These cells were like minute flowers or crystals and they vibrated constantly in their rank and circumstance, no one of them falling out of place, for the order of the whole was held together by the interdependence of each infinitesimal spark. And I learned that there is no single equilibrium anywhere in existence, and that the meaning and essence of balance is that it depends upon neighboring organisms, one leaning upon the other, one touching another, holding together, reinforcing the whole, creating form and defeating chaos which is the hellish realm of unattached and unassimilated atoms.

A full realization of all this broke upon me in a new way not just apprehended as an idea but experienced in my body, so that oddly I felt that the singing and the pattern that it was composed of was also the description of my own organism and all other people's, and it was my blood that sang and my tissues that vibrated upon the ether, making a picture and a design. There was such a consolation in this discovery that I was strengthened and raised up, and I got to my feet and went out to the others.

The abandoned little village was all lighted and rosy, the flames of the big campfire ran high and showed up the farthest cabins with dim trees standing behind them, and there was a circle of people lying and sitting in the firelight.

The Indians sat upright, shoulder to shoulder, and their voices were perfectly in unison. They sang a phrase repeatedly, over and over until the waves of it spread rapidly out from them one after another and the surrounding night became filled with it. When it was packed and complete, they changed the phrase.

The waves of their living power ran out from them upon the vehicle of sound. They penetrated and passed through each listener, altering him a little, shaking old dead compactnesses of matter apart, awakening the paralyzed tissues. This kind of singing is mantric and has a magical influence. No one can lay himself open to it and not be imperceptibly altered by it. Few know and realize this, however; people constantly play in dangerously magnetic neighborhoods and never know what is happening to them.

I wrapped myself in my shawl and sat upon a log. Tony's eyes fell upon me across the blaze but they did not linger and he made no sign. I felt a vast peace all through me and a sense of secret knowledge.

Though I had just had a lesson in the invisible coherence of all human beings, it did not seem illogical that I felt entirely separated from the others out here. There was a new faculty of detachment from them dawning upon me, a different kind from the solitary, unbalanced attitude which was the only one I had ever known. It is difficult to define. There was the beginning of objectivity in it, a realization of our oneness and dependence upon all others, with, at the same time, the realization of the need for withdrawal, for independence, for nonidentification with the mass. In a new dimension one might, nay must, realize that one is related to and identified with this universe and all its aspects, and yet that one must become more than that, more than a bright neighborly cell in the great organism. One must know that one is that cell, seeing it flash, and sensing the quiver and vibration of being, one must observe and keep the order of creation, always understanding one is a part of that scheme, but the step beyond is to know that one is also more than that, and in the strict detachment from organic life that characterizes the newborn observer, he watches himself functioning as a material cell, and by this detachment he draws the material to nourish the infant soul up out of the observed activity of the organism. How this flash of revelation worked out into fact and substance took twenty years of living to be proved a reality.

The Indians sang for many hours until one by one our party slipped away, but I sat sleepless all night and I felt fresh and made over when morning came.

That long, wakeful night was the most clarifying I had ever had, and the momentary glimpse of life I was given by an expansion of consciousness always remained with me, though it was often forgotten.

Just before dawn when I was lying down again in the bare room, Juan Concha returned and knelt beside me, and he said in the kind, gentle Indian way, "Come now! Drink again and you be well and strong." He put the cup to my lips and I drank the hot infusion obediently. Then he left me, and soon I heard the camp awakening outside, someone chopping wood, and low voices speaking together in the high, clear morning stillness. I had never had an awakening like that one. Though I had not actually slept, it was as though I had, as though I had always been asleep and was awake now for the first time.

The release from the troubled, senseless, nightmarish night my life had been, the relief at coming back to the reality of the bright, confident day, was overwhelming. I could feel my quivering nerves and my loud, frightened heart gradually compose themselves after a lifetime of concealed apprehension and alarm.

I lay there and gave myself up to the luxury of being at peace within the framework of a vast, beautiful creation. Safe. Nothing mattered. Knowing what I knew now, nothing mattered, everything was taken care of. I was taken care of, and what we saw about us was a mask for something else far more meaningful than anyone knew.

iv

THE CREATIVE
ECOLOGY

This incredible exchange of energy
goes on onstage, where you're almost
transported. For me, the spark comes,
very emotional, from the shared experience of what I'm singing about. It's the
band when we really lock in and the
audience knows you're locking in. I wish
I could lose myself more when I play by
myself. It's easy to do with an audience,
but I tend to be too self-conscious and
judgmental when I'm alone. The audience is more unconditional, as if the
channel is more open.

BONNIE RAITT

It takes a village to survive.

ISABEL ALLENDE

"Men work together," I told him from the heart,
Whether they work together or apart.

ROBERT FROST

Like all phenomena of nature, creativity lives and dies within an ecology. There are creatogenic ecologies, but there are also creatopathic ones; the former are favorable to creativity, generative, while the latter are pathological and destructive. In all ecologies, periods of relative stability alternate with instabilities—sometimes shattering disequilibria that alter the ecological niche and change the landscape of the creative surround. Whether stable or unstable, heterogeneous or homogeneous, a creative human ecology is made up of a multiplicity of natural phenomena, people, experiences, and actions.

The specifically creative ecology may extend backward in time as well as laterally in space. We may find inspiration in the work of our predecessors from other ages, or colleagues in other locations. The Renaissance drew heavily on the golden age of Greece, and we still draw heavily on both. Modern art has roots in the work of artists in other cultures, from Africa to Asia. The creative ecology is both here and now, and long ago and far away.

Friendships are an important part of creative human ecologies. Think how many artistic and intellectual movements have begun in cafes, with friends pondering problems, outlining constraints and possibilities, and embarking on a collective journey of exploration. The symposia described by Plato, the source of Western philosophy, were lively events with considerable eating and quite heroic drinking (to loosen the discussion), ending in the wee hours of the morning. There went Socrates, there went Alcibiades, there went Anaxagoras, a veritable creative ecology in the golden age of Greece.

Almost all creation is a collaboration. Many of the most creative activities that have blossomed in this century, whether moviemaking or musical performance in jazz and pop bands, the development of business ventures, or new social movements, required constant collaboration. The great research and development laboratories of our century have witnessed an outpouring of group creativity, of work conducted with others under the auspices (and usually with the financial backing) of others.

The big corporations are now recognizing the need for creative teams, for people who can work together cooperatively and creatively to produce those things that a single person simply cannot make alone.

As in all creative phenomena, the relationship between the creative person, the creative product, and the environment is full of seeming paradox. Creative persons benefit from support, from encouragement, from even a lone voice backing them in the face of adversity. Many creative persons have benefited from mentors, role models who guide them along the way to developing their own uniqueness. And yet the creative mind also needs a degree of solitude to match its immersion in the world, a time to mull things over and get down to the work of composing, painting, or writing alone. In that solitude we are perhaps never totally alone, wrestling as we are with ideas, debates, beliefs, and the notions of others. But in that solitude we can shape them, reorganize them, work with them, digest them, and make them our own.

So here again we find the constantly paradoxical nature of creativity, for as they internalize the work of others—their mentors, colleagues, friends, and enemies—creative persons are also developing their individual view of the world. They must! Yet the more unique and autonomous they become, the more dependent they become on their ecology. By alternating immersion and isolation, openness and closure, creative persons and creative environments co-evolve.

20.

the shape
of music

MAURICE SENDAK

The term synesthesia *describes the uncanny ability to "hear" colors and "see" sounds. In the movie* Fantasia, *for example, Walt Disney attempts to show us what sounds might look like. Maurice Sendak, famous children's author and illustrator, draws his illustrations with music in mind. In this instance, Sendak draws his illustrations while listening to music. Thus, he encourages synesthesia in his own creative ecology.*

Vivify, quicken, and *vitalize*—of these three synonyms, *quicken,* I think, best suggests the genuine spirit of animation, the breathing to life, the swing into action, that I consider an essential quality in pictures for children's books. *To quicken* means, for the illustrator, the task first of comprehending the nature of his text and then of giving life to that comprehension in his own medium, the picture.

The conventional techniques of graphic animation are related to this intention only in that they provide an instrument with which the artist can begin his work. Sequential scenes that tell a story in pictures, as in the comic strip, are an example of one form of animation. It is no difficult matter for an artist to simulate action, but it is something else to *quicken,* to create an inner life that draws breath from the artist's deepest perception.

The word *quicken* has other, more subjective associations for me. It suggests something musical, something rhythmic and impulsive. It suggests a beat—a heartbeat, a musical beat, the beginning of a dance. This association proclaims music as one source from which my own pictures take life. For me, "to conceive musically" means to quicken the life of the illustrated book.

All of my pictures are created against a background of music. More often than not, my instinctive choice of composer or musical form for the day has the galvanizing effect of making me conscious of my direction. I find something uncanny in the way a musical phrase, a sensuous vocal line, or a patch of Wagnerian color will clarify an entire approach or style for a new work. A favorite occupation of mine, some years back, was sitting in front of the record player as though possessed by a dybbuk, and allowing the music to provoke an automatic, stream-of-consciousness kind of drawing. Sometimes the pictures that resulted were merely choreographed episodes, imagined figures dancing imagined ballets. More interesting to me, and much more useful for my work, are the childhood fantasies that were reactivated by the music and explored uninhibitedly by the pen.

Music's peculiar power of releasing fantasy has always fascinated me. An inseparable part of my memories of childhood, music was the inevitable, animating accompaniment to the make-believe. No childhood fantasy of mine was complete without the restless, ceaseless sound of impromptu humming, the din of unconscious music-making that conjured up just the right fantastical atmosphere. All children seem to know what the mysterious, the riding-fiercely-across-the-plains (accompanied by hearty, staccato thigh slaps), and the plaintive conventionally sound like; and I have no doubt that this kind of musical contribution enriches each particular fantasy. The spontaneous breaking into song and dance seems so natural and instinctive a part of childhood. It is perhaps the medium through which children best express the inexpressible; fantasy and feeling lie deeper than words—beyond the words yet available to a child—and both demand a more profound, more biological expression, the primitive expression of music. Recently I watched a mother tell her little boy a familiar, ritualistic story while he embellished the tale with an original hummed score. He kept up a swinging motion "in time" to the story, then punctuated the end with a series of sharp, imitation bugle sounds and a wild jungle jump.

My intention is not to prove music the sole enlivening force behind the creation of pictures for children. But music is the impulse that most stimulates my own work and I invariably sense a musical element in the work of the artists I admire, those artists who achieve the authentic liveliness that is the essence of the picture book, a movement that is never still, and that children, I am convinced, recognize and enjoy as something familiar to themselves.

21.

A Life in the Day of Maya Angelou

MAYA ANGELOU*

Creativity may be chaos, disorder, and the unexpected: yet there has to be a method to the madness—even a routine, at times. But nobody says the routine has to be ordinary. Here poet Maya Angelou gives us an example: she writes in hotel rooms all morning long with a yellow note pad and a glass of sherry. The editing's done at night.

I wake usually about six and get immediately out of bed. Then I begin to wonder why. I have a fiendish attachment to something called Rose Geranium from Floris so I take a shower with a cloth which is green with the stuff—it's so aromatic that people down the street know that I've taken a shower and somehow I feel I've been pretty good to myself. I make very strong coffee and sit in the sunroom with the newspaper, the *Winston-Salem Journal*, the only paper in town.

I love to read the letters to the editor. I like to see what angers people; only one in a hundred says "I love what you're doing," the other 99 say they hate the paper or this is nonsense or that is absolutely wrong. I feel as if I've just met eight people, little human vignettes. And I look outside, I live in a wooded area and I don't think, I just look.

At about 8:30 I start looking at the house because the housekeeper arrives at nine and I'm still too well brought-up to offer Mrs. Cunningham a house in too much disarray so I straighten up before she comes in. She has been my housekeeper for six years now—my sister has suggested that in another life she was a staff-sergeant. I give to her and she gives to me and we live together with a lot of laughter. My secretary, Mrs. Garris, also comes at nine and that's

*This essay is adapted from an interview with Maya Angelou by Carol Sarler.

when real life begins. Mrs. Garris is a lovely southern black lady with efficiency and grace vying for dominance in her spirit. She says, "Ms. Angelou, you've got to sign this, send that, agree to that, deny this . . ." and I say, "Mrs. Garris, I will talk to you in an hour."

At ten I deal with my correspondence; I get about 300 letters a week. People send me all sorts of things, especially manuscripts. It's not fair, everybody's work deserves the attention of a qualified editor and I'm not that, so Mrs. Garris writes back to explain that and to say that I don't read unsolicited manuscripts. Then she goes off to lunch and I usually invite friends over. I'm a very serious cook and I prepare what to me is a fabulous lunch for two or three people like breadcrumbed turkey-breast cooked in butter, wine and lemon, served with rice and zucchini and there's my home-made bread. I offer good wine and we laugh and talk. I cook in competitions around the United States to raise money for Cancer Research, the American Jewish Association, Sickle Cell Anemia—we have these events where celebrities get together and people pay up to $250 to eat the food.

In the afternoon I read—if I'm teaching I read works coming out of the theme of my class and I put on the music to complement the reading. For instance, if I'm doing a course on African culture's impact on the world I will read Basil Davidson's *Last Kingdoms of Africa* and I'll put on tapes of African music, Odetta singing 19th-century slave songs, Mahalia Jackson singing anything—and I turn it up very loud, it's all over my house, that insistence of the music which helps to entrench me into the era. Unless I'm involved in something really important, Mrs. Garris and Mrs. Cunningham come up to say goodbye at five—really sweet—and then I have my house back.

At the time I suppose its tea-time for other people, I help myself to a very nice drink—Dewar's White Label whiskey—and I look at my paintings. I'm a collector of black American art and I have paintings throughout my house, wonderful paintings that sing. It's a big house and I keep extending it. I always use the same builder and he says he's waiting for me to stretch down to the next street just to give me more walls for the paintings.

I'm convinced that black American art, while it is graphic, is rooted in music. Romare Bearden, who is the most expensive but is considered the leading living black artist in the United States, also writes about blues. I collect Bearden and I collect John Biggers as well and he is an aficionado of African music—when you see the work you can hear the music. Some paintings I pass right by and two weeks later they will stop me and say, "Haven't you been listening to me lately?"

About seven I start to prepare dinner for myself; I drink more than I eat, but I prepare a proper dinner and put on candles and pretty music—all for me. If I'm not good to myself, how can I expect anyone else to be good to me? Then I read again, unless there's something on the television. Often something meaningless—sometimes I just don't want to be informed, increased, elevated, developed, I want something like an old Hollywood musical. Now that's really precious when the world is exploding in South Africa and Northern Ireland and the Middle East, but I know that the next morning the phone will ring and I will be asked to be involved and within hours I could be in jail or on a picket line, so I have to stop when I can.

If I do go out I like to go to friends—however, unless there is an issue which calls for immediate discussion, I don't like cocktail chit-chat over Israel, or the Arabs. I think everyone young should do that with lots of cheap wine, sitting on the floor and shouting and arguing, but I don't do it now.

The issues have too much importance to be minimalized by someone saying, "Now where *is* Syria?" I love good stories, funny stories, told by the person against him or herself. That's what I want of an evening, then I go home to bed by 12:00. If my gentleman friend is there, that's different. My gentleman friend visits every two or three months for four or five days from Ohio. I don't worry what he does when he's not there, I hope he has a good time. If he ever didn't come back, then he wasn't for me.

When I'm writing, none of anything I've said applies. When I'm writing, everything shuts down. I get up about five, take a shower and don't use the Floris—I don't want that sensual gratification. I get in my car and drive off to a hotel room: I can't write in my house, I take a hotel room and ask them to take everything off the walls so there's me, the Bible, *Roget's Thesaurus* and some good, dry sherry and I'm at work by 6:30. I write on the bed lying down—one elbow is darker than the other, really black from leaning on it— and I write in longhand on yellow pads. Once into it, all disbelief is suspended, it's beautiful. I hate to go, but I've set for myself 12:30 as the time to leave, because after that it's an indulgence, it becomes stuff I'm going to edit out anyway.

Then back home, shower, fresh clothes, and I go shopping for nice food and pretend to be sane. I don't see Mrs. Cunningham or Mrs. Garris or my gentleman friend, nobody. I play a lot of solitaire—in a month when I'm writing I use two or three decks of cards. After dinner I re-read what I've written . . . if April is the cruellest month, then eight o'clock at night is the cruellest hour because that's when I start to edit and all that pretty stuff I've written gets axed out. So if I've written 10 or 12 pages in six hours, it'll end up as three or four if I'm lucky.

But writing really is my life. Thinking about it when I'm not doing it is terribly painful but when I'm doing it . . . it's a lot like if I was a long-distance swimmer and had to jump into a pool covered with ice: it sounds terrible, but once in it and two or three laps done, I'm home and free.

22.

The Magic Lantern

INGMAR BERGMAN

In this extract, director Ingmar Bergman writes about the process of moviemaking and the complex interactions of the participants. Bergman's essay is particularly important because it deals with a topic that has not received much scholarly or public attention, creativity as a group process. Social creativity is an integral part of many of the most highly visible art forms of the twentieth century, such as cinema and popular music.

I have chosen a day's filming in 1982. According to my notes, it was cold—twenty degrees Celsius below zero. I woke up as usual at five o'clock, which means I was woken, drawn as if in a spiral by some evil spirit out of my deepest sleep, and I was wide awake. To combat hysteria and the sabotage of my bowels, I got out of bed immediately and for a few moments stood quite still on the floor with my eyes closed. I went over my actual situation. How was my body, how was my soul and, most of all, what had got to be done today? I established that my nose was blocked (the dry air), my left testicle hurt (probably cancer), my hip ached (the same old pain), and there was a ringing in my bad ear (unpleasant but not worth bothering about). I also registered that my hysteria was under control, my fear of stomach cramp not too intensive. The day's work consisted of the scene between Ismael and Alexander, in *Fanny and Alexander,* and I was worried because the scene in question might be beyond the capacity of my brave young actor in the title role, Bertil Guve. But the coming collaboration with Stina Ekblad as Ismael gave me a jolt of happy expectation. The first inspection of the day was thus completed and had produced a small but nevertheless positive profit: if Stina is as good as I think, I can manage Bertil-Alexander. I had already thought out two strategies: one with equally good actors, the other with a principal actor and a secondary actor.

Now it was a question of taking things calmly, of being calm.

At seven o'clock, my wife Ingrid and I had breakfast together in friendly silence. My stomach was acquiescent and had forty-five minutes in which to create hell. While I was waiting for it to decide on its attitude, I read the morning papers. At a quarter to eight, I was fetched and driven to the studio, which at that particular time was in Sundbyberg and was owned by Europafilm Ltd.

Those once so reputable studios were decaying. They produced mainly videos, and any staff left from the days of film were disoriented and downhearted. The actual film studio was dirty, not sound-proof, and badly maintained. The editing room, at first sight comically luxurious, turned out to be useless. The projectors were wretched, incapable of keeping either definition or stills. The sound was bad, the ventilation did not function and the carpet was filthy.

At exactly nine o'clock, the day's filming started. It was important that our collective start was punctual. Discussions and uncertainties had to take place *outside* this innermost circle of concentration. From this moment on, we were a complicated but uniformly functioning machine, the aim of which was to produce living pictures.

The work quickly settled into a calm rhythm, and intimacy was uncomplicated. The only thing to disturb this day was the lack of sound-proofing and the lack of respect for the red lamps outside in the corridor and elsewhere. Otherwise it was a day of modest delight. From the very first moment, we all felt Stina Ekblad's remarkable empathy with the ill-fated Ismael and, best of all, Bertil-Alexander had at once accepted the situation. In that strange way children have, he gave expression to a complicated mixture of curiosity and fear with touching genuineness.

The rehearsals moved on smoothly and a quiet cheerfulness reigned, our creativity dancing along. Anna Asp had created a stimulating set for us. Sven Nykvist had done the lighting with that intuition which is difficult to describe, but which is his hallmark and makes him one of the leading lighting camera men in the world, perhaps the best. If you asked him how he did it, he would point out some simple ground rules (which have been of great use to me in my work in the theatre). He could not—or had no wish to—describe the actual secret. If for some reason he was disturbed, pressurized or ill at ease, everything went wrong and he would have to start all over again from the beginning. Confidence and total security prevailed in our collaboration. Occasionally I grieve over the fact that we shall never work together again. I grieve when I think back to a day such as the one I have depicted. There's a sensual satisfaction in working in close union with strong, independent and creative people: actors, assistants, electricians, production staff, props people, makeup staff, costume designers, all those personalities who populate the day and make it possible to get through.

Sometimes I really feel the loss of everything and everyone concerned. I understand what Fellini means when he says filming to him is a way of life and I also understand his little story about Anita Ekberg. Her last scene in *La Dolce Vita* took place in a car erected in the studio. When the scene had been taken and filming was over as far as she was concerned, she started crying and refused to leave the car, gripping firmly onto the wheel. She had to be carried out of the studio with gentle force.

Sometimes there is a special happiness in being a film director. An unrehearsed expression is born just like that, and the camera registers that expression. That was exactly what happened that day. Unprepared and unrehearsed, Alexander turned very pale, a look of sheer agony appearing on his face. The camera registered the moment. The agony, the intangible, was there for a few seconds and never returned. Neither was it there earlier, but the strip of film caught the moment. That is when I think days and months of predictable routine have paid off. It is possible I live for those brief moments.

Like a pearl fisher.

23.

The second line

SIDNEY BECHET

Jazz saxophonist Sidney Bechet reminisces about New Orleans and the wealth of music he was exposed to as a child. In those days parades were made up "for the pleasure," as he puts it, not always to celebrate a particular event. The rich cultural milieu, the diverse cauldron that was New Orleans, produced one of America's greatest contributions to world culture: jazz.

Everyone in our house liked music. When they heard it played right, they answered to it from way down inside themselves. If my brothers weren't around the house playing, they was out playing somewhere else. My father, my mother, and me too—we was all the same about music. Even when I was just a little kid I was always running out to where the music was going on, chasing after the parades. Sometimes I'd get into the second line of the parade and just go along.

The second line of the parade, that was a thing you don't see any more. There used to be big parades all over New Orleans—a band playing, people dancing and strutting and shouting, waving their hands, kids following along waving flags. One of those parades would start down the street, and all kinds of people when they saw it pass would forget all about what they was doing and just take off after it, just joining in the fun. You know how it is—a parade, it just makes you stop anything you're doing; you stop working, eating, any damn thing, and you run on out, and if you can't get in it you just get as close as you can.

In those days people just made up parades for the pleasure. They'd all get together and everyone would put some money into it, maybe a dollar, and they'd make plans for stopping off at one place for one thing, and at some other place for something else—drinks or cake or some food. They'd have maybe six places they was scheduled to go to.

And those that didn't have money, they couldn't get in the parade. But they enjoyed it just as much as those that were doing it—more, some of them. And those people, they were called "second liners." They had to make their own parade with broomsticks, kerchiefs, tin pans, any old damn thing. And they'd take off shouting, singing, following along the sidewalk, going off on side streets when they was told they had no business being on the sidewalks or along the kerbs like that, or maybe when the police would try to break them up. Then they'd go off one way and join the parade away up and start all over again. They'd be having their own damn parade, taking what was going on in the street and doing something different with it, tearing it up kind of, having their fun. They'd be the second line of the parade.

When I was just a kid I used to get in on a lot of those second lines, singing, dancing, hollering—oh, it just couldn't be stopped! But sometimes you had to watch out: the police, sometimes they did nothing but smile, other times they just weren't taking anything for pleasure.

The police would come by sometimes and, like I say, some of them didn't do nothing to stop what was going on, but others used to beat up the people and break them up and get them moving away from there. You'd just never knew which it would be with those police. But somehow they never did touch the musicianers; I never did see that happen.

Once, I remember, Buddy Bolden was out there singing and playing. He was singing a song of his that got to be real famous, "I Thought I Heard Buddy Bolden Say." The words to that, they wasn't considered too nice. A lot of mothers would hear their kids singing when they came home:

> I thought I heard Buddy Bolden say,
> "Funky Butt, Funky Butt, take it away. . . ."

And if the kids were scratched up at all or hurt some, the mothers they'd know right away where their kids had been, because as often as not someone did get scratched up when they hung around listening to these contests or to the advertising the bands did for some dance hall or something. This time I remember, I was down there around Canal Street somewheres—I was awful little then—and a policeman come along and he looked at my head and he looked at my ass, and he smacked me good with that stick he was carrying. I ran home then and I was really hurting some, I couldn't even sit down for dinner that night; and my mother, she took one look at me and she knew right away where I'd been.

Then there were the funerals. There used to be a lot of clubs in New Orleans, social clubs. They used to meet regular. They had nights for ladies;

they played cards, they had concerts—a piano player or two or three musicians; it all depended what night in the week it was. Sometimes they used to have very serious meetings, and talk about how to do something good for members and the club and different things. When a member died, naturally all the members would meet at the club. They would have a brass band, the Onward Brass Band or Allen's Brass Band, and they would go from the club to the house of the member which was dead, and would play not dance music but mortuary music until they got to be about a block from the residence of the dead person. Then the big drum would just give tempo as they approached. The members would all go in to see the corpse, and then they would take him out to the cemetery with funeral marches. And they'd bury him, and as soon as he was buried they would leave the cemetery with that piece "Didn't He Ramble." That was a lovely piece and it's really the story about a bull. This bull, all through his life he rambled and rambled until the butcher cut him down. Well, that really meant that this member he rambled till the Lord cut him down; and that was the end of that.

Sometimes we'd have what they called in those days "bucking contests"; that was long before they talked about "cutting contests." One band, it would come right up in front of the other and play at it, and the first band it would play right back, until finally one band just had to give in. And the one that didn't give in, all the people, they'd rush up to it and give it drinks and food and holler for more, wanting more, not having enough. There just couldn't be enough for those people back there. And that band was best that played the best *together*. No matter what kind of music it was, if the band could keep it together, that made it the best. That band, it would know its numbers and know its foundation and it would know *itself*.

And those bands, they could play anything that was wanted—waltzes, shorties, marches, *anything*. Lots of times it was the Creole musicianers. They'd be the ones, their band, who'd win. And like I say, they had to be ready for anything. You take a band like Manuel Perez's; they'd have engagements at dance halls, theatres, for churches even. And they'd have to play tunes that could fit in, tunes like maybe "Have You Seen My Lovin' Henry?," "Fiddle Up on Your Violin," or "I'm Gonna See My Sweetie Tonight." Tunes like that you could one-step to. You had to have a reserve of knowing how to play anything with a lot of feeling and understanding. And one thing—that one thing you just can't describe—the feeling there was to a good band that made it able to do anything better than the next band, knowing how to do something without being told.

Some bands, they played compositions, some of Scott Joplin's numbers what had been arranged already. Or they played stand-bys like "Maple Leaf" or "High Society," pieces they had memorized, they had them put down in a fixed way.

But if a band could play numbers that weren't arranged, or even numbers that were, but do them in their own way, free and sure, with a kind of inspired improvising—that was the band that would naturally win in the bucking contests.

In Perez's band they used to play all kinds of numbers. Numbers like "Black Smoke," "Pineapple Rag," "Canadian Capers." Those were shorties really. In a way of speaking they were more of a challenge. Or not a challenge exactly, but they made what they were doing fuller just because they *could* play them too when other bands they didn't know how. Those were numbers for people to dance to. Their mood, it was different, the kind of feeling they demanded. Perez, he had a band could do anything. There was one number, it was English. It's one everybody knows. "Lightning Bug" it's called. Perez, he'd three-time that until it was really beautiful to hear.

Well, the people listening to them, they'd follow wherever they marched along playing, and finally they'd just win out. It was always the public who decided. You was always being judged. It would make you tremble when one of those bands, it came into sight. Say you was somebody standing there, a spectator—you'd be hearing two bands maybe advertising for different theatres or a dance or just being out there. One of them it would come up in front of the other and face it, and you'd hear both of them. There'd be the two. And then you'd start noticing onliest the one. Somehow you'd just hear it better. Maybe it was clearer, maybe it was just giving you a lot more feeling. That band, it would be so gay and fine—the men in it, there was nothing they was depending on but themselves. They didn't have to play after some arrangement. Almost it was like they was playing ahead of themselves. And so they'd have more confidence and there would be a richness to what they were doing. And so you'd want to hear it closer and you'd get up nearer. And then, it seemed it was *all* you was hearing. It was the only one that came through. And the other band, it would get away farther and farther until finally you just didn't hear it at all.

There was another kind of bucking contest too. There'd be those parades of different clubs and often times it would happen that two or three clubs, they would be parading the same day and they'd have engaged these different brass bands. Allen's Brass Band, it was one that was very well known. The Onward, that used to be another. The Excelsior, that was one. And those bands, the men in them, waiting for that parade to start, they'd all have that excited feeling, knowing they could play good, that they was going to please the people who would be about there that day. They had no fears. But the musicianers from other bands, bands that had just been gotten up for that day—they were just a bunch of men who was going to play, and that was a difference; they wouldn't have that sure feeling inside. Bands like the ones I named, they were organized and they had the preference at these club parades.

And those clubs, maybe the Lions Clubs or the Odd Fellows or the Swells or the Magnolias, the men who were their members, they'd all have their full dress suits on with sashes that would go down to their knees, and they'd have this Grand Marshal who was the leader of the club. He'd have the longest sash. He'd have a sash that would go right down to his shoe tops and it would have gold bangles on it. And on his shoulder, he'd have an emblem, maybe a gold lion. That was his badge. But most of all, the way you could tell the Marshal, it was from how he walked. The Marshal, he'd be a man that really could strut.

It was really a question of that: the best strutter in the club, he'd be the Grand Marshal. He'd be a man who could prance when he walked, a man that could really fool and surprise you. He'd keep time to the music, but all along he'd keep a strutting and moving so you'd never know what he was going to be doing next. Naturally, the music, it makes you strut, but it's *him* too, the way he's strutting, it gets you. It's what you want from a parade: you want to *see* it as well as hear it. And all those fancy steps he'd have—oh, that was really something!—ways he'd have of turning around himself. People, they got a whole lot of pleasure out of just watching him, hearing the music and seeing him strut and other members of the club coming behind him, strutting and marching, some riding on horses but getting down to march a while, gallivanting there in real style. It would have your eyes just the same as your ears for waiting.

And people everywhere, they'd be coming from every direction. They'd just appear. It was like Congo Square again, only modern, different. The times, they had changed. But the happiness, the excitement—that was the same thing all the time.

And so these parades march along. You'd be in the band for this one club say, you'd be stationed to be somewhere at a certain time, and another band it would be stationed at some other place, maybe somewhere almost on the other side of town. And the time would come you'd have fixed to start both, and you'd move off and start by going to some member of the club's house, stopping off there for a drink or a talk or to eat and have a little fun, and then go on again. The other band, it would be doing the same. Both of you would be moving to the meeting place. And the people, they'd be up by Claiborne Avenue and St. Philip. They know you'd be coming there. You *had* to pass some time. It was a parade and you'd be going to where the people were because naturally if you have a parade you were going out to be seen. And you timed it to reach there the same time as another band. And that's where the hell starts, because if two bands meet, there's got to be this bucking contest.

The way it was fixed, one of the bands, it would stop, face around, and then go up close to the other, go right through it, one band going uptown and the other downtown.

The Grand Marshal, he'd be leading the club and when he got to some corner or some turn, he'd have a way of tricking his knee, of turning all around, prancing—he'd fool you. You wouldn't be knowing if he was going left or right. Oftentimes, the second lines running along after the parade, they'd go complete right after he'd turned left. And that was a big part of it— him stepping and twisting and having you guessing all along. The way he could move, that was doing something for you. He led it.

And people they'd be singing along, dancing, drinking, toasting. That Marshal, he'd lead his club's band up to the other one, and the leader, he'd go through with him. Manuel Perez, for example, he had his Onward Band—other bands, they'd tremble to face him. A brass band, it was twenty pieces, you know. And the leader, he'd take his band right in amongst the other, and he'd stop. You'd be standing there on Claiborne Avenue and the bands, they'd come closer to each other, keep coming closer, and you'd be hearing the two of them, first one in a way, then the next. And then they'd get closer and you couldn't make them out any more. And then they'd be right in together, one line between another, and then it was just noise, just everything all at once. They'd be forty instruments all bucking at one another. And then you'd have to catch your breath: they'd be separating themselves.

Then came the beauty of it. That was the part that really took something right out of you. You'd hear mostly one band, so clear, so good, making you happier, sadder, whatever way it wanted you to feel. It would come out of the bucking and it would still be playing all together. None of the musicians would be confused, none of them would have mixed up the music, they would all be in time.

And that other band, getting scared, knowing it couldn't go on further, it was finished. It couldn't be trying any harder, it was there still doing its best, but hearing the other band, say some good band like the Onward—it had thrown them off. It wasn't a band any more. It was just some excited musicians. It would have three or six different tempos going. The men, they didn't know their music and they didn't know their feeling and they couldn't hear the next man. Every man, he'd be thrown back on his own trying to find whatever number it was they had started out to play. But that number, it wasn't there any more. There was nothing to be recognized.

And the people, they just let that band be. They didn't care to hear it. They'd all be gone after the other band, crowding around it, cheering the musicianers, waiting to give them drinks and food. All of them feeling good about the music, how that band it kept the music together.

And being able to play in that kind of band, it was more than a learning kind of thing. You know, when you learn something, you can go just as far. When you've finished that, there's not much else you can do unless you know how to get hold of something inside you that isn't learned. It has to be there inside you without any need of learning. The band that played what it knew, it didn't have enough. In the end it would get confused; it was finished. And the people, they could tell.

But how it was they could tell—that was the music too. It was what they had of the music inside themselves. There wasn't any personality attraction thing to it. The music, it was the onliest thing that counted. The music, it was having a time for itself. It was moving. It was being free and natural.

24.

IS IT A FICTION
THAT PLAYWRIGHTS
CREATE ALONE?

TONY KUSHNER

Playwright Tony Kushner, "author" of the play Angels in America, *questions the very notion of authorship in this philosophical essay. Kushner argues that there were in fact many people who made important contributions to the final product, the performance of the play. The performing arts, with the interactive nature of social creativity visible on stage and behind the scenes, are an ideal place to begin to understand creativity as a collaborative process. In this essay Kushner not only traces his many collaborators in the project but explores the cultural, political, and philosophical reasons why collaboration in the creative has been downplayed. American individualism has led us to focus on creativity almost exclusively as the acts of individual genius, and diverted our attention from the relationships and collaborations that occur along the way. Capitalism, with its focus on ownership, also plays a part in this. We conceive of creativity as a cultural product, and this concept shapes the way we think about the who, what, where, and when of creativity.*

Angels in America, Parts 1 and 2, has taken five years to write, and as the work nears completion I find myself thinking a great deal about the people who have left their traces in these texts. The fiction that artistic labor happens in isolation, and that artistic accomplishment is exclusively the provenance of individual talents, is politically charged, and, in my case at least, repudiated by the facts.

While the primary labor on *Angels* has been mine, more than two dozen people have contributed words, ideas and structures to these plays, including actors, directors, audiences, one-night stands, my former lover and many friends. Two in particular, my closest friend, Kimberly T. Flynn

(*Perestroika* is dedicated to her), and the man who commissioned *Angels*, helped shape it and co-directed the Los Angeles production, Oskar Eustis, have had profound influence. Had I written these plays without the participation of my collaborators, they would be entirely different—would, in fact, never have come to be.

Americans pay high prices for maintaining the Myth of the Individual: we have no system of universal health care, we don't educate our children, we can't pass sane gun-control laws, we hate and fear inevitable processes like aging and death.

Way down, close to the bottom of the list of the evils individualism visits on our culture is the fact that in the modern era it isn't enough to write; you must also be a Writer and play your part as the protagonist in a cautionary narrative in which you will fail or triumph, be in or out, hot or cold. The rewards can be fantastic; the punishment dismal; it's a zero-sum game, and its guarantor of value, its marker, is that you pretend you play it solo, preserving the myth that you alone are the wellspring of your creativity.

When I started to write these plays I wanted to attempt something of ambition and size even if that meant I might be accused of straying too close to ambition's ugly twin, pretentiousness. Given the bloody opulence of this country's great and terrible history, given its newness and its grand improbability, its artists are bound to be tempted toward large gestures and big embraces, a proclivity de Tocqueville deplored as a national artistic trait more than 150 years ago. Melville, my favorite American writer, strikes inflated, even hysterical chords on occasion. It's the sound of the individual ballooning, overreaching. We are all children of the "Song of Myself."

Anyone interested in exploring alternatives to Individualism and the political economy it serves, Capitalism, has to be willing to ask hard questions about the ego, both as abstraction and as exemplified in oneself.

Bertolt Brecht, while he was still in Weimar-era Berlin and facing the possibility of participating in a socialist revolution, wrote a series of remarkable short plays, his Lehrstucke, or learning plays. The principal subject of these plays was the painful dismantling, as a revolutionary exigency, of the individual ego. His metaphor for this dismantling is death.

(Brecht, who never tried to hide the dimensions of his own titanic personality, didn't sentimentalize the problems such personalities present, or the process of loss involved in attempting to let go of the richness, and the riches, that accompany such successful self-creation.)

He simultaneously claimed and mocked the identity he'd won for himself, "a great German writer," raising important questions about the means of literary production, challenging the sacrosanctity of the image of the solitary artist and, at the same time, openly, ardently wanting to be recognized as a genius. That he was a genius is inarguably the case. For a man deeply committed to collectivity as an ideal and an achievable political goal, this blazing singularity was a mixed blessing at best and at worst an obstacle to a blending of radical theory and practice.

In the lower-right-hand corner of the title page of many of Brecht's plays you will find, in tiny print, a list of names under the heading collaborators. Sometimes these people contributed little, sometimes a great deal. One cannot help feeling that those who bore those minuscule names, who expended the considerable labor the diminutive typography conceals, have had a bum deal. Many of these collaborators, Ruth Berlau, Elisabeth Hauptmann, Margarete Steffin, were women. In the question of shared intellectual and artistic labor, gender is always an issue.

On the day last spring when the Tony nominations were being handed out, I left the clamorous room at Sardi's thinking gloomily that here was another source of anxiety, another obstacle to getting back to work rewriting *Perestroika.* In the building's lobby I was introduced to the producer Elizabeth I. McCann, who said to me: "I've been worried about how you were handling all this till I read that you have an Irish woman in your life. Then I knew you were going to be fine." Ms. McCann was referring to Kimberly T. Flynn. An article in *The New Yorker* last year about *Angels in America* described how certain features of our shared experience dealing with her prolonged health crisis, caused by a serious cab accident several years ago, had a major impact on the plays.

Kimberly and I met in 1978 when I was a student at Columbia and she was a student at Barnard. We share Louisiana childhoods (she is from New Orleans, I grew up in Lake Charles); different but equally complicated, powerful religious traditions and an ambivalence toward those traditions; leftist politics informed by, among other things, liberation struggles (she as a feminist, I as a gay man); and a belief in the effectiveness of activism and the possibility of progress.

From the beginning Kimberly was my teacher. Though largely self-taught, she was more widely read and she helped me understand both Freud and Marx. She introduced me to the writers of the Frankfurt School and their early attempts at synthesizing psychoanalysis and Marxism; and to the German philosopher and critic Walter Benjamin, whose importance for me rests primarily in his introduction into these "scientific" disciplines a Kabbalist-inflected mysticism and a dark, apocalyptic spirituality.

As both writer and talker, Kimberly employs a rich variety of rhetorical strategies and effects, even while expressing deep emotion. She identifies this as an Irish trait; it's evident in O'Neill, Yeats, Beckett. This relationship to language, blended with Jewish and gay versions of the same strategies, is evident in my plays, in the ways my characters speak.

More pessimistic than I, Kimberly is much less afraid to look at the ugliness of the world. She tries to protect herself far less than I do and consequently she sees more. She feels safest, she says, knowing the worst, while most people I know, myself included, would rather be spared and feel safer encircled by a measure of obliviousness.

She is capable of teasing out fundamental concerns from their camouflage of words; at the same time she uses her analysis, her learning, her emotions, her lived experience, to make imaginative leaps, to see the deeper connections between ideas and historical developments. Through her example I learned to trust that such leaps can be made; I learned to admire them, in literature, in theory, in the utterances people make in newspapers. And certainly it was in part her example that made the labor of synthesizing disparate, seemingly unconnected things become for me the process of writing a play.

Since the accident Kimberly has struggled with her health, and I have struggled to help her, sometimes succeeding, sometimes failing. It's always been easier talking about the way in which I used what Kimberly and I lived through to write *Angels*, even though I sometimes question the morality of the act (while at the same time considering it unavoidable if I was to write at all), than it has been to acknowledge the intellectual debt. People seem to be more interested in the story of the accident and its aftermath than in the intellectual genealogy, the emotional life being privileged over the intellectual life in the business of making plays, and the two being regarded, incorrectly, as separable.

A great deal of what I understand about health issues comes from what Kimberly has endured and triumphed over and the ways she has articulated those experiences. But "Angels" is more the result of our intellectual friendship than it is autobiography, and her contribution was as teacher, editor, adviser, not muse.

Perhaps other playwrights don't have similar relationships or similar debts; perhaps they have. In a wonderful recent collection of essays on creative partnerships, *Significant Others*, edited by Isabelle De Courtivron and Whitney Chadwick, the contributors examine both healthy and deeply unhealthy versions of artistic interdependence in such couples as the Delaunays, Kahlo and Rivers, Hammett and Hellman, and Jasper Johns and Robert

Rauschenberg—and in doing so strike forcefully at what the editors call "the myth of solitariness."

Since this myth is all-important to our view of artistic work, we have no words for the people to whom we are indebted. I call Oskar Eustis a dramaturgist, sometimes a collaborator; but collaborator implies co-authorship and nobody knows what dramaturgist implies. *Angels* began in a conversation, real and imaginary, with Oskar. A romantic-ambivalent love for American history and belief in what one of the plays' characters calls "the prospect of some sort of radical democracy spreading outward and growing up" are things Oskar and I share, part of the discussions we had for nearly a year before I started writing Part 1. Oskar continues to be for me, intellectually and emotionally, what the developmental psychologists call "a secure base of attachment" (a phrase I learned from Kimberly).

The play is indebted, too, to writers I've never met. It's ironical that Harold Bloom, in his introduction to *Musical Variations on Jewish Thought* by Olivier Revault D'Allones, provided me with a translation of the Hebrew word for "blessing"—"More life"—which subsequently became key to the heart of *Perestroika*. Professor Bloom is also the author of *The Anxiety of Influence*, his oedipalization of the history of Western literature, which, when I first encountered it years ago, made me so anxious my analyst suggested I put it away. Recently I had the chance to meet Professor Bloom and, guilty over my appropriation of "more life," I fled from the encounter as one of Freud's *Totem and Taboo* tribesmen might flee from a meeting with that primal father, the one with the big knife. (I cite Professor Bloom as the source of the idea in the published script.)

Guilt, of course, plays a part in this confessional account; and I want the people who helped me make these plays to be identified because their labor was consequential. Many important names have not been mentioned, lest this begin to sound like a thank-you note or, worse, an acceptance speech. I have been blessed with remarkable comrades and collaborators: together we organize the world for ourselves, or at least we organize our understanding of it; we reflect it, refract it, criticize it, grieve over its savagery, and help one another to discern, amidst the gathering dark, paths of resistance, pockets of peace and places from whence hope may be plausibly expected.

Marx was right: the smallest divisible human unit is two people, not one; one is a fiction. From such nets of souls societies, the social world, human life spring. And also plays.

25.

odyssey

IRVING OYLE

Changing our environment, being exposed to radically different ways of doing and being, can lead to outbursts of creativity. Exposed to a different culture, we can see how it is possible to live in ways that are dramatically different from those we take for granted in our own culture. Worlds of possibilities are opened to us in these creative encounters. Irving Oyle, a physician from Long Island, tells the fascinating story of his encounter with the Tarahumara Indians, and how it gave him a completely different perspective on health and healing.

The invitation from a group of physician flyers to spend two weeks practicing medicine and distributing medical supplies among cave-dwelling Mexican Indians was impeccably timed. It arrived on the day I decided to take a two-week vacation. Little did I realize that that invitation was in reality a passport to a totally new professional and personal world!

Sisoguichi, Chihuahua, Mexico is an island in time. Perhaps the place might be more accurately labeled a warp in time. The folks who frequent the town are mostly local corn farmers. Tilling the soil with teams of oxen, pulling wooden plows, they live in caves, weave woolen blankets, and practice a lifestyle which hasn't changed in the past 35,000 years.

The outside world is brought to the *indígenas*, the natives, by the Society of Jesus, a religious group whose principles and practices date back some 400 years. The Jesuits run the local hospital and clinic, a movie house, auto repair shop, and the local school system.

The church women come in three colors according to habit. "White" nuns devote themselves to care of the body; white-robed sisters run the clinic, nurse in the hospital, and run the lab; "black" nuns, dedicated to care of the mind, run the schools, and accompany the priests on the weekly missionary expeditions to remote troglodyte communities. The town also has its "scarlet" women, Sisters of Perpetual Adoration, dressed in bright red habits; having renounced the material world, devoted entirely to the Spirit, the "red" nuns spend all their waking hours in continuous prayer.

Into this scene, in a single-engined Cessna, piloted by an incompetent, dropped the doctor from Long Island. When we slammed down onto the rutted cow pasture which doubles as the Sisoguichi Municipal Airport, I was convinced that I was about to die. In a sense, I did.

It would be difficult to create a greater change of environment for a medical practice than from the middle-class Long Island community to the remote mountains of Mexico, where the patient load consisted mostly of cave-dwelling Tarahumara Indians. Instead of house calls, we made cave calls. This was man in his natural habitat, creating life for himself under the most primitive conditions.

The healing science of Western medicine was being transported to Cro-Magnon man. Life among these people had not changed in thousands of years. While many of the Indians died young from a variety of causes, the survivors lived to remarkable ages.

In response to a radio message from the local priest, another Jesuit *padre* flew us to a village located on a 10,000-foot mountain. There we treated a man of indeterminate age and were directed by an 88-year-old lady to her mother's home. Her mother had suffered from heart failure and was being maintained on digitalis. More important, the village matriarch, 107 years old, was interested in seeing the new "gringo" doctor. Showing me a suspension of peyote buttons in tequila, she said, "If I rub this on my limbs, pain leaves me; if I eat it, illusion leaves me."

Another trait besides longevity which was demonstrated by these primitive people was that of physical stamina. A common sport among the younger Tarahumara is the game of *bola*. This is a race which lasts as long as two days and nights, covering enormous distances. The families of the contestants run alongside carrying food and water. At night these helpers carry torches through the forest to keep visible the wooden ball which must be kicked from the starting line to the finish point. In another instance, a father walked 40 miles daily for a week to visit his six-year-old son in the mission hospital, returning home in time to give the evening penicillin dose to his wife and four other children—all of whom had pneumonia.

It was apparent that the subjective living experience of these people (how they felt from the time they awoke in the morning to the time they retired for the night) was very different from what I had seen in Farmingdale! It seemed that 35,000 years of evolution had done very little to change their subjective life experience.

That summer among the Tarahumara was a pivotal experience, a ful-
crum upon which the life of the doctor from Farmingdale turned. He under-
went an ego-death. Renouncing property owners' associations, brick facades,
and pregnant telephones, I determined to totally alter my image—the manner in which I play my role. (When I say "I," I refer to that part of me which
answers to the name "Irving"—my personality, the puppeteer.) Four incidents precipitated my change of lifestyle.

I. PENETRATING THE VENEER
In which the puppeteer undertakes a role reappraisal

Seven hours after leaving base at Sisoguichi, our driver stopped the vehicle
saying, *"Ya estamos"*—We are here. Motioning his passengers to get out, he
began to crank the handle of the siren mounted on the fender of his World
War II four-wheel-drive Dodge army ambulance. The venerable vehicle carried several cartons of assorted drug company samples collected from the
mailboxes of physicians all over the United States. Her cargo also included an
ear-nose-and-throat man, a surgeon, and a general practitioner from Farmingdale.

Drawn by the wail of the siren, our patients moved cautiously out of the
caves dotting the hillside. Surrounding the green machine with the red cross
and white passengers, they chatted amiably with the driver, speaking a tongue
which was ancient when the Greek Democritus postulated a physical reality
composed of atoms.

Standing there contemplating the proceedings, I was struck by a thought.
I wondered how these ancient humans saw us. Take away the trappings, strip
away civilized society's ultra-thin veneer, and what's left? What, aside from su-
perficialities—the right kind of house, car, costume, and demeanor—constitutes the crux of the Medicine Man's role?

I spent the afternoon treating runny noses, sore throats, and a variety of
complaints not unlike those endemic to Farmingdale. That day's doctoring
produced no answers to my questions. It did, however, induce in me a sense
of joy and satisfaction which brought back the excitement of my first years of
practice. The spectacular sunset which signaled the end of that exhilarating
afternoon foreshadowed the end of the Farmingdale phase of my medical
career.

"Out here," I thought, "I'm not a suburban GP. I'm a medicine man." To this day, while I still practice medicine, the word on my state licenses has taken on a broader meaning.

II. Medicine Man as Conduit
In which the doctor acquires a new perspective

"Could you stop over at the hospital for a moment? There's a problem with a childbirth. Perhaps you can help." All my colleagues having returned to civilization, I was the only physician present. Leading me into the delivery room, the Mother Superior hurried off to attend other pressing matters.

On the delivery table lay an Indian woman who had just given birth. Wrapped and cared for, a healthy baby boy slept in his cradle. Beside the mother, on his knees, was a Mexican medical student who had assisted in the child's birth. Tears streaming down his cheeks, he rocked slowly back and forth in quiet prayer. "*Madre de Dios, ayudenos*"—Mother of God, help us— he murmured over and over as he gazed imploringly up at the operating room ceiling. Eyes wide with fear, severed umbilical cord protruding from her birth canal, the young mother responded with a prayer of her own. In a soft contrapuntal chant, she pleaded, "Help me, dear Jesus, dear Jesus, please help me." Faced with a life-threatening situation, these people placed all their faith in Mary and Jesus, just as my patients place all their faith in science and the doctor.

"It's been three hours and the afterbirth hasn't come out," said the distraught student, becoming aware of my presence. "If it doesn't come out she will die." I hadn't done a delivery in ten years. I had never dealt with a case of retained placenta. "It is necessary to reach inside and peel it off. I am only a student, señor. The wall of her womb is soft like butter; the placenta it sticks like glue. If either tears, she will bleed to death. If we don't get it all out, it will rot and she will be poisoned. I cannot attempt it. I have too much fear." Still on his knees, he clasped his hands and resumed rocking, praying, and sobbing.

At that moment the Mother Superior bustled into the room, carrying an anesthesia mask. "I will put her to sleep, you will take out the placenta." Sensing my hesitation, she added, "She will live or die according to God's will. You are but an instrument, a tool like this mask." Sinking into merciful oblivion, the frightened young mother continued to chant, "Jesus, help me, dear Jesus, please help me."

Reaching gently into the gaping uterine opening, I felt my fingers probing for the edge of the afterbirth. There, that must be it. Slowly, delicately, as though they had a mind of their own, my fingers insinuated themselves between the jellylike placenta and the swollen, delicate uterine wall.

Ten minutes later, the placenta lay in a pan. The student examined it and found it intact. Uttering a heartfelt thanks to the Virgin Mary, he turned and left the room, too overwhelmed to say anything else. The patient, recovered from her light anesthesia, whispered something to the Mother Superior who passed it on to me: "She wants to thank you for allowing Jesus to use your fingers to save her life."

III. DEATH AND THE ONE-LEGGED INDIAN
In which the doctor battles the Grim Reaper . . . and loses

A flatbed truck, raising a great cloud of dust, horn honking frantically, raced toward us as rapidly as road conditions would allow. "There goes my afternoon siesta," observed Hector, the newly arrived surgeon from Mexico City. Hector was in the habit of pouring two eight-ounce bottles of orange soda down his gullet, directly into his stomach without swallowing, every afternoon. Following this feat, he would curl up in fetal position on his desktop to sleep for two hours.

Shuddering to a stop, the flatbed disgorged its occupants. Supported by his comrades, ashen face twisted with pain, a man about twenty-four crumpled into unconsciousness as he stepped onto the ground. His useless right leg bore a tourniquet which staunched the flow of blood from a bullet wound high on the front of his thigh. "Julio was cleaning his *pistola* and it went off," said his distraught brother.

"The entry wound is located directly over the femoral artery," mused Hector as we headed for the marginally adequate operating room of the ramshackle Sisoguichi General Hospital. "If he's cut the main artery to the leg, we'll have to amputate immediately before gangrene begins."

"Better to let him die," murmured Mother Superior as she prepared the patient for surgery.

We took off Julio's leg, transfused ten pints of blood collected from his neighbors and relatives, supported his circulation with intravenous fluids, administered antibiotics in huge doses, all to no avail. Our patient never regained consciousness. "God has been merciful," said Mother Superior crossing herself.

"Why do you say that?" wondered the physician from Farmingdale as he climbed out of his green operating gown.

"To be a one-legged Indian in the Sierra is to suffer greatly," responded the white-robed *Madre*. "Your struggle against the death of Julio showed compassion. It also showed your fear. You fought against death as though he were Julio's enemy, and your foe as well. Death, señor, like the medicine man— like yourself—is but a tool serving the will of God."

"I am sworn to preserve human life, Madre."

"That is not the same as resisting death, señor."

IV. HEALING POTIONS AND PENICILLIN PILLS
In which the doctor sees the tangible in the ritual

The fourth incident affecting the course of my career occurred the following year during a similar work period with the Mayas in Yucatan. These people lived in a more advanced state of civilization than did the Tarahumara and depended on native healing rituals as did the Indians of Central Mexico. In Chomula, I met a Mexican doctor in a small government clinic. When I asked to see his medical equipment, he smiled and showed me a modern treatment room which was in an advanced state of neglect. Some of the equipment showed signs of rust. "There is no need to maintain the stuff I never use. The Indian people do not use my services; they hardly recognize the existence of the Mexican government. They don't need me because their own medicine men are more effective healers; their methods get better results. I can't do for them what they can."

Here was a group of humans who, given a free choice between 20th-century medicine and ancient Mayan medicine, chose the latter. The doctor was a Western-trained physician who had learned both systems firsthand, and made the same choice. "We work things out," he said. "The medicine man will sometimes add penicillin powder to his potions. I can't honestly say that it makes any difference in their therapeutic efficacy."

The comparison of these two healing systems and their effectiveness was, for me, enlightening. If you consult a modern American physician for a complaint, he performs a ritual which consists of X-rays, blood tests, and physical examination with medical tools. When he is finished he may say, for example, "You have an ulcer." He then proceeds to describe in detail an ulcerated area in the lining of your stomach which, being constantly bathed in hydrochloric acid, is prevented from healing. He may even explain with pic-

tures or three-dimensional models how the process can eat into a blood ves-
sel and cause bleeding or penetrate the wall to cause perforation—a catastro-
phe requiring immediate surgical intervention.

Having made the diagnosis and given the process a name, the physician
recommends a program based on established practice. Even if it fails and the
patient gets worse or dies, he is usually satisfied that he has earned his fee and
discharged his responsibility to his patient. The patient, on the other hand,
does not really know what initiated the chain of events, or how to alter their
compelling course. Having a clear picture of impending disaster, he worries
about it, thus stimulating its materialization.

I had been taught in medical school (and had practiced as a physician)
that all I could do is create the conditions under which healing can take
place. The Indian medicine man sees himself as a channel for cosmic healing energy. After all, the body is a self-repairing mechanism—it *has* the power
to heal itself. Apparently some kind of ritual is necessary. Medicine men
transmit religious or magical powers through ritual while the modern physician initiates healing through a rather formalized examination, diagnosis,
and therapy. In either case the patient receives information, processes it, and
accepts or rejects the ritual as the truth. Some patients decide that only the
proper herb can heal while others put childlike faith in the power of a pill;
still others insist that salvation can be achieved by mastering a particular yoga
position, or by repeating a mantra. *Whatever you put your trust in can be the
precipitating agent for your cure.*

Recently, Dr. William Kroger made the following prediction: "[The]
arthritics, then the asthmatics, the neurotics, and then the cancerous . . .
Help will seem imminent to these—they will journey off to the Lourdes of
acupuncture and throw down their crutches and their canes, not realizing
that it's not the rock that cures, but their own inner belief." Any ritual accepted by the patient as reality can be substituted for the word *acupuncture*.

So it is possible that this inner belief is a vital factor in any healing
process regardless of the ritual employed by the therapist healer. In the
course of two decades of family medical practice, I became aware of two factors which are essential to the therapeutic relationship: The physician must
have the complete confidence in his healing system or ritual, and the patient
must trust that the physician knows what he is doing. If either aspect of this
inner belief is missing, the healing process is adversely affected.

‡6.

the magic of words

N. SCOTT MOMADAY

*In this interview, novelist and poet N. Scott Momaday discusses the nature and rel-
evance of Native American culture in the context of his writing. He comments on
nature, landscape, words, and dreams, from a perspective that is radically different
from most Western literary discourse. Continuity, and the importance of the land
and of tradition, play an important part in his work, and he contrasts this practice
with the Euro-American tendency to want to break from the past and move into
new, uncharted territories.*

JB: Did it affect your writing when you worked in another country?

MOMADAY: I think it did. I'm not sure that I can say how, exactly. There was
a great compulsion there to write, and that surprised me; I could not have anticipated that. But when I got there and had been there a while and had begun to understand a little bit about my isolation and my distance from my
native land, this somehow became a creative impulse for me, and so I wrote
much more than I thought I would. And I wrote about things I saw and felt in
the Soviet Union. "Krasnopresnenskaya Station" is an example. The little
poem called "Anywhere is a Street into the Night" is a comment upon my
understanding of that distance that I mentioned a moment ago. But I also
found myself writing about my homeland, the Southwest—perhaps as a kind
of therapy. I wrote the poem that I dedicated to Georgia O'Keeffe ("Forms of
the Earth at Abiquiu") there, for example, and it is very much an evocation of
the Southwest, isn't it?

JB: This southwestern landscape which turns up in your poems throughout
your writing . . . how do you define that landscape? What are the important
qualities of it for you? The qualities of life in the Southwest which are important . . .

MOMADAY: Well, I think it's a much more spiritual landscape than any other that I know personally. And it is beautiful, simply in physical terms. The colors in that landscape are very vivid, as you know, and I've always been greatly moved by the quality of light upon the colored landscape of New Mexico and Arizona.

JB: Yes, that's evident in your work.

MOMADAY: And I think of it as being inhabited by a people who are truly involved in it. The Indians of the Southwest, and the Pueblo people, for example, and the Navajos with whom I grew up, they don't live on the land; they live *in* it, in a real sense. And that is very important to me, and I like to evoke as best I can that sense of belonging to the earth.

JB: I think that idea of belonging is also of central importance. In *The Names* or even in some of your poems, you present us with situations where there is a possibility for distance, or a possibility for alienation. But I don't see that alienation coming about. I see, rather, a motion in a different direction — toward a kind of resolution. Am I correct in seeing this?

MOMADAY: I think that's a fair statement.

JB: Why is that so? Why are you not an existentialist, for example, a "modern" man looking at the world as separate from the person?

MOMADAY: Well, I'm a product of my experience, surely, of what I have seen and known of the world. I've had, by the way, what I think of as a very fortunate growing up. On the basis of my experience, trusting my own perceptions, I don't see any validity in the separation of man and the landscape. Oh, I know that the notion of alienation is very widespread, in a sense very popular. But I think it's an unfortunate point of view and a false one, where the relationship between man and the earth is concerned. Certainly it is one of the great afflictions of our time, this conviction of alienation, separation, isolation. And it is certainly an affliction in the Indian world. But there it has the least chance of taking hold, I believe, for there it is opposed by very strong forces. The whole worldview of the Indian is predicated upon the principle of harmony in the universe. You can't tinker much with that; it has the look of an absolute.

JB: Do you differentiate between prose and poetry in a strict sense?

MOMADAY: When I talk about definitions, yes. Prose and poetry are opposed in a certain way. It's hard to define poetry. Poetry is a statement concerning the human condition, composed in verse. I did not invent this definition, skeletal as it is. I think I may be repeating something I heard in class years ago. In that refinement, in that reservation, "composed in verse," is really, finally, the matter that establishes the idea of poetry and sets it apart.

JB: I wonder, because I see in the work of a number of American Indian writers, for example, Leslie Silko, places where prose suddenly breaks into what appears to be verse in parts of *Ceremony.* There the stories that are told are in a form I would describe as verse. I see, also, in a number of other writers who are American Indians, if not a blurring of that distinction, a passing back and forth, rather freely, between verse and prose. I see it, also, in your work . . . your prose in such books as *House Made of Dawn,* and especially *The Way to Rainy Mountain.* There are sections which one could read as poems. Is this observation a good one? Why do you think it's like this, with yourself and other American Indian prose writers?

MOMADAY: That's a large question, and I've thought about it before. The prose pieces in *The Way to Rainy Mountain* are illustrations of the very thing that I was talking about before, the lyrical prose, the thing that is called the prose poem. The oral tradition of the American Indian is intrinsically poetic in certain, obvious ways. I believe that a good many Indian writers rely upon a kind of poetic expression out of necessity, a necessary homage to the native tradition, and they have every right and reason to do so. . . .

JB: I have noticed that certain themes appear to turn up again and again in your work. What are those themes? Do you think about them or are they there subconsciously?

MOMADAY: I would say that much of my writing has been concerned with the question of man's relationship to the earth, for one thing. Another theme that has interested me is man's relationship to himself, to his past, his heritage. When I was growing up on the reservations of the Southwest, I saw people who were deeply involved in their traditional life, in the memories of their blood. They had, as far as I could see, a certain strength and beauty that I find missing in the modern world at large. I like to celebrate that involvement in my writing.

JB: You don't think of yourself, though, as a person who is sort of conserving something that's disappearing, do you? I've heard that description of their work given by many non-Indian writers who have written about Indian ways. And I'm not just talking about anthropologists, but also some of the novelists of the early part of the century who thought of themselves as both celebrating and preserving—almost like an artifact—something which was vanishing. Yet I don't think that is characteristic of your approach.

MOMADAY: No, I wouldn't say so. There is an aspect of this matter that has to do with preservation, of course—with a realization that things are passing. I feel this very keenly. But I'm not concerned to preserve relics and artifacts. Only superficially have things changed in the world I knew as a child. I can enumerate them. When I was growing up at Jemez Pueblo—I lived there for several years from the time I was twelve—I saw things that are not to be seen now. I wrote about some of them in *The Names*. I remember one day looking out upon a dirt road and seeing a caravan of covered wagons that reached as far as the eye could see. These were the Navajos coming in from Torreon to the annual Jemez feast on November 12, 1946. It was simply an unforgettable sight. But the next year it had changed considerably; there were fewer wagons, and there were some pickups, and the year after that there were still fewer wagons and more pickups, and the year after that there were no wagons. And I had later the sense that I had been in the right place at the right time, that I had seen something that will not be seen again, and I thank God for that. But the loss is less important to me than the spirit which informs the remembrance, the spirit that informs that pageantry across all ages and which persists in the imagination of every man everywhere.

JB: Yes, that's a great example. Are words magical?

MOMADAY: Oh, yes.

JB: How so?

MOMADAY: Well, words are powerful beyond our knowledge, certainly. And they are beautiful. Words are intrinsically powerful, I believe. And there is magic in that. Words come from nothing into being. They are created in the imagination and given life on the human voice. You know, we used to believe—and I'm talking now about all of us, regardless of our ethnic backgrounds—in the magic of words. The Anglo-Saxon who uttered spells over his fields so that the seeds would come out of the ground on the sheer strength of his voice, knew a good deal about language, and he believed absolutely in the efficacy of language. That man's faith—and may I say, wisdom—has been lost upon modern man, by and large. It survives in the poets of the world, I suppose, the singers. We do not now know what we can do with words. But as long as there are those among us who try to find out, literature will be secure; literature will remain a thing worthy of our highest level of human being.

JB: You mention poets and singers. Are they related or are they different?

MOMADAY: I think they are the same thing. You might make this sort of superficial distinction. The poet is concerned to construct his expression according to traditional and prescribed forms. The singer, too, composes his expression according to strict rules, but he is a more religious being, on the whole, less concerned with form than with the most fundamental and creative possibilities of language. The American Indian would be in the second of these categories. This distinction, of course, requires elucidation, but, for the time being, I shall spare you that.

JB: And do you think there are some Indian poets who are still singers or vice versa?

MOMADAY: Yes. . . .

JB: The idea of dreams, then . . . what are dreams?

MOMADAY: Yeah, what are dreams? Has there ever been an answer to that? There is so much we have yet to know about dreams and dreaming. Dreams are prophetic, meaningful, revealing of inmost life. But no one knows how they work, as far as I know. I have powerful dreams, and I believe they determine who I am and what I do. But how, I'm not sure. Maybe that is how it ought to be. Mystery is, perhaps, the necessary condition of dreams.

JB: The term, "the great mystery," is often used by some of the Plains people to describe the Creator or that life force which is beyond and above all human, in other life. That's not a mystery that, I sense, native people wish to pierce. It's a mystery which they live in the knowledge of, without wanting to know "what" it is. It seems rather counter to the Western approach to things. The Anglo approach is to *always* know.

MOMADAY: Yes, yes. I don't know.

JB: I was talking about the contrast between the Western, Anglo, view and the American Indian view. I'd like to take that back directly to literature and ask what you think the difference is between, let's say, an Indian view of what literature is, and I don't mean just a traditional Indian person, but, let's say someone who has been raised in the twentieth century and who is writing still as an Indian, as opposed to that writer who is non-Indian.

MOMADAY: I think there is only one real difference between the two, and that is that the Indian has the advantage of a very rich spiritual experience. As much can be said, certainly, of some non-Indian writers. But the non-Indian writers of today are culturally deprived, I think, in the sense that they don't have the same sense of heritage that the Indian has. I'm told this time and time again by my students, who say, "Oh, I wish I knew more about my grandparents; I wish I knew more about my ancestors and where they came from and what they did." I've come to believe them. It seems to me that the Indian writer ought to make use of that advantage. One of his subjects ought certainly to be his cultural investment in the world. It is a unique and complete experience, and it is a great subject in itself.

JB: One thing which I'm concerned with is a sense of the continuance and the survival of various things which seem to be central to a number of American Indian writers. Do you see your work as continuing some tradition?

MOMADAY: Yes. I think that my work proceeds from the American Indian oral tradition, and I think it sustains that tradition and carries it along. And vice versa. And my writing is also of a piece. I've written several books, but to me they are all parts of the same story. And I like to repeat myself, if you will, from book to book, in the way that Faulkner did—in an even more obvious way, perhaps. My purpose is to carry on what was begun a long time ago; there's no end to it that I can see.

JB: That's a question that I was going to ask. I'm glad you led into it. In *House Made of Dawn* there is a sermon which is given by a Kiowa character. He's not terribly likable in some ways. Yet those words turn up again in *The Way to Rainy Mountain* out of, I assume, your own lips. The things that happen in *The Gourd Dancer* also seem to be a continuance of that same voice and, of course, in *The Names* you have that repetition. I've heard some people say, "Momaday's repeating himself. Doesn't he have any new material?" But I've suspected this repetition was a conscious thing.

MOMADAY: Oh, yes. In a sense I'm not concerned to change my subject from book to book. Rather, I'm concerned to keep the story going. I mean to keep the same subject, to carry it farther with each telling.

JB: Some traditional songs and stories begin each new movement by repeating. They repeat and then go a bit further. That's the structure in your work?

MOMADAY: Yes, indeed, and I believe that is a good way in which to proceed. It establishes a continuity that is important to me.

JB: What are the links in your everyday life to American Indian traditions?

MOMADAY: Well, I have the conviction that I am an Indian. I have an idea of myself as an Indian, and that idea is quite secure. My father was Huan-toa; my grandfather was Mammedaty; my great-grandfather was Guipagho. How can I not be an Indian? I'm a member of the Gourd Dance society in the Kiowa tribe, and when I can, I go to the annual meeting of that society, and it is a great thing for me, full of excitement and restoration, the deepest meaning. Since I've returned to the Southwest I feel new and stronger links with the Indian world than I felt in California, where I was for twenty years in exile. Then, too, I have children. And my children are, much to my delight, greatly interested in their stake in the Indian world. So that's another link for me as well as for them. Of course I have Indian relatives. I lost my father, who was my closest tie with the Kiowa world; he died last year. But there are others who sustain me. I keep in touch.

JB: You could say then, perhaps, of "The Gourd Dancer," of your poem, although it's dedicated to your grand-father, that Gourd Dancer is also you.

MOMADAY: Oh, yes, yes. Again the continuity. That part of the poem which refers to the giving away of a horse: I wasn't there, of course. But it really did happen; my father was only eight years old, but it remained in his memory as long as he lived. And I absorbed it when I was the same age, so that it became my memory as well. This is a profound continuity, something at the very center of the Indian perception of the world. We are talking about immortality, or something very close to it, though the American Indian would not have that name for it. He would say, perhaps, if he were Kiowa, *Akeahde*, "they were camping." In that word is the seed of the same idea.

JB: The American writer some people might link you most closely to who is non-Indian is Walt Whitman. Whitman's life was a single work, *Leaves of Grass*, which went through different stages of development. Vine Deloria and Geary Hobson have both pointed out (Geary in an article in *New America Magazine* and Vine in that *Sun Tracks* interview), that there have been cycles of interest in American Indians and in the publication of American Indian literary work. As you know D'arcy McNickle more or less stopped being published after a certain point in the late thirties and only was published just before his death in the current resurgence in the late seventies. In the thirties, it was Luther Standing Bear, twenty years before that Charles Eastman. Do you think that this kind of cycle will happen again with American Indian literature or is there something different about the current surge of writing by American Indians and interest in their writing?

MOMADAY: I really don't know the answer to that. Oh, I suppose there will be cycles; the popularity of books by and about American Indians will pass, and then there will be regenerations of interest, *ad infinitum*. That's the nature of the publishing world, isn't it? I'm not worried about it. The American Indian is indispensable to the soil and the dream and the destiny of America. That's the important thing. He always was and always will be a central figure in the American imagination, a central figure in American literature. We can't very well do without him.

JB: I also wonder if it might not be different this time because we now have more Indian people who are literate, who do read. We now have also our own audience as opposed to an audience of people who are non-Indian.

MOMADAY: I'm sure that's true.

JB: What is it that contemporary American Indian poetry has to offer to the world of literature or to the world as a whole?

MOMADAY: Well, I think it's a legitimate and artistic expression in itself, first of all. Here is my voice, and my voice proceeds out of an intelligence that touches upon the inexorable motions of the world. There is design and symmetry in the pattern of my speech, my words. That in itself is a noteworthy thing. Another such thing is the perception that we were talking about a moment ago. I believe that the Indian has an understanding of the physical world and of the earth as a spiritual entity that is his, very much his own. The non-Indian can benefit a good deal by having that perception revealed to him.

why world music?

BRIAN ENO

Brian Eno discusses the role of world music and the potential that musical cross-pollination has for bringing people of diverse cultures together as it builds bridges between normally separate worlds. Eno writes of several changes in the way music is understood, and how the differences between all cultures, "high" and "low," "us" and "them," and "Western" and "other," are collapsing. This heralds the potential for a new openness and empathy for different sounds and different worlds, judged not on the basis of pre-established Western codes, but by new, emerging criteria, which include consideration of the way different forms of music personally affect us and of their sources worldwide.

The last decade has seen a huge upsurge of interest in what is now called "World Music." The technical reason for this is that records have become available allowing people to participate in the music of other cultures with an ease and breadth that was not possible earlier. But actually, that situation has existed for a long time—since the "ethnic" recordings of the forties and fifties. But it is only comparatively recently that this has interested more than a handful of specialists.

I believe that this new, widening popularity results from something other than simple availability. One of these factors is the increasing ability of people to listen to songs without being concerned to know what they mean: the "language barrier," in the past always cited as the main reason that "ethnic" music could not become popular, has suddenly fallen. It now seems that nobody minds if Salif Keita sings in Arabic, Youssou N'Dour in Wolof and Zvuki Mu in Russian. Perhaps this means that people are listening to music now, rather than specifically to songs: perhaps it also means that the composers and musicians of the world are making new forms of music that do not depend on language as much as they used to.

But perhaps a more important reason is the breakdown of a world view

that says: "We, and our values, are the hub, the norm, the center, and everyone else is a kind of aberration from us." Of course, this view would lead one
to regard other musics as, at best, curiously exotic and at worst, proof of all the
nasty things people like to think about each other. And within this "us and
them" distinction, there was another subdivision. Our version of it was called
the Western classical tradition, and it maintained that there was High Music—the type that the people who wrote the history books liked—and there
was all the rest, the stuff that everyone else liked. This picture maintained
that innovation always worked from the top downwards—that the pure ideas
of the great composers found their way, in degenerate form, into the popular
music, and that, therefore, these popular musics were necessarily dilute and
comparatively less "valuable" and "enduring." Occasionally there was an acknowledgment that this flow could be reversed—Kodály and Bartók, for example, borrowed from rustic folk dances—but then it was assumed that the
raw material of folk culture would be enhanced and ennobled in the hands
of a great composer.

Distinctions of this kind are interesting because they notify us about the
limits of our empathy. If we really have no feeling whatsoever for the music
that so deeply moves somebody else, surely this indicates that there is a part
of their psyche that is closed to us. How important is that part? What does music represent in this sense?

Take a particular case: what does it tell you about somebody that they begin to like (for example) West African music? Well, it tells you that their focus
of attention as a listener is starting to shift. Nigerian music downplays harmony and melody in favour of extremely rich and complex rhythmic meshes.
These engage a different part of you: they are extremely physical, sexual and
movement-oriented. They deal with the body, an area that Western classical
music (for example) rarely addresses. When a listener is moved by this music,
and is allowing herself to accept the idea that her body is a fit focus for artistic attention, she is saying (in the words of the artist Peter Schmidt) that the
body is the large brain. Our cultures, which have made such a big distinction
between "men of action" and "men of thought," might find this hard to accept; all our hierarchies are based upon the idea that the brain is good and
the body inferior. I believe that in the process of being moved by Nigerian
music, you begin to empathize with another view of the universe, another
picture of how things work and how they fit together. And in noticing how
you have the capacity to empathize with that, perhaps you take a further step
and begin to suppose that the cultural values are also "possible" for you. It
doesn't mean that you are going to become Nigerian, but might mean that

you can begin to get a feeling of what it is like to be Nigerian, what kind of world you might be looking at, through what kind of eyes.

It would be naive to assume that this broadening of understanding automatically leads to something like world peace. (It is, after all, standard operating behavior in the subversion industry to know your enemy at the deepest cultural level so that you can eliminate him!) No, I wouldn't make any such happy predictions—understanding, like a knife, has many uses.

My hope for the future is not that everyone will sit around the lunar campfire discussing, in Esperanto, the bad old days of division and strife. I wouldn't expect that. What I want to see is the demise of fundamentalism in favour of pragmatism.

By fundamentalism I mean any philosophy that thinks it has the final and unique answer, that believes that there is one essential plan underlying the workings of the universe, and that seeks to make sure everyone else gets persuaded to fall in line with it.

By pragmatism I mean improvisation: the belief that there are many approaches, that whatever works in the light of our present knowledge is a good course of action, and that what is the best course of action for us, here and now, might not be for someone else, there or then.

I want to see societies (and people) who know how to improvise, who can throw together a social mode (tuxedo and black Thai) just for the evening, who can move fluently and easily between different social and personal vocabularies as the situation changes, who don't feel lost without the religious reassurance of "thisism" and "thatism." I see these people as hunter-gatherers in the great flux of the world's cultures, enjoying a rich diet of ideas and techniques and styles, creating their own special mixes. There is no snobbism in this picture—no material too common or too exotic to be used, no simple distinction between real and make-believe. This kind of improvisational flexibility entails a continuous questioning of boundaries and categories, a refusal to accept that names necessarily fit accurately onto what is being named. When languages are developing and changing as rapidly as they do now, and everyone is a rap artist, you need all the voices you can get.

V

THE DEDICATION
TO MASTERY

Work is more fun than fun.

NOEL COWARD

I have very joyful dreams which I cannot bring to paper, much less to any approach to practice, and I blame myself not at all for my reveries, but that they have not yet got possession of my house and barn.

RALPH WALDO EMERSON

The experience of doing anything well — from the minor scale to the Hammerklavier Sonata — is an irreplaceable event of the spirit.

ROBERT GRUDIN

The creative process involves a tension between opposites, and nowhere is that tension more apparent than in the need to balance freedom and exploration with the disciplined fine-tuning of our craft. Creativity is a gift, some say, but not a gift that survives without practice.

Talent always plays a part, but to get really good at something you have to practice. It need not be a practice imposed from without; the exercise of a talent gives us practice in it. The best way to learn to read is to read. The best way to learn to run is to run.

According to their own accounts, the great creators practice incessantly. They start early and keep going until late. Concentration, hard work, the learning of craft as well as art, dedication to the goal of excellence, and willingness to accept the mentorship of others all play a part in creativity that makes its mark.

There is evidence that if you break down creativity into its factors, ability in those factors can be increased by training. If creativity itself cannot be taught, perhaps we can create the conditions in which it can flourish. And creativity is in part a matter of attitude. If you place a positive value on the creativity of yourself and others, you will dedicate yourself to practicing it. But the right attitude alone won't do it. Creativity needs to be expressed through a medium, the knowledge of which is essential if we are to see our dreams become a reality. We must acquire the necessary knowledge, through study and practice.

This leads us to a paradox. Creativity, the sublime expression of human freedom, needs discipline and routine. It takes time and energy and organization to produce something great.

But the discipline and routine of creativity do not have to be boring. Even our disciplined routines can be creative. They can allow our personal differences and idiosyncrasies to emerge. If we are to organize our creativity, we can make that organization itself creative. The two elements most important are dedication and the drive toward mastery.

Organized creativity such as we find in dance, music, product development, or sports, to give just a few examples, requires a lot of practice to develop mastery—the mastery shown by the team player, finely attuned to the movements and needs of colleagues, sensitive to motion and possibility, as they create opportunities together. In a sports team, as in an orchestra or a jazz ensemble, we find each player an integral part of the team, yet possessed of her or his own unique qualities—a mastery of collaborative creation.

At times creativity cannot escape from simple hard labor—deadlines to be met, canvases to be stretched, scales to be learned and repeated endlessly so that our fingers may match our inspiration. The dedication to mastery needs the mastery of practice, and the exhilaration of creativity is sometimes counteracted by drudgery. Yet the drudgery of practice takes on a different light when we see our plodding efforts turn into mastery.

28.

HOW TO MANAGE AN
ADVERTISING AGENCY

DAVID OGILVY

Acclaimed British advertising executive David Ogilvy discusses his early training in a different field—a great Parisian restaurant. He was taught by a master, who, along with the tricks of the trade, stressed the importance of character. Like so many creative individuals, Ogilvy transferred what he learned in one field to another.

Managing an advertising agency is like managing any other creative organization—a research laboratory, a magazine, an architect's office, a great kitchen.

Thirty years ago I was a chef at the Hotel Majestic in Paris. Henri Soulé of the Pavillon tells me that it was probably the best kitchen there has ever been.

There were thirty-seven chefs in our brigade. We worked like dervishes, sixty-three hours a week—there was no trade union. From morning to night we sweated and shouted and cursed and cooked. Every man jack was inspired by one ambition: to cook better than any chef had ever cooked before. Our *esprit de corps* would have done credit to the Marines.

I have always believed that if I could understand how Monsieur Pitard, the head chef, inspired such white-hot morale, I could apply the same kind of leadership to the management of my advertising agency.

To begin with, he was the best cook in the whole brigade, and we knew it. He had to spend most of his time at his desk, planning menus, scrutinizing bills, and ordering supplies, but once a week he would emerge from his glass-walled office in the middle of the kitchen and actually *cook* something. A crowd of us always gathered around to watch, spellbound by his virtuosity. It was inspiring to work for a supreme master.

(Following Chef Pitard's example, I still write occasional advertisements myself, to remind my brigade of copywriters that my hand has not lost its cunning.)

M. Pitard ruled with a rod of iron, and we were terrified of him. There he sat in his glass cage, the *gros bonnet*, the arch symbol of authority. Whenever I made a mistake in my work, I would look up to see if his gimlet eye had noticed it.

Cooks, like copywriters, work under ferocious pressures, and are apt to be quarrelsome. I doubt whether a more easygoing boss could have prevented our rivalries from breaking into violence. M. Bourgignon, our *chef saucier*, told me that by the time a cook is forty, he is either dead or crazy. I understood what he meant the night our *chef potagier* threw forty-seven raw eggs across the kitchen at my head, scoring nine direct hits; his patience had been exhausted by my raids on his stock pot in search of bones for the poodles of an important client.

Our *chef pâtissier* was equally eccentric. Every night he left the kitchen with a chicken concealed in the crown of his Homburg hat. When he went on vacation he made me stuff two dozen peaches into the legs of his long underwear. But when the King and Queen of England were given a state dinner at Versailles, this roguish genius was chosen from all the *pâtissiers* in France to prepare the ornamental baskets of sugar and the *petits fours glacés*.

M. Pitard praised very seldom, but when he did, we were exalted to the skies. When the President of France came to a banquet at the Majestic, the atmosphere in our kitchen was electric. On one of these memorable occasions, I was covering frogs' legs with a white *chaud-froid* sauce, decorating each little thigh with an ornate leaf of chervil. Suddenly I became aware that M. Pitard was standing beside me, watching. I was so frightened that my knees knocked together and my hands trembled. He took the pencil from his starched toque and waved it in the air, his signal for the whole brigade to gather. Then he pointed at my frogs' legs and said, very slowly and very quietly, "That's how to do it." I was his slave for life.

(Today I praise my staff as rarely as Pitard praised his chefs, in the hope that they too will appreciate it more than a steady gush of appreciation.)

M. Pitard gave us all a great sense of occasion. One evening when I had prepared a Soufflé Rothschild (with three liqueurs) he took me upstairs to the door of the dining room and allowed me to watch President Paul Doumer eat it. Three weeks later, on May 7, 1932, Doumer was dead.*

---

*Not from my *soufflé*, but from the bullet of a mad Russian.

(I find that people who work in my agency get a similar charge out of state occasions. When a crisis keeps them working all night, their morale is high for weeks afterward.)

M. Pitard did not tolerate incompetence. He knew that it is demoralizing for professionals to work alongside incompetent amateurs. I saw him fire three pastry-cooks in a month for the same crime: they could not make the caps on their brioches rise evenly. Mr. Gladstone would have applauded such ruthlessness; he held that the "first essential for a Prime Minister is to be a good butcher."

M. Pitard taught me exorbitant standards of service. For example, he once heard me tell a waiter that we were fresh out of the *plat du jour*—and almost fired me for it. In a great kitchen, he said, one must always honor what one has promised on the menu. I pointed out that the dish in question would take so long to cook that no client would wait for a new batch to be prepared. Was it our famous *coulibiac de saumon*, a complicated kedgeree made with the spine marrow of sturgeon, semolina kache, salmon collops, mushrooms, onions, and rice, rolled up in a brioche paste and baked for fifty minutes? Or was it our still more exotic Karoly Éclairs, stuffed with a purée of woodcocks' entrails cooked in champagne, covered with a brown *chaud-froid* sauce and masked with game jelly? At this distance of time, I do not remember, but I remember exactly what Pitard said to me: "Next time you see that we are running out of a *plat du jour*, come and tell me. I will then get on the telephone to other hotels and restaurants until I find one which has the same dish on its menu. Then I will send you in a taxi to bring back a supply. Never again tell a waiter that we are fresh out of anything."

(Today I see red when anybody at Ogilvy, Benson & Mather tells a client that we cannot produce an advertisement or a television commercial on the day we have promised it. In the best establishments, promises are always kept, whatever it may cost in agony and overtime.)

Soon after I joined M. Pitard's brigade I was faced with a problem in morality for which neither my father nor my schoolmasters had prepared me. The *chef garde-manger* sent me to the *chef saucier* with some raw sweetbreads which smelled so putrid that I knew they would endanger the life of any client who ate them; the sauce would mask their condition, and the client would eat them. I protested to the *chef garde-manger*, but he told me to carry out his order; he knew that he would be in hot water if M. Pitard discovered that he had run out of fresh sweetbreads. What was I to do? I had been brought up to believe that it is dishonorable to inform. But I did just that. I took the putrid sweetbreads to M. Pitard, and invited him to smell them.

Without a word to me, he went over to the *chef garde-manger* and fired him. The poor bastard had to leave, then and there.

In *Down and Out in Paris and London* George Orwell told the world that French kitchens are dirty. He had never worked at the Majestic. M. Pitard was a martinet in making us keep the kitchen clean. Twice a day I had to scrape the wooden surface of the larder table with a sharp plane. Twice a day the floor was scrubbed, and clean sawdust put down. Once a week a bug-catcher scoured the kitchen in search of roaches. We were issued clean uniforms every morning.

(Today I am a martinet in making my staff keep their offices shipshape. A messy office creates an atmosphere of sloppiness, and leads to the disappearance of secret papers.)

We cooks were badly paid, but M. Pitard made so much from the commissions which his suppliers paid him that he could afford to live in a château. Far from concealing his wealth from the rest of us, he drove to work in a taxi, carried a cane with a gold head, and dressed, when off-duty, like an international banker. This flaunting of privilege stimulated our ambition to follow in his footsteps.

The immortal Auguste Escoffier had the same idea. When he was *chef des cuisines* at the Carlton in London before the First World War, he used to drive to the Derby on the box of a coach-and-four, dressed in a gray frock coat and top hat. Among my fellow cooks at the Majestic, Escoffier's *Guide Culinaire* was still the definitive authority, the court of last appeal in all our arguments about recipes. Just before he died he emerged from retirement and came to luncheon in our kitchen; it was like Brahms lunching with the musicians of the Philharmonic.

During the service of luncheon and dinner, M. Pitard stationed himself at the counter where we cooks handed our dishes to the waiters. He inspected every single dish before it left the kitchen. Sometimes he sent it back to the cook for more work. Always he reminded us not to put too much on the plate — "*pas trop!*" He wanted the Majestic to make a profit.

(Today I inspect every campaign before it goes to the client, and send back many of them for more work. And I share M. Pitard's passion for profit.)

Perhaps the ingredient in M. Pitard's leadership which made the most profound impression on me was his industry. I found my sixty-three hours bending over a red-hot stove so exhausting that I had to spend my day off lying on my back in a meadow, looking at the sky. But Pitard worked *seventy-seven* hours a week, and took only one free day a fortnight.

(That is about my schedule today. I figure that my staff will be less reluctant to work overtime if I work longer hours than they do. An executive who recently left my agency wrote in his farewell letter, "You set the pace on doing homework. It is a disconcerting experience to spend a Saturday evening in the garden next door to your house, carousing for four hours while you sit, unmoving, at your desk by the window doing your homework. The word gets around.")

29.

anatomy

LEONARDO DA VINCI

Leonardo da Vinci, the prototypical Renaissance man, embodied what was later to blossom as the scientific spirit of inquiry, and he vigorously describes his approach in these pages. Leonardo's meticulous and painstaking research into human anatomy (among other things) contributed greatly to art and science, and pointed the way to a new way of thinking and a new method of inquiry.

The mental matters which have not passed through the sense are vain, and they produce no other truth than the injurious one; and as such discourses spring from poverty of genius, such discoursers are always poor, and if they are born rich they shall die poor in their old age; because it seems that nature revenges itself on those who wish to work miracles that they shall possess less than other more quiet men; and those who want to grow rich in a day live for a long time in great poverty, as always happens, and to all eternity will happen, to alchemists, the would-be creators of gold and silver, and to engineers who would have dead water stir itself into life and perpetual motion, and to those supreme fools, the necromancer and the enchanter.

And you, who say that it would be better to watch an anatomist at work than to see these drawings, you would be right, if it were possible to observe all the things which are demonstrated in such drawings in a single figure, in which you, with all your cleverness, will not see nor obtain knowledge of more than some few veins, to obtain a true and perfect knowledge of which I have dissected more than ten human bodies, destroying all the other members, and removing the very minutest particles of the flesh by which these veins are surrounded, without causing them to bleed, excepting the insensible bleeding of the capillary veins; and as one single body would not last so long, since it was necessary to proceed with several bodies by degrees, until I came to an end and had a complete knowledge; this I repeated twice, to learn the differences.

And if you should have a love for such things you might be prevented by loathing, and if that did not prevent you, you might be deterred by the fear of living in the night hours in the company of those corpses, quartered and flayed and horrible to see. And if this did not prevent you, perhaps you might not be able to draw so well as is necessary for such a demonstration; or if you had the skill in drawing, it might not be combined with knowledge of perspective; and if it were so, you might not understand the methods of geometrical demonstration and the method of the calculation of forces and of the strength of the muscles; patience also may be wanting, so that you lack perseverance. As to whether all these things were found in me or not, the hundred and twenty books composed by me will give verdict. Yes or No. In these I have been hindered neither by avarice nor negligence, but simply by want of time. Farewell.

30.

composing
a symphony

PETER ILICH TCHAIKOVSKY

In these excerpts from his three thousand letters, the composer Tchaikovsky sum-marizes his creative process. In a few brief pages he encapsulates some of the cru-cial issues, from the nature of inspiration to the importance of continuing to work even if one feels uninspired, from the birth of an idea in concrete rather than abstract form to the need to be ruthless in the pruning, editing, and criticizing of one's work. Whereas much of the popular literature on creativity emphasizes so-called right-brain, uncritical, nonjudgmental acceptance of our creative process, Tchaikovsky reminds us that this is only one part of it.

FLORENCE, 17 FEBRUARY (1 MARCH) 1878

You ask if in composing this symphony I had a special programme in view. To such questions, regarding my symphonic works I generally answer: nothing of the kind. In reality it is very difficult to answer this question. How interpret those vague feelings which pass through one during the composition of an in-strumental work, without reference to any definite subject? It is a purely lyri-cal process. A kind of musical shriving of the soul, in which there is an encrustation of material which flows forth again in notes, just as the lyrical poet pours himself out in verse. The difference consists in the fact that music possesses far richer means of expression, and is a more subtle medium in which to translate the thousand shifting moments in the mood of a soul. Gen-erally speaking, the germ of a future composition comes suddenly and unex-pectedly. If the soil is ready—that is to say, if the disposition for work is there—it takes root with extraordinary force and rapidity, shoots up through the earth, puts forth branches, leaves and, finally, blossoms. I cannot define the creative process in any other way than by this simile. The great difficulty is that the germ must appear at a favourable moment, the rest goes of itself. It would be vain to try to put into words that immeasurable sense of bliss which comes over me directly a new idea awakens in me and begins to assume a definite form. I forget everything and behave like a madman. Everything within me starts pulsing and quivering; hardly have I begun the sketch ere one thought follows another. In the midst of this magic process it frequently happens that some external interruption wakes me from my somnambulistic state: a ring at the bell, the entrance of my servant, the striking of the clock, reminding me that it is time to leave off. Dreadful, indeed, are such interruptions. Sometimes they break the thread of inspiration for a considerable time, so that I have to seek it again—often in vain. In such cases cool head-work and technical knowledge have to come to my aid. Even in the works of the greatest master we find such moments, when the organic sequence fails and a skillful join has to be made, so that the parts appear as a completely welded whole. But it cannot be avoided. If that condition of mind and soul, which we call inspiration lasted long without intermission, no artist could survive it. The strings would break and the instrument be shattered into fragments. It is already a great thing if the main ideas and general outline of a work come without any racking of brains, as the result of that supernatural and inexplicable force we call inspiration. . . .

CLARENS, 5 (17) MARCH 1878

It is delightful to talk to you about my own methods of composition. So far I have never had any opportunity of confiding to anyone these hidden utterances of my inner life; partly because very few would be interested, and partly because, of these few, scarcely one would know how to respond to me properly. To you, and you alone, I gladly describe all the details of the creative process, because in you I have found one who has a fine feeling and can understand my music.

Do not believe those who try to persuade you that composition is only a cold exercise of the intellect. The only music capable of moving and touching us is that which flows from the depths of a composer's soul when he is stirred by inspiration. There is no doubt that even the greatest musical geniuses have sometimes worked without inspiration. This guest does not always respond to the first invitation. We must always work, and a self-respecting artist must not fold his hands on the pretext that he is not in the mood. If we wait for the mood, without endeavouring to meet it half-way, we easily become indolent and apathetic. We must be patient, and believe that inspiration will come to those who can master their disinclination. A few days ago I told you I was working every day without any real inspiration. Had I given way to my disinclination, undoubtedly I should have drifted into a long period of idleness. But my patience and faith did not fail me, and to-day I felt that inexplicable glow of inspiration of which I told you; thanks to which I know beforehand that whatever I write to-day will have power to make an impression, and to touch the hearts of those who hear it. I hope you will not think I am indulging in self-laudation, if I tell you that I very seldom suffer from this disinclination to work. I believe the reason for this is that I am naturally patient. I have learnt to master myself, and I am glad I have not followed in the steps of some of my Russian colleagues, who have no self-confidence and are so impatient that at the least difficulty they are ready to throw up the sponge. This is why, in spite of great gifts, they accomplish so little, and that in an amateur way.

You ask me how I manage my instrumentation. I never compose in the abstract; that is to say, the musical thought never appears otherwise than in a suitable external form. In this way I invent the musical idea and the instrumentation simultaneously. Thus I thought out the scherzo of our symphony—at the moment of its composition—exactly as you heard it. It is inconceivable except as pizzicato. Were it played with the bow, it would lose all its charm and be a mere body without a soul. . . .

KAMENKA, 25 JUNE (7 JULY) 1878

Yesterday, when I wrote to you about my methods of composing, I did not sufficiently enter into that phase of work which relates to the working out of the sketch. This phase is of primary importance. What has been set down in a moment of ardour must now be critically examined, improved, extended, or condensed, as the form requires. Sometimes one must do oneself violence, must sternly and pitilessly take part against oneself, before one can mercilessly erase things thought out with love and enthusiasm. I cannot complain of poverty of imagination, or lack of inventive power; but, on the other hand, I have always suffered from my want of skill in the management of form. Only after strenuous labour have I at last succeeded in making the form of my compositions correspond, more or less, with their contents. Formerly I was careless and did not give sufficient attention to the critical overhauling of my sketches. Consequently my seams showed, and there was no organic union between my individual episodes. This was a very serious defect, and I only improved gradually as time went on; but the form of my works will never be exemplary because, although I can modify, I cannot radically alter the essential qualities of my musical temperament. But I am far from believing that my gifts have yet reached their ultimate development. I can affirm with joy that I make continual progress on the way of self-development, and am passionately desirous of attaining the highest degree of perfection of which my talents are capable. Therefore I expressed myself badly when I told you yesterday that I transcribed my works direct from the first sketches. The process is something more than copying; it is actually a critical examination, leading to correction, occasional additions and frequent curtailments.

31.

The Genesis
of Orpheus

MURIEL RUKEYSER

The poet Muriel Rukeyser was attracted to the myth of Orpheus and Eurydice, and she wrote a long poem, Orpheus, in free verse, inspired by a personal spiritual crisis. She had fallen in love with a man who betrayed her and left her alone to bear their child by herself. In this beautiful narrative the poet reflects on her work and unpacks the many layers of meaning in art and experience.

The laws of exchange of consciousness are only suspected. Einstein writes, "Now I believe that events in nature are controlled by a much stricter and more closely binding law than we recognize today, when we speak of one event being the *cause* of another. We are like a child who judges a poem by the rhyme and knows nothing of the rhythmic pattern. Or we are like a juvenile learner at the piano, *just* relating one note to that which immediately precedes or follows. To an extent this may be very well when one is dealing with very simple and primitive compositions; but it will not do for an interpretation of a Bach fugue."

I believe that one suggestion of such law is to be found in the process of poetry.

Essentials are here, as in mathematical or musical creation—we need no longer distinguish, for we are speaking of the process itself, except for our illustrations. Only the essential is true: Joseph Conrad, in a letter of advice, drives this home by recommending deletions, explaining that these words are "not essential and therefore not true to the fact."

The process has very much unconscious work in it. The conscious process varies: my own experience is that the work on a poem "surfaces" several times, with new submergence after each rising. The "idea" for the poem, which may come as an image thrown against memory, as a sound of words that sets off a traveling of sound and meaning, as a curve of emotion (a form) plotted by certain crises of events or image or sound, or as a title which evokes a sense of inner relations; this is the first "surfacing" of the poem. Then a period of stillness may follow. The second surfacing may find the poem filled in, its voices distinct, its identity apparent, and another deep dive to its own depth of sleep and waiting. A last surfacing may find you ready to write. You may have jotted down a course of images, or a first line, or a whole verse, by now. This last conscious period finds you with all the work on yourself done—at least this is typical of the way I write a fairly sustained poem—and ready for the last step of all, the writing of the poem. Then the experience is followed, you reach its conclusion with the last word of your poem. One role is accomplished. At this point, you change into the witness. You remember what you may, and much or little critical work—re-writing—may be done.

I know most clearly the process of writing a recent, fairly extended poem, *Orpheus.** The beginnings go far back, to childhood and a wish for identity, as rebirth, as co-ordination, as form. My interests here are double: a desire for form, and perhaps a stronger desire to understand the wish for form. The figure of Orpheus stands for loss and triumph over loss, among other things: the godhead of music and poetry, yes, in a mythology I was always familiar with at a distance at which it could be better dealt with than the mythology, say, of the Old Testament. In a poem written when I was nineteen, after a long hospitalization for typhoid fever contracted in an Alabama station-house during the second Scottsboro trial—a poem called "In Hades, Orpheus," I focussed the poem on Eurydice, the ill woman who yearns backward from the burning green of the world to the paleness and rest—and death—of the hospital. Then the interest in Orpheus himself took precedence: I was at the brilliant performance of Gluck's *Orpheus* which Tchelitchew designed for the Metropolitan Opera, and was moved by that play of loss and the dragging loves and the music and thorny volcanic Hell; so moved and disturbed that, years later, I wished to go on from there, not to revisit those scenes of Hell.

On Forty-Second Street, late one night, I saw the nightwalkers go past the fifth-run movie houses, the Marine Bar, the Flea Circus, not as whole people, but as a leg, part of a shoulder, an eye askew. Pieces of people. This went into notes for a poem that never was written. They say, "MARINE BAR, portraits of an eye and the mouth, blue leg and half a face." This was eight years before the poem was written. Then there was a period of writing other poems

---

Orpheus, Centaur Press, San Francisco, 1949.

and prose, of being away from New York and returning, and then a time
of great scattering, a year later, when I wrote what became the beginning of
"The Antagonists":

> Pieces of animals, pieces of all my friends
> prepare assassinations while I sleep. . . .

This was a poem that began with the tearing of the "I" and moved on to
a reconciliation in love and intensity. Near the phrases, in my notebook, I
wrote "bringing the dead back to life."

Four years later, reading Thomson and Geddes' *Life*, I became interested
again in morphology and specifically in the fact that no part of the body lives
or dies to itself. I read what I could about the memory and lack of memory of
fragments, of amputees, and of dislocated nerve centers. And at the same
time I was writing as part of another poem,

> Orpheus in hell remembered rivers
> and a music rose
> full of all human voices;
> All words you wish are in that living sound.
> And even torn to pieces
> one piece sang
>> Come all ye torn and wounded here
>> together
>> and one sang to its brother
>> remembering.

There, in Carmel, the course of the poem suddenly became clear. It did
not concern Eurydice—not directly—it was of a later time. The murder of
Orpheus began it; that early unsolved murder. Why did the women kill him?
Reinach has written a paper about the murder. Was it because he loved Eurydice and would not approach them? Was it because he was homosexual,
and they were losing their lovers to him? Was it because he had seen their or-
gies without taking part? All these theories had been advanced. But my poem
started a moment later. I had it now! *Pieces of Orpheus*, I wrote: that would be
the title. The scene is the mountain top, just after the murder. The hacked
pieces lie in their blood, the women are running down the slope, there is only
the mountain, the moon, the river, the cloud. He was able to make all things
sing. Now they begin: "the voice of the Cloud to the killers of Orpheus," I

wrote. I knew what would follow. The pieces of the body would begin to talk, each according to its own nature, but they would be lost, they would be nothing, being no longer together. Like those in love, apart, I thought. No, not like anything. Like pieces of the body, knowing there had been pain, but not able to remember what pain—knowing they had loved, but not remembering whom. They know there must be some surpassing effort, some risk. The hand moves, finds the lyre, and throws it upward with a fierce gesture. The lyre flies upward in night, whistling through the black air to become the constellation; as it goes up, hard, the four strings sing *Eurydice*. And *then* the pieces begin to remember; they begin to come together; he turns into the god. He is music and poetry; he is Orpheus.

I was not able to write the poem. I went back to Chicago and to New York that winter, and, among a hundred crucial pressures, looked up some of the Orphic hymns in the New York Public Library. I wrote "The mountaintop, in silence, after the murder" and "lions and towers of the sky" and "The pieces of the body begin to remember" and "He has died the death of the god." Now there begin to be notes. This is the middle of winter, six years after the night on Forty-Second Street.

Again in California, in a year of intense physical crisis, threat, renewal, loss, and beginning. Now the notes begin to be very full. He did not look at Eurydice. He looked past her, at Hell. Now the wounds are the chorus: Touch me! Love me! Speak to me! This goes back to the yearning and self-pity of early love-poems, and a way must be found to end the self-pity.

Months later, the phrases begin to appear in fuller relationship. "The body as a circus, these freaks of Orpheus." Body Sonnets is one rejected notion. "Air-trees, nerve-trees, bloodmaze"; Pindar said of him "Father of Songs."

"Sing in me, days and voices," I write; and a form takes shape. I will solve a problem that has been moving toward solution. My longer poems, like the "Elegies" and "The Soul and Body of John Brown," contained songs. This poem will move toward its song: its own song and Orpheus' song. A poem that leads to a song! The pieces that come together, become a self, and sing.

Now I was ready to write. There were pages of notes and false starts, but there was no poem. There were whole lines, bits of drawing, telephone messages in the margin. Now something was ready; the poem began, and the first section was written.

It was slower to come to the second and third sections; as they were finished, the song too was ready; but now I turned into reader. The resurrection itself needed sharpening. These symbols must not be finished; the witness himself wants to finish. But this friend is right, the women must be part of his song, the god must include his murderers if murder is part of his life. And this correspondent is right, pain is not *forgotten*. All of this re-writing is conscious throughout, as distinct from the writing of the poem, in which suggestions, relations, images, phrases, sailed in from everywhere. For days of reminder and revery, everything became Orpheus. Until it was time to go back to the title. The working title was "Pieces of Orpheus." But that was for myself. No longer the pieces, but the rebirth, stands clear. The name alone should head the poem. So: two words are crossed out: it is ready.

poetics
of music

IGOR STRAVINSKY

Composer Igor Stravinsky discusses the element of craftsmanship involved in the production of music, the pleasure he experienced in arranging materials, and the security provided by the constraints of having to work within the existing framework of the seven notes of a scale and its chromatic intervals. It is telling that Stravinsky, known as a musical innovator, should be so explicitly concerned with the role of craftsmanship, work, tradition, and constraints. Indeed, he writes that "should the impossible happen and my work suddenly be given to me in a perfectly completed form, I should be embarrassed and nonplussed by it, as by a hoax." In these few pages Stravinsky touches on a number of important issues, from the rise of the concept of the artist (as opposed to the artisan) during the Renaissance to the difference between invention and imagination, the role of accident, and the pleasure of work.

I was made a revolutionary in spite of myself. Now, revolutionary outbreaks are never completely spontaneous. There are clever people who bring about revolutions with malice aforethought. . . . It is always necessary to guard against being misrepresented by those who impute to you an intention that is not your own. For myself, I never hear anyone talk about revolution without thinking of the conversation that G. K. Chesterton tells us he had, on landing in France, with a Calais innkeeper. The innkeeper complained bitterly of the harshness of life and increasing lack of freedom: "'It's hardly worthwhile,' concluded the innkeeper, 'to have had three revolutions only to end up every time just where you started.'" Whereupon Chesterton pointed out to him that a revolution, in the true sense of the word, was the movement of an object in motion that described a closed curve, and thus always returned to the point from where it had started . . .

The tone of a work like the *Rite* may have appeared arrogant, the language that it spoke may have seemed harsh in its newness, but that in no way implies that it is revolutionary in the most subversive sense of the word.

If one only need break a habit to merit being labelled revolutionary, then every musician who has something to say and who in order to say it goes beyond the bounds of established convention would be known as revolutionary. Why burden the dictionary of the fine arts with this stertorous term, which designates in its most usual acceptation a state of turmoil and violence, when there are so many other words better adapted to designate originality? . . .

All creation presupposes at its origin a sort of appetite that is brought on by the foretaste of discovery. This foretaste of the creative art accompanies the intuitive grasp of an unknown entity that will not take definite shape except by the action of a constantly vigilant technique.

This appetite that is aroused in me at the mere thought of putting in order musical elements that have attracted my attention is not at all a fortuitous thing like inspiration, but as habitual and periodic, if not as constant, as a natural need.

This premonition of an obligation, this foretaste of a pleasure, this conditioned reflex, as a modern physiologist would say, shows clearly that it is the idea of discovery and hard work that attracts me.

The very act of putting my work on paper, of, as we say, kneading the dough, is for me inseparable from the pleasure of creation. So far as I am concerned, I cannot separate the spiritual effort from the psychological and physical effort; they confront me on the same level and do not present a hierarchy.

The word *artist* which, as it is most generally understood today, bestows on its bearer the highest intellectual prestige, the privilege of being accepted as a pure mind—this pretentious term is in my view entirely incompatible with the role of the *Homo faber*.

At this point it should be remembered that, whatever field of endeavour has fallen to our lot, if it is true that we are intellectuals, we are called upon not to cogitate, but to perform.

The philosopher Jacques Maritain reminds us that in the mighty structure of medieval civilization, the artist held only the rank of an artisan. "And his individualism was forbidden any sort of anarchic development, because a natural social discipline imposed certain limitative conditions upon him from without." It was the Renaissance that invented the artist, distinguished him from the artisan and began to exalt the former at the expense of the latter.

At the outset the name artist was given only to the Masters of Arts:

philosophers, alchemists, magicians; but painters, sculptors, musicians and poets had the right to be qualified only as artisans.

> *Plying divers implements*
> *The subtile artizan implants*
> *Life in marble, copper, bronze.*

says the poet Du Bellay. And Montaigne enumerates in his *Essays* the "painters, poets and other artizans." And even in the seventeenth century, La Fontaine hails a painter with the name of *artisan* and draws a sharp rebuke from an ill-tempered critic who might have been the ancestor of most of our present-day critics.

The idea of work to be done is for me so closely bound up with the idea of the arranging of materials and of the pleasure that the actual doing of the work affords us that, should the impossible happen and my work suddenly be given me in a perfectly completed form, I should be embarrassed and nonplussed by it, as by a hoax.

We have a duty towards music, namely, to invent it. I recall once during the war when I was crossing the French border a gendarme asked me what my profession was. I told him quite naturally that I was an inventor of music. The gendarme, then verifying my passport, asked me why I was listed as a composer. I told him that the expression "inventor of music" seemed to me to fit my profession more exactly than the term applied to me in the documents authorizing me to cross borders.

Invention presupposes imagination but should not be confused with it. For the act of invention implies the necessity of a lucky find and of achieving full realization of this find. What we imagine does not necessarily take on a concrete form and may remain in a state of virtuality, whereas invention is not conceivable apart from its actual being worked out.

Thus, what concerns us here is not imagination in itself, but rather creative imagination: the faculty that helps us to pass from the level of conception to the level of realization.

In the course of my labours I suddenly stumble upon something unexpected. This unexpected element strikes me. I make a note of it. At the proper time I put it to profitable use. This gift of chance must not be confused with that capriciousness of imagination that is commonly called fancy. Fancy implies a predetermined will to abandon one's self to caprice. The aforementioned assistance of the unexpected is something quite different. It is a collaboration which is immanently bound up with the inertia of the creative process and is heavy with possibilities which are unsolicited and come most appositely to temper the inevitable over-rigorousness of the naked will. And it is good that this is so.

"In everything that yields gracefully," G. K. Chesterton says somewhere, "there must be resistance. Bows are beautiful when they bend only because they seek to remain rigid. Rigidity that slightly yields, like Justice swayed by Pity, is all the beauty of earth. Everything seeks to grow straight, and happily, nothing succeeds in so growing. Try to grow straight and life will bend you."

The faculty of creating is never given to us all by itself. It always goes hand in hand with the gift of observation. And the true creator may be recognized by his ability always to find about him, in the commonest and humblest thing, items worthy of note. He does not have to concern himself with a beautiful landscape, he does not need to surround himself with rare and precious objects. He does not have to put forth in search of discoveries: they are always within his reach. He will have only to cast a glance about him. Familiar things, things that are everywhere, attract his attention. The least accident holds his interest and guides his operations. If his finger slips, he will notice it; on occasion, he may draw profit from something unforeseen that a momentary lapse reveals to him.

One does not contrive an accident: one observes it to draw inspiration therefrom. An accident is perhaps the only thing that really inspires us. A composer improvises aimlessly the way an animal grubs about. Both of them go grubbing about because they yield to a compulsion to seek things out. What urge of the composer is satisfied by this investigation? The rules with which, like a penitent, he is burdened? No: he is in quest of his pleasure. He seeks a satisfaction that he fully knows he will not find without first striving for it. One cannot force one's self to love; but love presupposes understanding, and in order to understand, one must exert one's self.

It is the same problem that was posed in the Middle Ages by the theologians of pure love. To understand in order to love; to love in order to understand: we are here not going around in a vicious circle; we are rising spirally, providing we have made an initial effort, have even just gone through a routine exercise.

Pascal has specifically this in mind when he writes that custom "controls the automaton, which in its turn unthinkingly controls the mind. For there must be no mistake," continues Pascal, "we are automatons just as much as we are minds. . . ."

So we grub about in expectation of our pleasure, guided by our scent, and suddenly we stumble against an unknown obstacle. It gives us a jolt, a shock, and this shock fecundates our creative power.

The faculty of observation and of making something out of what is observed belongs only to the person who at least possesses, in his particular field of endeavour, an acquired culture and an innate taste. A dealer, an art-lover who is the first to buy the canvases of an unknown painter who will be famous twenty-five years later under the name of Cézanne—doesn't such a person give us a clear example of this innate taste? What else guides him in his choice? A flair, an instinct from which this taste proceeds, a completely spontaneous faculty anterior to reflection.

As for culture, it is a sort of upbringing which, in the social sphere, confers polish upon education, sustains and rounds out academic instruction. This upbringing is just as important in the sphere of taste and is essential to the creator who must ceaselessly refine his taste or run the risk of losing his perspicacity. Our mind, as well as our body, requires continual exercise. It atrophies if we do not cultivate it.

It is culture that brings out the full value of taste and gives it a chance to prove its worth simply by its application. The artist imposes a culture upon himself and ends by imposing it upon others. That is how tradition becomes established.

Tradition is entirely different from habit, even from an excellent habit, since habit is by definition an unconscious acquisition and tends to become mechanical, whereas tradition results from a conscious and deliberate acceptance. A real tradition is not the relic of a past that is irretrievably gone; it is a living force that animates and informs the present. In this sense the paradox which banteringly maintains that everything which is not tradition is plagiarism, is true. . . .

A mode of composition that does not assign itself limits becomes pure fantasy. The effects it produces may accidentally amuse but are not capable of being repeated. I cannot conceive of a fantasy that is repeated, for it can be repeated only to its detriment.

Let us understand each other in regard to this word fantasy. We are not using the word in the sense in which it is connected with a definite musical form, but in the acceptation which presupposes an abandonment of one's self to the caprices of imagination. And this presupposes that the composer's will is voluntarily paralysed. For imagination is not only the mother of caprice but the servant and handmaiden of the creative will as well.

The creator's function is to sift the elements he receives from her, for human activity must impose limits upon itself. The more art is controlled, limited, worked over, the more it is free.

As for myself, I experience a sort of terror when, at the moment of setting to work and finding myself before the infinitude of possibilities that present themselves, I have the feeling that everything is permissible to me. If everything is permissible to me, the best and the worst; if nothing offers me any resistance, then any effort is inconceivable, and I cannot use anything as a basis, and consequently every undertaking becomes futile.

Will I then have to lose myself in this abyss of freedom? To what shall I cling in order to escape the dizziness that seizes me before the virtuality of this infinitude? However, I shall not succumb. I shall overcome my terror and shall be reassured by the thought that I have the seven notes of the scale and its chromatic intervals at my disposal, that strong and weak accents are within my reach, and that in all of these I possess solid and concrete elements which offer me a field of experience just as vast as the upsetting and dizzy infinitude that had just frightened me. It is into this field that I shall sink my roots, fully convinced that combinations which have at their disposal twelve sounds in each octave and all possible rhythmic varieties promise me riches that all the activity of human genius will never exhaust.

33.

All about music

FRANK ZAPPA

In this essay, musician and composer Frank Zappa describes his understanding of the process of composition. Despite his obvious genius and his rather facile description of the compositional process, Zappa insisted on reminding people that what he was doing might look like fun, and in fact was fun, but was also hard work. Furthermore, he also asked his audience to do a little bit of work, as opposed to just settling for those tried and trusted familiar sounds. Question authority, he shouted, but think, and think for yourself.

What Do You Do for a Living, Dad?

If any of my kids ever asked me that question, the answer would have to be: *"What I do is composition."* I just happen to use material other than *notes* for the pieces.

Composition is a process of organization, very much like architecture. As long as you can conceptualize what that organizational process is, you can be a "composer"—**in any medium you want.**

You can be a "video composer," a "film composer," a "choreography composer," a "social engineering composer"—whatever. Just give me some *stuff*, and I'll organize it for you. That's what I do.

Project/Object is a term I have used to describe the overall concept of my work in various mediums. Each project (in whatever realm), or interview connected to it, is part of a larger object, for which there is no "technical name."

Think of the connecting material in the Project/Object this way: A novelist invents a character. If the character is a good one, he takes on a life of his own. Why should he get to go to only one party? He could pop up anytime in a future novel.

Or: Rembrandt got his "look" by mixing just a little brown into every other color—he didn't do "red" unless it had brown in it. The brown itself wasn't especially fascinating, but the result of its obsessive inclusion was that "look."

In the case of the *Project/Object*, you may find a little *poodle* over here, a little *blow job* over there, etc., etc. I am not obsessed by *poodles* or *blow jobs*, however; these words (and others of equal insignificance), along with pictorial images and melodic themes, recur throughout the albums, interviews, films, videos (and this book) for no other reason than to unify the "collection."

THE FRAME

The most important thing in art is **The Frame.** For painting: literally; for other arts: figuratively—because, without this humble appliance, you can't **know** where *The Art* stops and *The Real World* begins.

You have to put a "box" around it because otherwise, **what is that shit on the wall?**

If John Cage, for instance, says, *"I'm putting a contact microphone on my throat, and I'm going to drink carrot juice, and that's my composition,"* then his gurgling qualifies as **his composition** because he put a frame around it and said so. *"Take it or leave it, I now* **will** *this to be* **music."** After that it's a matter of taste. Without the frame-as-announced, it's a guy swallowing carrot juice.

So, if *music is the best*, what **is** music? Anything **can** be music, but it doesn't **become music** until someone **wills** it to be music, and the audience listening to it decides to **perceive it as music.**

Most people can't deal with that abstraction—or don't want to. They say: *"Gimme* **the tune.** *Do I like this* **tune?** *Does it sound like another* **tune that I like?** *The more* familiar *it is,* **the better I like it.** *Hear those three notes there? Those are the three notes I can sing along with. I like those notes very, very much. Give me a beat. Not a fancy one. Give me a* **GOOD BEAT**—*something I can dance to. It has to go* boom-bap, boom-boom-**BAP.** *If it doesn't, I will* **hate** *it* very, very much. *Also, I want it* **right away**—*and then, write me some more songs like that*—*over and over and over again, because I'm* really *into* **music."**

WHY BOTHER?

I used to love putting little black dots on music paper. I'd sit for sixteen hours at a time, hunched over in a chair with a bottle of India ink, and draw beams and dots.

No other activity could have enticed me away from the table. I'd maybe get up for coffee or to eat, but, other than that, I was glued to the chair for weeks and months on end, writing music.

I thought it was fun, because I could hear everything in my head, and I kept telling myself how *thoroughly bitchen* it was.

To be able to write a piece of music and hear it in your head is a completely different sensation from the ordinary listening experience.

I don't write "music on paper" anymore. The incentive to continue was removed by having to deal with symphony orchestras. . . .

LET'S <u>ALL</u> BE COMPOSERS!

A composer is a guy who goes around forcing his will on unsuspecting air molecules, often with the assistance of unsuspecting musicians.

Want to be a composer? You don't even have to be able to **write it down.** The stuff that gets written down is only a recipe, remember?—like the stuff in Ronnie Williams's *MACHA* book. If you can **think design,** you can **execute design**—it's only a bunch of air molecules, who's gonna check up on you?

Just Follow These Simple Instructions:

1. Declare your **intention** to create a "composition."

2. **Start** a piece at **some time.**

3. Cause **something to happen over a period of time** (it doesn't matter what happens in your "time hole"—we have critics to tell us whether it's any good or not, so we won't worry about that part).

4. **End the piece at some time** (or keep it going, telling the audience it is a *"work in progress"*).

5. Get a part-time job so you can continue to do stuff like this.

34.

zen in the art
of archery

EUGEN HERRIGEL

Eugen Herrigel was a German philosophy professor who studied archery in Japan. In this excerpt he discusses the importance of relaxation and concentration, and the role of the teacher in allowing the student to realize for himself or herself what is needed to engage in the process of archery (or any other learning process) in a spiritual manner.

That the way of the "artless art" is not easy to follow we were to learn during the very first lesson. The Master began by showing us various Japanese bows, explaining that their extraordinary elasticity was due to their peculiar construction and also to the material from which they are generally made, namely bamboo. But it seemed even more important to him that we should note the noble form which the bow—it is over six feet long—assumes as soon as it is strung, and which appears the more surprising the further the bow is drawn. When drawn to its full extent, the bow encloses the "All" in itself, explained the Master, and that is why it is important to learn how to draw it properly. Then he grasped the best and strongest of his bows and, standing in a ceremonious and dignified attitude, let the lightly drawn bowstring fly back several times. This produces a sharp crack mingled with a deep thrumming, which one never afterwards forgets when one has heard it only a few times: so strange is it, so thrillingly does it grip the heart. From ancient times it has been credited with the secret power of banishing evil spirits, and I can well believe that this interpretation has struck root in the whole Japanese people. After this significant introductory act of purification and consecration the Master commanded us to watch him closely. He placed, or "nocked," an arrow on the string, drew the bow so far that I was afraid it would not stand up to the strain of embracing the All, and loosed the arrow. All this looked not only very beautiful, but quite effortless. He then gave us his instructions: "Now you do the same, but remember that archery is not meant to strengthen the muscles. When drawing the string you should not exert the full strength of your body, but must learn to let only your two hands do the work, while your arm and shoulder muscles remain relaxed, as though they looked on impassively. Only when you can do this will you have fulfilled one of the conditions that make the drawing and the shooting 'spiritual.'" With these words he gripped my hands and slowly guided them through the phases of the movement which they would have to execute in the future, as if accustoming me to the feel of it.

Even at the first attempt with a medium-strong practice-bow I noticed that I had to use considerable force to bend it. This is because the Japanese bow, unlike the European sporting bow, is not held at shoulder level, in which position you can, as it were, press yourself into it. Rather, as soon as the arrow is nocked, the bow is held up with arms at nearly full stretch, so that the archer's hands are somewhere above his head. Consequently, the only thing he can do is to pull them evenly apart to left and right, and the further apart they get the more they curve downwards, until the left hand, which holds the bow, comes to rest at eye level with the arm outstretched, while the right hand, which draws the string, is held with arm bent above the right shoulder, so that the tip of the three-foot arrow sticks out a little beyond the outer edge of the bow—so great is the span. In this attitude the archer has to remain for a while before loosing the shot. The strength needed for this unusual method of holding and drawing the bow caused my hands to start trembling after a few moments, and my breathing became more and more labored. Nor did this get any better during the weeks that followed. The drawing continued to be a difficult business, and despite the most diligent practice refused to become "spiritual." To comfort myself, I hit upon the thought that there must be a trick somewhere which the Master for some reason would not divulge, and I staked my ambition on its discovery.

Grimly set on my purpose, I continued practicing. The Master followed my efforts attentively, quietly corrected my strained attitude, praised my enthusiasm, reproved me for wasting my strength, but otherwise let me be. Only, he always touched on a sore spot when, as I was drawing the bow, he called out to me to "Relax! Relax!"—a word he had learned in the meantime—though he never lost his patience and politeness. But the day came when it was I who lost patience and brought myself to admit that I absolutely could not draw the bow in the manner prescribed.

"You cannot do it," explained the Master, "because you do not breathe right. Press your breath down gently after breathing in, so that the abdominal wall is tightly stretched, and hold it there for a while. Then breathe out as slowly and evenly as possible, and, after a short pause, draw a quick breath of air again—out and in continually, in a rhythm that will gradually settle itself. If it is done properly, you will feel the shooting becoming easier every day. For through this breathing you will not only discover the source of all spiritual strength but will also cause this source to flow more abundantly, and to pour more easily through your limbs the more relaxed you are." And as if to prove it, he drew his strong bow and invited me to step behind him and feel his arm muscles. They were indeed quite relaxed, as though they were doing no work at all.

The new way of breathing was practiced, without bow and arrow at first, until it came naturally. The slight feeling of discomfort noticeable in the beginning was quickly overcome. The Master attached so much importance to breathing out as slowly and steadily as possible to the very end, that, for better practice and control, he made us combine it with a humming note. Only when the note had died away with the last expiring breath were we allowed to draw air again. The breathing in, the Master once said, binds and combines; by holding your breath you make everything go right; and the breathing out loosens and completes by overcoming all limitations. But we could not understand that yet.

The Master now went on to relate the breathing, which had not of course been practiced for its own sake, to archery. The unified process of drawing and shooting was divided into sections: grasping the bow, nocking the arrow, raising the bow, drawing and remaining at the point of highest tension, loosing the shot. Each of them began with breathing in, was sustained by firm holding of the down-pressed breath, and ended with breathing out. The result was that the breathing fell into place spontaneously and not only accentuated the individual positions and hand-movements, but wove them together in a rhythmical sequence depending, for each of us, on the state of his breathing-capacity. In spite of its being divided into parts the entire process seemed like a living thing wholly contained in itself, and not even remotely comparable to a gymnastic exercise, to which bits can be added or taken away without its meaning and character being thereby destroyed.

I cannot think back to those days without recalling, over and over again, how difficult I found it, in the beginning, to get my breathing to work out right. Though I breathed in technically the right way, whenever I tried to keep my arm and shoulder muscles relaxed while drawing the bow, the muscles of my legs stiffened all the more violently, as though my life depended on a firm foothold and secure stance, and as though, like Antaeus, I had to draw strength from the ground. Often the Master had no alternative but to pounce quick as lightning on one of my leg muscles and press it in a particularly sensitive spot. When, to excuse myself, I once remarked that I was conscientiously making an effort to keep relaxed, he replied: "That's just the trouble, you make an effort to think about it. Concentrate entirely on your breathing, as if you had nothing else to do!" It took me a considerable time before I succeeded in doing what the Master wanted. But—I succeeded. I learned to lose myself so effortlessly in the breathing that I sometimes had the feeling that I myself was not breathing but—strange as this may sound—being breathed. And even when, in hours of thoughtful reflection, I struggled against this bold idea, I could no longer doubt that the breathing held out all that the Master had promised. Now and then, and in the course of time more and more frequently, I managed to draw the bow and keep it drawn until the moment of release while remaining completely relaxed in body, without my being able to say how it happened. The qualitative difference between these few successful shots and the innumerable failures was so convincing that I was ready to admit that now at last I understood what was meant by drawing the bow " spiritually."

So that was it: not a technical trick I had tried in vain to pick up, but liberating breath-control with new and far-reaching possibilities. I say this not without misgiving, for I well know how great is the temptation to succumb to a powerful influence and, ensnared in self-delusion, to overrate the importance of an experience merely because it is so unusual. But despite all equivocation and sober reserve, the results obtained by the new breathing—for in time I was able to draw even the strong bow of the Master with muscles relaxed—were far too definite to be denied.

In talking it over with Mr. Komachiya, I once asked him why the Master had looked on so long at my futile efforts to draw the bow "spiritually," why he had not insisted on the correct breathing right from the start. "A great Master," he replied, "must also be a great teacher. With us the two things go hand in hand. Had he begun the lessons with breathing exercises, he would never have been able to convince you that you owe them anything decisive. You had to suffer shipwreck through your own efforts before you were ready to seize the lifebelt he threw you. Believe me, I know from my own experience that the Master knows you and each of his pupils much better than we know ourselves. He reads in the souls of his pupils more than they care to admit."

VI

THE COURAGE
TO GO NAKED

It's like going out there naked every night. Any one of us can screw the whole thing up because he just had a fight with his wife before the gig or because he's just not with it that night for any number of reasons. I mean, we're out there improvising. The classical guys have their scores, whether they have them on stand or have memorized them. But we have to be creating, or trying to, anticipating each other, transmuting our feelings into the music, taking chances every goddamned second. That's why, when jazz musicians are really putting out, it's an exhausting experience. It can be exhilarating too, but always there's that touch of fear, that feeling of being on a very high wire without a net below.

ANONYMOUS JAZZ BASS PLAYER

He was a bold man that first ate an oyster.

JONATHAN SWIFT

τaking ouɾ cɾeaτive ideas out of the shelter of the studio, the workshop, the laboratory, or the manuscript and sending them out into the world for its judgment is often a threatening proposition. Many of us fear public exposure of our creative ideas because we then feel naked in front of others, and believe we may end up scorned, rejected, or laughed at in our vulnerability.

Our creative products usually mean something special to us. They express something that we have been quietly nurturing in our inner self, away from the eyes and ears of others. It seems risky to go public with them. Suddenly we're out there, and despite layers of clothes we feel naked.

We must balance the need to expose our creation to public consideration and criticism with fear that we may find our offering cheapened, devalued, and even stolen. It is especially awful to put forth a personal observation, have your hearer disagree with it, and then hear it soon thereafter presented as another person's idea.

Despite persistent and nagging stage fright, many of us continue to seek the thrill of performing in public. It can be both a fearsome and an exhilarating process. It can be rewarding, being in front of others, thriving on the attention and the rush of adrenaline. Perhaps there is a healthy exhibitionism tucked away beneath the courage to go naked—but we had better have something to back it up!

And after a while there can be the shock of realizing that what was once an experience that induced trepidation and excitement has turned into another humdrum "gig." What for some might be the experience of a lifetime has become routine for others. We need the courage to go naked, but it is much more than simply overcoming first night jitters. Perhaps the stage fright is not just a fear of seeming to be out there naked, but a desire to be there and be *really* naked. As we present our creative product to others, perhaps we also need the knowledge that we are pushing our own boundaries along with those of our audience. We are naked to ourselves as well as to others.

Creativity involves a degree of risk-taking, if only because we have invested so much in our product that we do not want to see it flop. We have pinned our hopes on our creative ideas, and we want some degree of recognition and reward, whether social or financial.

The moral is, get out there and do it! Take it off! In the realization of the dream is self-realization, in its impact is its proof, in our creations we complete ourselves.

35.

The Mother Cry
of Creation

ISADORA DUNCAN

In this extraordinary piece from her autobiography, the revolutionary dancer Isadora Duncan (1878–1927) writes of the nature of memory, of dance, of life and death, and of creation. In exposing her nature through movement, she risked, and received, ridicule. However, generations of dancers have since been inspired by her courage.

My Art is just an effort to express the truth of my Being in gesture and movement. It has taken me long years to find even one absolutely true movement. Words have a different meaning. Before the public which has thronged my representations I have had no hesitation. I have given them the most secret impulses of my soul. From the first, I have only danced my life. As a child, I danced the spontaneous joy of growing things. As an adolescent, I danced with joy turning to apprehension of the first realization of tragic undercurrents; apprehension of the pitiless brutality and crushing progress of life.

When I was sixteen, I danced before an audience without music. At the end, someone suddenly cried from the audience, "It is Death and the Maiden," and the dance was always afterwards called "Death and the Maiden." But that was not my intention; I was only endeavouring to express my first knowledge of the underlying tragedy in all seemingly joyous manifestation. The dance, according to my comprehension, should have been called "Life and the Maiden."

Later on, I danced my struggle with this same life, which the audience had called death, and my wresting from it its ephemeral joys . . .

Lying here on my bed at the Negresco, I try to analyze this thing that they call memory. I feel the heat of the sun of the Midi. I hear the voices of children playing in a neighbouring park. I feel the warmth of my own body. I look down on my bare legs—stretching them out. The softness of my breasts, my arms that are never still but continually waving about in soft undulation, and I realize that for twelve years I have been weary. This breast has harbored a never-ending ache, these hands before me have been marked with sorrow, and when I am alone these eyes are seldom dry. The tears have flowed for twelve years, since that day, twelve years ago, when, lying on another couch, I was suddenly awakened by a great cry and, turning, saw L. like a man wounded: "The children have been killed."

I remember a strange illness came upon me, only in my throat I felt a burning as if I had swallowed some live coals. But I could not understand. I spoke to him very softly; I tried to calm him; I told him it could not be true. Then other people came, but I could not conceive what had happened. Then entered a man with a dark beard. I was told he was a doctor. "It is not true," he said. "I will save them."

I believed him. I wanted to go with him, but people held me back. I know since that this was because they did not wish me to know that there was indeed no hope. They feared the shock would make me insane, but I was, at that time, lifted to a state of exaltation. I saw everyone about me weeping, but I did not weep. On the contrary, I felt an immense desire to console every one. Looking back, it is difficult for me to understand my strange state of mind. Was it that I was really in a state of clairvoyance, and that I knew that death does not exist—that those two little cold images of wax were not my children but merely their cast-off garments? That the souls of my children lived on in radiance, but always lived? Only twice comes that cry of the mother which one hears as without one's self—at Birth and at Death—for when I felt in mine those little cold hands that would never again press mine in return, I heard my cries—the same cries as I had heard at their births. Why the same—since one is the cry of supreme Joy and the other of Sorrow? I do not know why, but I know they are the same. Is it that in all the Universe there is but one Great Cry containing Sorrow, Joy, Ecstasy, Agony, the Mother Cry of Creation?

36.

License
for Madness

KAREN FINLEY

Performance artist Karen Finley is known for her outrageous and provocative work. In this brief extract from an interview she describes a particularly dramatic experience in San Francisco (at J. C. Penney's, of all places). Finley raises a host of important issues, including the relationship between life and art, what art "really" is, the importance of shock, and the role of gender, and she still manages to be funny—no mean feat.

When I was twenty-one, I performed in the window of [an abandoned] J. C. Penney store in San Francisco. . . . There was no language in it, because people couldn't hear me, but I was kissing the window and putting my breasts up there. I was fully clothed but I put my body up there, it was supposed to be a joke—the woman as a sex symbol. And then I took all these bananas and I put my head up to the window and I was mushing them in my mouth, really close up there. Someone called the police and said there was this woman who's on drugs, insane, and nude, let loose in this J. C. Penney window. . . .

And these two officers came and dragged me off and put me in a squad car, and what I decided to do was continue my performance in the squad car. So I was on the seat, kissing all the windows. I think that was sort of funny, that I continued doing this show, and I never broke the energy. That was the first time my gender helped me . . . being a woman, and being young.

The curator came up and he said to the police that he was a curator and this was art. "This is part of a performance, it's part of a series." He had asked me to perform there, at J. C. Penney's. What struck me was that this was art and it was okay, I could go. And I thought that was funny, or odd; I felt sad.

What if I was a person who didn't go to art school and wasn't given that educational privilege? I would have been arrested, if I was just a person expressing myself that way, and didn't have a curator. I thought what about if I *was* on drugs, or insane? It made me start thinking of things in a different way: that art is a shelter.

37·

Lessons from the past

LAURENCE OLIVIER

Actor Laurence Olivier describes his relationship to stage fright, something one does not typically associate with a consummate performer thought by many to have been the greatest actor in the world. Fear, over-excitement, and performance anxiety are quite common for artists, no matter how brilliant they are, and should not discourage anybody from performing. Indeed, it's when we approach the stage without any feeling, whether of anxiety or excitement, that we should wonder if we have not turned a creative process into a routine activity.

It was during the run of *The Merchant* that I suffered badly from the actor's nightmare: *stage fright*. I wonder if that had anything to do with my performance's becoming fresh, open and naked again. It's always possible.

Let me give you a brief insight into stage fright. It comes in all sorts of forms; I suppose it's always there, but most of the time it hovers unseen. It is an animal, a monster which hides in its foul corner without revealing itself, but you know that it is there and that it may come forward at any moment. A shadow in a lightless room, it's lurking there in the back of your brain cells, an insubstantial presence that refuses to go away. At any moment it will push a finger forward and knock over the "operator" who is waiting at your "exchange" for the next message to be received, translated and sent to another part of your body. The next message can't get through. Stage fright is like the character in *The Turn of the Screw* who never appears: he is always waiting outside the door, any door, waiting to get you. You either battle or walk away.

For people who haven't had it it is very difficult to understand. To the young actor who is full of optimism and energy it is a joke. I'm certain I didn't believe in it when I was young and hopeful. I don't suppose I even gave it a thought. But suddenly there he is: the bogey-man comes along and tries to rob you of your living. He can come at any time, in any form. The dark shadow of fear.

Sometimes the process can begin in bed at night, the night before a performance. Hot and cold sweats suddenly wake you; your brain leaps into top gear, thinking of the performance to come. The logical fighting the illogical.

"I don't know the lines. Dear God, I don't know the lines."

"Of course you do. You know them backwards."

"That's not the point. I don't want to know them backwards. I just want to know them."

"You know them. You know you know them."

"Let me just go through them again."

"What's the point? Sleep—you really must sleep."

"To hell with sleep. I'll go through the whole blasted script, that's what I'll do. I'll go through the whole thing."

"It's pointless."

"I'll write it all out in longhand. I'll go through it syllable by syllable."

> *How like a fawning publican he looks!*
> *I hate him for he is a Christian. . . .*

"Next—what's next? For God's sake, what comes next?"

"Relax."

"I'll get up . . . I'll get up and walk round the house. I'll recite the whole play out loud until it is so bored with me, it will reside in my memory box forever."

And up I'd get, the hot sweat having turned to cold.

"Panic . . . that's all it is. People get like this in the early hours of the morning . . . it's a well-known fact."

"Come on back to bed . . . you'll feel better in the morning."

"Maybe you're right . . . maybe. I'm really very tired. . . . I need to sleep."

Back to bed, feeling cold now, blankets pulled up round the ears. Sleeping in fits and starts. Suddenly moments of wide-awakeness, and other moments of deep sleep. Nightmares . . . black holes . . . bright colors . . . Suddenly it's morning.

As I have said, it comes in many forms, creeps up and swamps you like a shadow, and just when you think you've conquered it, there it is sitting at the end of the bed grinning at you.

There is the kind of stage fright that begins when you are waiting in the wings and you can hear your cue approaching. The heart starts to pound and you can feel it at the base of your spine. It is nothing like first-night nerves—it is way beyond that. The breathing becomes affected: the breath becomes shorter when you want to make it longer and deeper; and all the time this wretched cue is getting nearer. You try to calm down, but the sweat breaks out again. The voice in the head starts to ramble.

"I should have stayed in the dressing room . . . why do I subject myself to this? I've done it all . . . I've done everything . . . why don't I stop now, while I'm on top?"

The cue is getting nearer.

"I'm not going to be able to go on . . . I'm rooted to the spot. Somebody has nailed my shoes to the floor. My legs are made of lead. I'm alone—oh, God, how alone I am! Nobody understands this . . . nobody."

Cue nearly here.

"I'm going to walk out into that bright glare and be utterly exposed. Walk out? Nonsense. I can't leave here. I'll never move again. I'm going to be rooted to this spot forever."

> PORTIA . . . *If he have the condition of a saint*
> *and the complexion of a devil . . .*

"If I don't go on now I'll never go on again."

> PORTIA . . . *I had rather he should shrive me than wive me . . .*

"This is the theater where I have played Hamlet, Richard, Henry. . . . This is my theater . . . my beloved theater. This can't happen here . . . I will not let it happen here . . . I am in control . . . I have to got to be in control . . . I am . . . I am . . ."

> PORTIA . . . *Come, Nerissa. Sirrah, go before.*
> *Whiles we shut the gate upon one wooer,*
> *another knocks at the door.*

"Now . . . that's it . . . *now*. The next lines to be spoken are mine. Move . . . move . . ."

The thumping at the base of the spine is now almost painful. This is what it must be like to give birth.

I go forward. Slowly I go forward.

"Shylock . . . you're Shylock. Am I? Am I really? I'm not . . . I'm just me . . . stage-frightened me."

Suddenly I'm there. The wing is left behind and I'm on.

I have given instructions to the other actors not to look me in the eyes.

My company—what a thing to do to them. But I had to. The one thing an actor must do is look his fellow actor in the eyes, and I have asked my fellow players not to.

> SHYLOCK. *Three thousand ducats—well.*

"I've said it . . . the line's out. I've said the first line. God, supposing I fall over? I've got the feeling I'm going to fall over."

> BASSANIO. *Ay, sir, for three months.*

"I mustn't fall over."

> SHYLOCK. *For three months—well.*

"Second line out . . . I've said two lines. Why can't I get rid of this lack of balance? Lack of sense of balance."

> BASSANIO. *For the which, as I told you,*
> *Antonio shall be bound.*

"Relax . . . that's all I've got to do . . . relax."

> SHYLOCK. *Antonio shall become bound—well.*

"What happens if I fall over now? Balance . . . come on, balance."

> BASSANIO. *May you stead me? Will you pleasure me?*
> *Shall I know your answer?*

"The lines are echoing. I'm in an echo chamber. . . . 'Shall I know your answer? What is my answer? Calm—stay calm. My heart is racing. Speak . . . it's your turn. What is it? What do I say? I know it . . . I know the lines. . . . What is it . . . what is it? Come on . . . come on. . . . I've been here for an hour . . . I've paused for an hour. Why aren't they coughing? Anything . . . just say anything. . . .'"

> SHYLOCK. *Three thousand ducats for three months,*
> *and Antonio bound.*

"I've done it . . . that's the right line. I've done it."

Once you have experienced stage fright, you are always aware that it could be just around the corner waiting for you, just waiting for you to get cocky and overconfident. So you treat the body and the brain with much more respect, and you remain conscious always of the shadow in the corner.

I find the play horrid and cruel, and none of the characters likeable. Shylock is just better-quality stuff than any of the Christians in the play, who are heartless, money-grubbing monsters. But I have much to thank the play for. It finally put down my stage fright. Now I can say, "I have been there, I have looked over the edge, and I have returned."

38.

creation myth

MAT CALLAHAN

Musician Mat Callahan tells a tale of music, inspiration, collaboration, and the social forces that impinge on creative expression in the music industry today. He briefly documents his evolution as an artist and thoughtful chronicler of the music scene. Many aspects of the production of music are hidden from the public, which is usually exposed to romanticized rags-to-riches success stories or pathographies of artists succumbing to the temptations of substance (and people) abuse. The realities are far more complex, and the term music industry is an indication of the market-driven, corporate powers that dominate the world of music and musicians today. In spite of it all, Callahan finds in the joys of the creative process more than enough inspiration to keep working and producing his critically acclaimed recordings.

The most terrifying thing was the noise. The roaring, squealing, grinding noise of scrap iron being brought dockside by a locomotive, lifted out of the railcars by giant magnets and then dropped from a height of a hundred feet or so down into the hold of a ship. The cranes were framed against the night sky by blazing lights that helped the operators see their targets. The ship was huge, hulking blackness, deeper than the blackness of the night, dotted by lights on its gangway, fo'castle, prow, stern and various points amidships where stevedores needed to see to avoid being crushed by flying metal. Lights on forklifts, helmets, in men's hands darted about the dock like fireflies as the workers made their way through the maze of tracks, steel cable, racing machines and other men. No one could hear a word unless it was shouted directly into an ear and signals were given by periodic blasts from horns, sirens and waving hands. This is where my father worked. This is where we'd visit him because he worked whenever there was scrap to ship, sometimes weeks on end, in those days. We'd rarely see him otherwise.

It always struck me how jovial and easygoing all the men were. Laughing, patting me on the head with their big, meaty workers' hands. Me clinging to my mother or father, scared out of my wits and these guys acting like hell was perfectly fine. None of them acted like it was strange when my father would insist on leading us two hundred feet up narrow, steel ladders to the tiny, glass-enclosed cab of the crane to meet the operator and show us what the dock looked like from up there. Maybe he thought it was a thrill for us. Maybe he was just proud of his family.

The irony didn't entirely escape my adolescent mind when my father forbade and then grudgingly accepted my first guitar insisting I would just make a lot of noise! That racket that all the other kids were listening to. Which I promptly did. And I practiced in the basement. And I woke him up when I forgot that he was home trying to sleep days because he worked nights. And he would storm down the stairs and literally chase me and my friends out into the street throwing slippers and curses as we fled.

Then we kept on running. Away from those docks. Away from all the deadend jobs our parents did. We ran from the draft. We ran from school. We ran from anything that symbolized the authority that was telling us it was wrong to enjoy living. And we ran into the embrace of the great angel who'd swept down among us on an electric storm. The Pied Piper who promised nothing but offered everything, beckoning us all to "Partake! Partake! This is life! This is music!"

Now there were heroes. Now there were codes. Now there was right and wrong. The drugs. The sex. The adventure. A way to live another way right now. And standing in a field, surrounded by thousands we bathed in the waves of glorious sound because at the center of all the turmoil, all the wildness, was music. That was the power. That was the magical essence that gave meaning to everything.

I dove into these waters headlong. I have never emerged. Playing in a dark, stinking pit of a nightclub, bloody feces smeared on the walls of the bathroom, one pathetic spotlight with cracked green gel to illuminate the band, trash piled alongside the stage all the way out the backdoor into the alley where rats boldly ran, there I have seen, I have made the transformation only an inspired performance can make. I have walked out into filthy, disease-ridden streets where everything that moves is suspicious and even stillness has a claw and I've felt the total exhilaration of a great night of music. Who needs faith when you have experience!

To go from that to the bar in one of the world's fanciest hotels to meet the man from the record company who wants to sign my band; to sit amongst the potted plants, the chandeliers, the walls of redwood hewn by robber barons a century ago, the tinkling glasses and the tinkling piano nobody listens to, the waiters asking me would I like a drink and me feeling like I'm going to be asked to leave any minute now and, "Holy shit!" here he comes . . . my future! Where is the music now? I sense this presence as mysterious and gripping as god. I don't know what to say that will convince him I am worthy. But, for a moment, everything in the universe seems to depend on this exchange. I have been told that a deal is likely. They "really believe" in my music. They're "really behind" this band.

Maybe it's my background. Maybe it's my dire poverty. But something somewhere inside makes me really despise this man. Something, my pride, my fear, I don't know, makes me feel utter contempt for whatever it is he's saying, the whole situation he's saying it in and the grime that's gradually piling up in thicker and thicker layers upon my soul. But I say none of this. My manager has warned me to be cool and just roll with it. "Don't say anything that would give the impression you're a 'problem artist,' OK? You don't have to do anything you don't believe in. Just get past this, take the money and make your album." Besides, I'm excited. This is what everyone works for: To get signed by a major label. Wow!

Thousands of hours in our basement. Taking a fragment of melody. A piece of a groove. Sometimes even a set of changes. Jamming endlessly. Listening back to the cassettes we make. Picking out the minute or so from each rehearsal that actually sounds good and turning that into a completed composition. Performing to our friends at parties. Testing the songs, the grooves and each other to see what works and what doesn't. We all know when it's right. We just know. Smiles break out on faces that scowl for publicity shots. Joy fills the room 'til you can taste it. You can be high for a week off that energy. I've sat on the stoop, hungry and broke, just listening, over and over, to sections of tapes we made because it felt so good. All the possibilities. How a change in the high-hat pattern could give the groove a lift. How an accidental interplay between the guitars was perfect if we repeated it as a break. Man, this shit is BAD! Yabbadabbadooza, Baby!

Way down river now. Headed out to the open sea. The phone is ringing and everybody wants to be my friend. Night after night the crowds get bigger. Everybody wants to see the next big thing. The press is cranking out the stories. My face is on the cover of magazines. I'm reading things I never said attributed to me. Lies and distortion are being stated as fact. I'm talking to people at decibel levels high enough to drown out a freight train but who's listening?

I know that many people do. I talk endlessly with friends, musicians, anyone who will, about what's going on. I hear their enthusiasm, the genuine respect, even love, for the music. At times I am deeply moved by how much what we're playing means to people. But this can't stop the sense of foreboding that is creeping into the atmosphere.

As events rush on I steal moments to check back on the muse. I work on songs. I fight for time to just jam again. To rekindle the spirit and generate new ideas. To go back to the source. This is difficult. We're working with a producer who has different ways of doing things. We want to learn. We want to improve our music. But who really knows? Often we spend days, weeks even, trying out new arrangements that go nowhere. Sometimes the "outside ear" helps us hear a better way in a flash. All the time tension mounts. Now there is a schedule to keep. And this record is forever. It's not a momentary trial like a live gig. This is etched in oxide, cast in metal, boxed and shipped out to the world. Besides, in the politics of the music business we have our moment. This is not on a calendar or a clock. It's in the continuum of life and culture and commerce and control. Embedded in the calluses on my fingertips are traces of the scepter of Pharaoh. No man is immortal. But this struggle is.

The promised land is having a hit.

With the album in the can, a release date and tour scheduled, we play a concert with Ladysmith Black Mambazo at Zellerbach Auditorium, among the best-sounding rooms I've ever heard. We're up, the music crackles sharply, clearly, the crowd is excited and the warmth of their applause carries us into that place that must be heaven 'cause there ain't nothing else I've ever felt that I could call holy. We run off the stage after it's over and down the stairs to the dressing rooms and our manager is waiting for us. I expect him to be beaming as he usually does on a night like this. But instead he pulls me out of the crowd of friends, roadies and well-wishers and says, "Come here, I've got to tell you something." I knew it was bad. "I didn't want to tell you this before you went on. I hate to tell you at all. But you've been dropped . . ." Silence. "I'm sorry, man."

The record hasn't even been released and the label's decided to shelve it, put us on the street with nary a wave or a fare-thee-well. Wham, bam, thank you ma'am! I'm standing there and I hear this sound. It's hidden in the din of the crowded, buzzing theater. It takes me a moment to sort it out. But then it's unmistakable. It's the sound of a plane that's been shot down, the crescendoing whine as it plummets, trailing flames down to the earth below. It mingles with the sound of that scrap iron crashing into the hold of the ship in a roaring, screeching crash that reverberates around my memory and my present and my future all at once; a barbed-wire tangle of time and emotion that fiercely grips me as I whisper to myself: "Life . . ."

For those not initiated into the mysteries of the Culture Industry it may seem odd that after all that the record did come out, we were reinstated, temporarily, by the record company, we did tour and ultimately garnered much favorable press for what was, in my view, a flawed but successful first effort. Not that this was a "happy ending." Not at all. It was a tortured, tormented series of maneuvers and manipulations through which we were driven by economic necessity, near-psychotic anxiety and vain hope. We survived both as an artistic unit (we made three more albums) and as individuals. I continue to write music, produce records and work on other creative projects. But that's not the point. Indeed, this is not even an attempt to be the "whole story."

My purpose here has been to describe, not define. Something as vaporous as creativity defies definition, resists quantification and refuses access to those who seek to possess it like a Thing. My life has presented me with two interconnected problems: to live a good life and to transform the world. I have found definitions useful only insofar as they enable people to act. Participation in the creative process is essential to knowing it. Its purpose, for me, is to transport the participants to another place from which to view and then to reengage with this one. To be moved, as the saying goes.

My experience has revealed no eternal, universal truths. But it has given meaning to words such as creative, sacred, life and community. The only constant has been struggle. For some reason, a poverty of means has engendered an abundance of spirit. Music has lifted me out of despair, purged me of bitterness and filled me with resolve. I don't have to believe in it. It happens.

Conversely, what has been revealed to me is the lie. Not eternal, not universal, but a large, gaudily festooned lie. Which is that the only reliable measure of the quality of anything is money. This hoax is perpetuated by capitalism for obvious reasons but its ability to fool people is nonetheless undiminished. I have never found any correlation between money and the effectiveness of the creative process or its results. Do I produce a demand for my creative work, in other words, do I produce marketable commodities? Maybe. Do I apply my energies to creative work, regardless? Certainly. Continuously. Why? Because of the satisfaction I derive from the process itself and the pleasure it brings to others. The marketplace calls this a hobby. I call it my life.

The implications of this revelation go beyond the scope of this piece. But suffice it to say that when I get ready to perform I don't count ducats, I count beats and FOUR has greater significance in the universe from the dollar sign and why that is may not be known nor does it have to be to understand how that number expressed in a rhythm can lift a body off its backside and into a dance of jubilation. Or how, in the desperate loneliness that engulfs us all from time to time, I have sung a song to no one that, in a very real sense, connects me with everyone. Or how a child, encouraged to sing, dance or paint, opens like a flower and speaks with the voice of all humanity. And that ain't commerce, pal, that is creativity as it lives and breathes.

39.

The Fisherwoman's Daughter

URSULA K. LE GUIN

Books or babies? Wrong question, writes science-fiction author Ursula K. Le Guin. Our conceptions of creativity—who can be creative, how they can be creative, and yes, even where they can be creative and with whom, are not written in stone. They are not the result of a commandment from on high, or a genetic imperative. In this brilliant essay, Le Guin challenges this either/or proposition, and shows how it is possible not only to be creative and have children, but to be creative about your own creativity.

The artist with the least access to social or aesthetic solidarity or approbation has been the artist-housewife. A person who undertakes responsibility both to her art and to her dependent children, with no "tireless affection" or even tired affection to call on, has undertaken a full-time double job that can be simply, practically, destroyingly impossible. But that isn't how the problem is posed—as a recognition of immense practical difficulty. If it were, practical solutions would be proposed, beginning with childcare. Instead the issue is stated, even now, as a moral one, a matter of ought and ought not. The poet Alicia Ostriker puts it neatly: "That women should have babies rather than books is the considered opinion of Western civilization. That women should have books rather than babies is a variation on that theme."

Freud's contribution to this doctrine was to invest it with such a weight of theory and mythology as to make it appear a primordial, unquestionable fact. It was, of course, Freud who, after telling his fiancée what it is a woman wants, said that what we shall never know is what a woman wants. Lacan is perfectly consistent in following him, if I as a person without discourse may venture to say so. A culture or a psychology predicated upon man as human and woman as other cannot accept a woman as artist. An artist is an autonomous, choice-making self: to be such a self a woman must unwoman herself. Barren, she must imitate the man—imperfectly, it goes without saying.

Hence the approbation accorded Austen, the Brontës, Dickinson, and Plath, who though she made the mistake of having two children compensated for it by killing herself. The misogynist Canon of Literature can include these women because they can be perceived as incomplete women, as female men.

Still, I have to grit my teeth to criticize the either-books-or-babies doctrine, because it has given real, true comfort to women who could not or chose not to marry and have children, and saw themselves as "having" books instead. But though the comfort may be real, I think the doctrine false. And I hear that falseness when a Dorothy Richardson tells us that other women can have children but nobody else can write *her* books. As if "other women" could have had *her* children—as if books came from the uterus! That's just the flip side of the theory that books come from the scrotum. This final reduction of the notion of sublimation is endorsed by our chief macho dodo writer, who has announced that "the one thing a writer needs to have is balls." But he doesn't carry the theory of penile authorship to the extent of saying that if you "get" a kid you can't "get" a book and so fathers can't write. The analogy collapsed into identity, the you-can't-create-if-you-procreate myth, is applied to women only.

I've found I have to stop now and say clearly what I'm not saying. I'm not saying a writer ought to have children, I'm not saying a parent ought to be a writer, I'm not saying any woman *ought* to write books *or* have kids. Being a mother is one of the things a woman can do—like being a writer. It's a privilege. It's not an obligation, or a destiny. I'm talking about mothers who write because it is almost a taboo topic—because women have been told that they *ought not* to try to be both a mother and a writer because both the kids and the books will *pay*—because it can't be done—because it is unnatural.

This refusal to allow both creation and procreation to women is cruelly wasteful: not only has it impoverished our literature by banning the housewives, but it has caused unbearable personal pain and self-mutilation: Woolf obeying the wise doctors who said she must not bear a child; Plath who put glasses of milk by her kids' beds and then put her head in the oven.

A sacrifice, not of somebody else but of oneself, is demanded of women artists (while the Gauguin Pose demands of men artists only that they sacrifice others). I am proposing that this ban on a woman artist's full sexuality is harmful not only to the woman but to the art.

There is less censure now, and more support, for a woman who wants both to bring up a family and to work as an artist. But it's a small degree of im-

provement. The difficulty of trying to be responsible, hour after hour, day after day for maybe twenty *years*, for the well-being of children and the excellence of books, is immense: it involves an endless expense of energy and an
impossible weighing of competing priorities. And we don't know much about
the process, because writers who are mothers haven't talked much about their
motherhood—for fear of boasting? for fear of being trapped in the Mom trap,
discounted?—nor have they talked much about their writing as in any way
connected with their parenting, since the heroic myth demands that the two
jobs be considered utterly opposed and mutually destructive. . . .

As for myself: I have flagrantly disobeyed the either-books-or-babies rule,
having had three kids and written about twenty books, and thank God it
wasn't the other way around. By the luck of race, class, money, and health, I
could manage the double-tightrope trick—and especially by the support of
my partner. He is not my wife; but he brought to marriage an assumption of
mutual aid as its daily basis, and on that basis you can get a lot of work done.
Our division of labor was fairly conventional; I was in charge of house, cooking, the kids, and novels, because I wanted to be, and he was in charge of being a professor, the car, the bills, and the garden, because he wanted to be.
When the kids were babies I wrote at night; when they started school I wrote
while they were at school; these days I write as a cow grazes. If I needed help
he gave it without making it into a big favor, and—this is the central fact—he
did not ever begrudge me the time I spent writing, or the blessing of my work.

That is the killer: the killing grudge, the envy, the jealousy, the spite that
so often a man is allowed to hold, trained to hold, against anything a woman
does that's not done in his service, for him, to feed his body, his comfort, his
kids. A woman who tries to work against that grudge finds the blessing turned
into a curse; she must rebel and go it alone, or fall silent in despair. Any artist
must expect to work amid the total, rational indifference of everybody else to
their work, for years, perhaps for life: but no artist can work well against daily,
personal, vengeful resistance. And that's exactly what many women artists get
from the people they love and live with.

I was spared all that. I was free—born free, lived free. And for years that
personal freedom allowed me to ignore the degree to which my writing was
controlled and constrained by judgments and assumptions which I thought
were my own, but which were the internalized ideology of a male suprema-
cist society. Even when subverting the conventions, I disguised my subver-
sions from myself. It took me years to realize that I chose to work in such
despised, marginal genres as science fiction, fantasy, young adult, precisely
because they were excluded from critical, academic, canonical supervision,

leaving the artist free; it took ten more years before I had the wits and guts to see and say that the exclusion of the genres from "literature" is unjustified, unjustifiable, and a matter not of quality but of politics. So too in my choice of subjects: until the mid-seventies I wrote my fiction about heroic adventures, high-tech futures, men in the halls of power, men—men were the central characters, the women were peripheral, secondary. Why don't you write about women? my mother asked me. I don't know how, I said, A stupid answer, but an honest one. I did not know how to write about women—very few of us did—because I thought that what men had written about women was the truth, was the true way to write about women. And I couldn't.

My mother could not give me what I needed. When feminism began to reawaken, she hated it, called it "those women's libbers"; but it was she who had steered me years and years before to what I would and did need, to Virginia Woolf. "We think back through our mothers," and we have many mothers, those of the body and those of the soul. What I needed was what feminism, feminist literary theory and criticism and practice, had to give me. And I can hold it in my hands—not only *Three Guineas*, my treasure in the days of poverty, but now all the wealth of *The Norton Anthology of Literature by Women* and the reprint houses and the women's presses. Our mothers have been returned to us. This time, let's hang on to them.

And it is feminism that has empowered me to criticize not only my society and myself but—for a moment now—feminism itself. The books-or-babies myth is not only a misogynist hang-up; it can be a feminist one. Some of the women I respect most, writing for publications that I depend on for my sense of women's solidarity and hope, continue to declare that it is "virtually impossible for a heterosexual woman to be a feminist," as if heterosexuality were heterosexism; and that social marginality, such as that of lesbian, childless, Black, or Native American women, "appears to be necessary" to form the feminist. Applying these judgments to myself, and believing that as a woman writing at this point I have to be a feminist to be worth beans, I find myself, once again, excluded—disappeared.

The rationale of the exclusionists, as I understand it, is that the material privilege and social approbation our society grants the heterosexual wife, and particularly the mother, prevent her solidarity with less privileged women and insulate her from the kind of anger and the kind of ideas that lead to feminist action. There is truth in this; maybe it's true for a lot of women; I can oppose it only with my experience, which is that feminism has been a lifesaving *necessity* to women trapped in the wife/mother "role." What do the privilege and approbation accorded the housewife-mother by our society in fact consist of? Being the object of infinite advertising? Being charged by psychologists with total answerability for children's mental well-being, and by the government with total answerability for children's welfare, while being regularly equated with apple pie by sentimental warmongers? As a social "role," motherhood, for any woman I know, simply means that she does everything everybody else does plus bringing up the kids.

To push mothers back into "private life," a mythological space invented by the patriarchy, on the theory that their acceptance of the "role" of mother invalidates them for public, political, artistic responsibility, is to play Old Nobodaddy's game, by his rules, on his side.

In *Writing Beyond the Landing,* Du Plessis shows how women novelists write about the woman artist: they make her an ethic force, an activist trying "to change the life in which she is also immersed." To have and bring up kids is to be about as immersed in life as one can be, but it does not always follow that one drowns. A lot of us can swim.

Again, whenever I give a version of this paper, somebody will pick up on this point and tell me that I'm supporting the Superwoman syndrome, saying that a woman *should* have kids write books be politically active and make perfect sushi. I am not saying that. We're all asked to be Superwoman; I'm not asking it, our society does that. All I can tell you is that I believe it's a lot easier to write books while bringing up kids than to bring up kids while working nine to five plus housekeeping. But that is what our society, while sentimentalizing over Mom and the Family, demands of most women—unless it refuses them any work at all and dumps them onto welfare and says, Bring up your kids on food stamps, Mom, we might want them for the army. Talk about superwomen; those are the superwomen. Those are the mothers up against the wall. Those are the marginal women, without either privacy or publicity; and it's because of them more than anyone else that the woman artist has a responsibility to "try to change the life in which she is also immersed."

And now I come back round to the bank of that lake where the fisherwoman sits, our woman writer, who had to bring her imagination up short because it was getting too deeply immersed . . . The imagination dries herself off, still swearing under her breath, and buttons up her blouse, and comes to sit beside the little girl, the fisherwoman's daughter. "Do you like books?" she says, and the child says, "Oh, yes. When I was a baby I used to eat them, but now I can read. I can read all of Beatrix Potter by myself, and when I grow up I'm going to write books, like Mama."

"Are you going to wait till your children grow up, like Jo March and Theodora?"

"Oh, I don't think so," says the child. "I'll just go ahead and do it."

"Then will you do as Harriet and Margaret and so many Harriets and Margarets have done and are still doing, and hassle through the prime of your life trying to do two full-time jobs that are incompatible with each other in practice, however enriching their interplay may be both to the life and the world?"

"I don't know," says the little girl. "Do I have to?"

"Yes," says the imagination, "if you aren't rich and you want kids."

"I might want one or two," says reason's child. "But why do women have two jobs where men only have one? It isn't reasonable, is it?"

"Don't ask me!" snaps the imagination. "I could think up a dozen better arrangements before breakfast! But who listens to me?"

The child sits and watches her mother fishing. The fisherwoman, having forgotten that her line is no longer baited with the imagination, isn't catching anything, but she's enjoying the peaceful hour; and when the child speaks again she speaks softly. "Tell me, Auntie. What is the one thing a writer has to have?"

"I'll tell you," says the imagination. "The one thing a writer has to have is not balls. Nor is it a child-free space. Nor is it even, speaking strictly on the evidence, a room of her own, though that is an amazing help, as is the good will and cooperation of the opposite sex, or at least the local, in-house representative of it. But she doesn't have to have that. The one thing a writer has to have is a pencil and some paper. That's enough, so long as she knows that she and she alone is in charge of that pencil, and responsible, she and she alone, for what it writes on the paper. In others words, that she's free. Not wholly free. Never wholly free. Maybe very partially. Maybe only in this one act, this sitting for a snatched moment being a woman writing, fishing the mind's lake. But in this, responsible; in this, autonomous; in this, free."

"Auntie," says the little girl, "can I go fishing with you now?"

editors' note

This work was a collaboration. Frank Barron wrote the introduction. Alfonso Montuori wrote the section and selection introductions, and compiled the suggested reading list. Anthea Barron conceptualized the overall structure of the collection, compiled and edited the essays, and produced the working manuscripts. Each contributed to all the elements of the anthology.

It was important that all three of us should have an individual say in each aspect of the work. The theme of creative collaboration is present throughout the book; in practice this has meant that Anthea's writing and criticism has been incorporated into the general and part introductions; Monty has been instrumental in the choice of readings; and Frank has contributed his expertise throughout. All in all, it has been a collaborative effort, with only the usual amount of civil warfare.

Further, the book would not be in its present form without the dedication of our editors, Dan Malvin and David Groff, and the help of friends and colleagues, especially Kimberly Chloros-Beer, Karen Tschanz, Angela Colette Turenne, Karen van Schaack, Steve D. White, Al Wiggins, and the reference librarians at the McHenry and Science libraries at the University of California, Santa Cruz.

suggested Readings

These selections represent only a few of the many important books that have been published on the subject of creativity, and they are in no way intended to represent an exhaustive bibliography. The interested reader is also referred to two excellent scholarly journals Creativity Research Journal *and the* Journal of Creative Behavior. *Among many others, the* Journal of Humanistic Psychology, World Futures, *and the* Journal of General Evolution *also regularly include scholarly discussions of creativity.*

Arieti, Silvano. 1976. *Creativity: The magic synthesis.* New York: Basic Books.

An accessible and stimulating introduction to creativity in art and science. A good introductory book for the more theoretically inclined.

Barron, Frank. 1969. *Creative person and creative process.* New York: Holt, Rinehart and Winston.

An opening of the little-understood relationship of the person to the process in creative thinking, experience, and behavior, this book is written in an easy-to-read popular style. It emphasizes educational, professional, and organizational applications.

Barron, Frank. 1963. *Creativity and psychological health.* Princeton, N.J.: D. Van Nostrand Co. Reprinted by Creative Education Foundation, 1991.

A detailed account of the psychological research on creativity at the Institute of Personality Assessment and Research described in the Introduction of this volume. Includes discussions of such issues as intelligence, motivation, altered states, complexity, personality, and so on.

Barron, Frank. 1995. *No rootless flower: An ecology of creativity.* Cresskill, N.J.: Hampton Press.

An accessible work about creativity as an ecological process, summarizing existing research and pointing to new directions. Includes discussions of autobiography from an ecological perspective, and updates many of the topics addressed in the author's *Creativity and Psychological Health.* Includes six chapters of his own autobiography.

Barron, Frank, and David Harrington. *Creativity, intelligence, and personality.* Palo Alto, CA: Annual Reviews, Inc.: *Annual Review of Psychology,* 32, 1981.

This is the most referenced professional review of research and theory at the intersection of creativity, intelligence, and personality. It continues to be seen as the best condensed synthesis of the topic.

Bateson, Mary Catherine. 1990. *Composing a life.* New York: Plume.

A beautifully written account of the creativity of five women by a leading anthropologist, developing the perspective that creativity can be embodied in everyday life as we compose our own lives.

Burke, James. 1978. *Connections.* Boston: Little, Brown.

A companion to the PBS series of the same title, in which Burke shows how creative products emerged through remarkable connections, with ideas in one field being applied in other areas. Burke beautifully illustrates the role of mental, social, economic, and political connections as a vital factor in innovation.

Burke, James. 1985. *The day the universe changed.* Boston: Little, Brown.

Also a companion to the PBS series. This time Burke discusses how knowledge and creativity have changed our view of ourselves and of the world around us. Burke focuses on eight specific examples, including the idea of progress and the birth of science.

Cameron, Julia. 1992. *The artist's way: A spiritual path to higher creativity.* Los Angeles: Tarcher.

A workbook presenting a twelve-week course in developing creativity. Filled with exercises, tasks, suggestions for keeping a creativity journal, and other useful processes; a favorite with many artists.

Chang, C. 1963. *Creativity and Taoism: A study of Chinese philosophy, art, and poetry.* New York: Harper Torchbooks.

In this somewhat dense at times but extremely worthwhile book, philosopher Chang's exploration of Chinese concepts of creativity provides the reader with a wealth of insights into a fundamentally different approach to creativity.

Csikszentmihalyi, Mikhail. 1990. *Flow: The psychology of optimal experience.* New York: Harper.

Csikszentmihalyi (chick-sent-me-highly) presents a useful discussion of the "flow" state, typically associated with optimal performance and with creativity. Not quite the same as Maslow's "peak experiences," flow states mercifully occur more often, usually when we're really absorbed in a task that offers just the right amount of challenge for our competence.

Davis, Catherine R. 1992. *The lived experience of creativity in nursing practice.* Long Island, N.Y.: Adelphi University.

This is a fascinating and down-to-earth phenomenological analysis of the creative experience of nurses in the actual day-to-day medical setting. The often innovative contribution of nursing to treatment is supported by many examples drawn from real life.

Gablik, S. 1984. *Has modernism failed?* New York: Thames and Hudson.

A thoughtful discussion of art and the modern/postmodern debate by a leading art critic. Covers such timely subjects as the role of individualism, the nature of art, and the role of the sacred. Useful for understanding some of the problems and potentials facing artists today.

Gardner, Howard. 1994. *Creating minds: An anatomy of creativity seen through the lives of Freud, Einstein, Picasso, Stravinsky, Eliot, Graham, and Gandhi.* New York: Basic Books.

A cognitive scientist and creativity researcher, Gardner uses his popular model of multiple intelligences to discuss the nature of creativity through a series of case studies.

Goleman, Daniel, P. Kaufman, and Michael Ray. 1992. *The creative spirit.* New York: Dutton.

A well-illustrated and lively companion to the PBS series of the same name, addressing such issues as creativity and children, creativity and work, and creativity and community. A good popular overview.

Harman, Willis, and H. Rheingold. 1984. *Higher creativity: Liberating the unconscious for breakthrough insights.* Los Angeles: Tarcher.

A transpersonal approach; discusses intuition, channeling, extrasensory perception, and other paranormal phenomena at times associated with creativity. Also uses a computer analogy to present a model through which the mind can be "programmed" for creative output through mental affirmations.

Kearney, Richard. 1988. *The wake of imagination: Toward a postmodern culture.* Minneapolis: University of Minnesota Press.

Philosopher Richard Kearney's history of the concept of imagination in western thought through Hebrew, Greek, medieval, modern, and postmodern times is a sometimes difficult but extremely rewarding book. Apart from providing one of the best available introductions to postmodernism, it gives the reader a much-needed historical and philosophical grounding that shows that we have not always thought about creativity in the same way, or, for that matter, engaged in the same creative practices.

Koestler, Arthur. 1964. *The act of creation: A study of the conscious and unconscious processes in humor, scientific discovery, and art.* New York: Macmillan.

A classic in the literature on creativity by one of the most eclectic and fascinating minds of the century. Koestler covers a vast range of topics from biology to literature, and brings them together with style, as only a former novelist and journalist could.

Krippner, Stanley, and J. Dillard. 1988. *Dreamworking: How to use your dreams for creative problem-solving.* Buffalo, N.Y.: Bearly.

A comprehensive and useful discussion of the relationship between dreams and creativity. Includes exercises to develop creativity, understand the use of dreams to foster creativity, and a comprehensive report of existing research.

May, Rollo. 1975. *The courage to create*. New York: W. W. Norton.

A highly readable work on creativity by a leading existential-humanistic psychologist. May discusses the importance of courage, risk-taking, and creativity as a process of self-discovery.

Montuori, Alfonso, and Ronald E. Purser, eds. 1996. *Social creativity*. 4 vols. Cresskill, N.J.: Hampton Press.

A series on the social dimensions of creativity including essays by psychologists, sociologists, philosophers, and artists. Volume 1 deals with theoretical issues, volume 2 with creativity in business, volume 3 with creative communities and cultures, and volume 4 with creativity in the arts.

Nachmanovitch, Steven. 1990. *Free play: Improvisation in life and art*. Los Angeles: Tarcher.

A lively discussion of a fascinating topic provides some insights into the nature of improvisation, a subject that has received scant attention in the literature thus far.

Ray, Michael, and R. Myers. 1986. *Creativity in business*. Garden City, N.Y.: Doubleday.

This volume, coauthored by Stanford professor Michael Ray, who teaches a course on creativity in business, presents the many applications of creative thinking to business, with many useful tips and exercises.

Root-Bernstein, R. S. 1989. *Discovering: Inventing and solving problems at the frontiers of scientific knowledge*. Cambridge: Harvard University Press.

A useful and informative discussion of scientific creativity, incorporating dialogues, research, and speculations about the process of scientific discovery.

Rothenberg, A., and C. R. Hausman. 1976. *The creativity question*. Durham, N.C.: Duke University.

An important collection of theoretical writings about creativity by philosophers and psychologists ranging from Aristotle and Plato to Freud and Jung. Provides a broad account of thinking about creativity through history; makes for excellent browsing.

Runco, Mark A., and Robert S. Albert, eds. 1990. *Theories of creativity*. Newbury Park, N.J.: Sage.

New theoretical perspectives on creativity in art and science by a number of leading figures in the field. An excellent companion volume to Sternberg's work.

Runco, Mark A., and Ruth Richards, eds. 1996. *Eminent creativity, everyday creativity, and l.ealth*. Norwood, N.J.: Ablex.

A collection of essays showing the diverse facets of, and connections between, creativity and health in the individual and society.

Stein, Morris I. 1984. *Making the point: Anecdotes, poems, and illustrations for the creative process*. Buffalo, N.Y.: Bearly.

In this entertaining and informative booklet, Morris Stein, a veteran of the golden age of creativity research (1950–1965) presents in a very accessible manner some of the most important dimensions of creativity, offering anecdotes, quotations, research findings, and tips on how to stimulate and nurture creativity.

Sternberg, Robert. 1988. *The nature of creativity: Contemporary psychological perspectives.* Cambridge: Cambridge University.

Sternberg's edited volume provides an overview of the literature on psychological approaches to creativity, with essays by some of the leading theorists in the field.

Tatsuno, S. 1990. *Created in Japan: From imitators to world-class innovators.* New York: Harper Business.

Tatsuno discusses the Japanese perspective on creativity, combining theoretical discussions with examples of how Japanese industry has applied creativity, and contrasting them with American approaches.

Wallace, D. B., and Howard E. Gruber. 1989. *Creative people at work.* New York: Oxford University Press.

Case studies of Jean Piaget, Anaïs Nin, Charles Darwin, William Wordsworth, and others. Shows how their creativity manifested itself in specific ways through the development of recurring themes, interests, ways of thinking and formulating problems, work patterns, and so on.

Wilson, Robert Anton. 1990. *Quantum psychology: How brain software programs you and your world.* Phoenix, Arizona: New Falcon.

Novelist and iconoclastic philosopher Robert Anton Wilson discusses how to become more creative by breaking out of mental and emotional traps. Contains useful exercises.

permissions

"A Life in the Day of Maya Angelou" adapted from an interview with Maya Angelou by Carol Sarler, *The Sunday Times Magazine* December 27, 1987 © Times Newspapers Limited, 1987. Reprinted by permission of the publisher.

Excerpt from *Treat It Gentle* by Sidney Bechet. Copyright © 1960 by Sidney Bechet. Reprinted by permission of Farrar, Straus & Giroux, Inc.

"Living in the Medium" from *Creative Thinking* (third edition, 1989) by J. G. Bennett, published by Claymont Communications. Reprinted by permission of the Bennett Family.

Excerpt from *The Magic Lantern* by Ingmar Bergman, translated by Joan Tate. Translation copyright © 1988 by Joan Tate. Original copyright © 1987 by Ingmar Bergman. Used by permission of Viking Penguin, a division of Penguin Books USA Inc.

"Creation Myth," published in *Komotion International*, 10. Copyright © Mat Callahan, 1994. Reprinted by permission of the author.

Excerpt reprinted by permission of the publishers from *Six Memos for the Next Millennium* by Italo Calvino, translated by Patrick Creagh, Cambridge, Mass: Harvard University Press. Copyright © 1988 by the Estate of Italo Calvino.

Specified excerpts from "Heaven and Earth in Jest" from *Pilgrim at Tinker Creek* by Annie Dillard. Copyright © 1974 by Annie Dillard. Reprinted by permission of Harper-Collins Publishers, Inc.

Excerpt reprinted from *My Life* by Isadora Duncan, with the permission of Liveright Publishing Corporation. Copyright © 1927 by Boni & Liveright, renewed 1955 by Liveright Publishing Corporation.

"Why World Music?" by Brian Eno, reprinted from *Whole Earth Review*, Spring 1992; subscriptions to WER are $20 a year (4 issues) from FULCO, 30 Broad St., Denville, NJ 07834, (800) 783-4903. Copyright © 1992 Opal Ltd., 3 Penbridge Mews, London W11 3EQ. Reprinted by permission of the author.

Excerpts from *Fellini on Fellini* by Federico Fellini, translated from the Italian by Isabel Quigley. Copyright © 1976 by Eyre Methuen Ltd. (Eng. trans.).

and renewed 1970 by Marjorie T. Parsons, executrix. Reprinted by permission of the publisher.

Excerpt reprinted with the permission of Simon & Schuster from *Essays and Introductions* by W. B. Yeats. Copyright © 1961 by Mrs. W. B. Yeats.

Reprinted with the permission of Simon & Schuster from *The Real Frank Zappa Book* by Frank Zappa. Copyright © 1989 by Frank Zappa.

contributors

MAYA ANGELOU (1928–), poet and novelist, is the author of such acclaimed works as *I Know Why the Caged Bird Sings, And Still I Rise*, and *I Shall Not Be Moved*. She received a Grammy award for her recording of "On the Pulse of the Morning: The Inaugural Poem," which she recited at the inauguration of President William J. Clinton in 1993.

SIDNEY BECHET (1897–1959), an African-American jazz musician, was a master of the soprano saxophone and was influential in his use of "note bending." He toured Europe with the Southern Syncopated Orchestra, became popular in America with his recording of "Summertime" in 1938, appeared on Broadway, and eventually moved to France.

J. G. BENNETT (1897–1974) was a British philosopher who wrote about esoteric philosophy in a four-volume series, *The Dramatic Universe*. He spread the ideas of the mystic-philosopher Georges Gurdjieff through the International Academy of Continuous Education and in the book *Gurdjieff: Making a New World*.

INGMAR BERGMAN (1918–), Swedish film director, playwright, and theater producer, has achieved international success with his films *The Seventh Seal, Wild Strawberries*, and *The Magic Flute*. He has received numerous awards, including Best Director, National Society of Film Critics; the Luigi Pirandello International Theatre Prize; the Gold Medal of the Swedish Academy; the European Film Award; Le Prix Sonning; and the Premium Imperiale Prize (Japan).

MAT CALLAHAN (1954–), leader of the band The Wild Bouquet, musician, author, and cofounder of the San Francisco artists' collective Komotion, is perhaps best known for his work with The Looters, a worldbeat band that released a number of highly acclaimed recordings in the late eighties and early nineties.

ITALO CALVINO (1923–1985) was an erudite and imaginative Italian novelist and essayist. Science, metaphysics, and images of the fantastic inspired his many writings, including *Cosmicomics* and *The Castle of Crossed Destinies*. His awards included the Viareggio Prize, the Bagutta Prize, the Veillon Prize, the Premio Feltrinelli per la Narrativa, the Austrian State Prize for European Literature, and the Nice Festival Prize.

ANNIE DILLARD (1945–), novelist, essayist, and memoirist, is the author of *Tickets for a Prayer Wheel, Holy the Firm, Living by Fiction, Teaching a Stone to Talk, Encounters with Chinese Writers*, and *The Writing Life*. She was awarded a Pulitzer Prize for *Pilgrim at Tinker Creek*.

ISADORA DUNCAN (1878–1927), American dancer, was one of the first to raise interpretive dance to the status of a creative art; she was the pioneer of modern dance. She founded dance schools in Germany, Russia, and the United States. The Isadora Duncan Hall of Fame has been established in her honor.

BRIAN ENO (1948–), musician, producer, and philosopher, cofounded the band Roxy Music. His many solo albums include *Taking Tiger Mountain (by Strategy)*, *Discreet Music*, and *Music for Airports*. He has produced popular albums for David Byrne, The Talking Heads, and U2. He recently published a semi-autobiography, *A Year (with Swollen Appendices)*.

FEDERICO FELLINI (1920–1993) was known for his brilliance as the writer-director of at least thirteen films. Initially part of Italy's neorealist movement, Fellini became known for his surreal imagination. He won Oscars for *La Strada*, *8½*, and *The Nights of Cabiria*; the Golden Palm at the Cannes Film Festival for *La Dolce Vita*; and the top prize at the Moscow Film Festival for *8½*.

RICHARD P. FEYNMAN (1918–1988) was a Nobel Prize–winning physicist noted for his simplicity in interpreting physical problems. He contributed to the theory of quantum electrodynamics using simple graphics, and illuminated elementary physics in his acclaimed *Feynman Lectures on Physics*. He also illustrated the cause of the *Challenger* disaster by dipping an O-ring into a glass of ice water.

KAREN FINLEY (1956–) is a provocative visual and performance artist. She has also recorded albums and appeared on film. She is the author and illustrator of *Shock Treatment*.

MICHEL FOUCAULT (1926–1984) was a French philosopher, sociologist, and linguist who was known for his analysis of power in relationships, in works such as *Madness and Civilization*; *The Order of Things*; *Discipline and Punish*; and *History of Sexuality*.

ANNA HALPRIN (1920–), dancer, choreographer, and writer, founded and directed the Dancers' Workshop of San Francisco and the Marin Dance Co-op, directed the Tamalpais Institute, and founded *Impulse* magazine. Among other awards she received the Guggenheim Award in 1970. She is honored in the Isadora Duncan Hall of Fame.

EUGEN HERRIGEL (1884–1955) was a German professor of philosophy at the University of Tokyo who approached Zen Buddhist mysticism through the rigorous practice of archery. He was able to translate his experience for a Western audience in *Zen in the Art of Archery* and *The Method of Zen*.

ALFRED EDWARD HOUSMAN (1859–1936) was an English classical scholar and poet and a professor of Latin at University College London and later at Cambridge. He is known mainly for his volumes of poetry—*A Shropshire Lad*, *Last Poems*, and the posthumous *More Poems*. His lectures on poetry at Cambridge are published in *The Name and Nature of Poetry*.

CATHY JOHNSON (1942–) is an author and artist whose written works include *On Becoming Lost: A Naturalist's Search for Meaning* and *The Naturalist's Cabin*. She runs a publishing company, Graphics/Fine Arts, in Missouri.

CARL G. JUNG (1875–1961) was a Swiss psychiatrist who collaborated with Freud until his own *The Psychology of the Unconscious* was published in 1913. He is known for his theories of psychological types, dream analyses, ethnology, comparative religion, archetypes, and the collective unconscious.

TONY KUSHNER (1956–) is a controversial playwright who received the 1993 Pulitzer Prize for Drama and the Tony Award for Best Play in 1993 and 1994 for his work *Angels in America: A Gay Fantasia on National Themes, Parts I and II.*

URSULA K. LE GUIN (1929–) is an author of novels, essays, screenplays, poems, and short stories. She is renowned for her science-fiction works, such as *A Wizard of Earthsea* and *The Left Hand of Darkness.* She has received the Hugo, Gandalf, and Kafka awards, and the 1972 National Book Award.

LEONARDO DA VINCI (1452–1519) was an Italian painter, draftsman, sculptor, musician, architect, engineer, philosopher, and, as such, an exemplary Renaissance man. His manuscripts reveal extraordinary scientific intuition. His most famous paintings are *La Gioconda* (the Mona Lisa) and *The Last Supper.*

MABEL DODGE LUHAN (1879–1962) was an author and patron of the arts. She established salons in New York City and Taos, New Mexico, which were famous for their encouragement of intellectual discourse. She vividly described these conversational evenings, as well as her experience of the American Southwest, in the four volumes of her *Intimate Memoirs.*

HENRY MILLER (1891–1980) was an American author who drew moral censure for his explicit accounts of life in *Tropic of Cancer; Tropic of Capricorn; Rosy Crucifixion; Black Spring; The Cosmological Eye; The Wisdom of the Heart; The Colossus of Maroussi;* and *Hamlet: A Philosophic Correspondence.*

MARION MILNER (1900–) is a psychoanalyst and author of numerous books on art, intelligence, and psychotherapy, including *On Not Being Able to Paint* and *A Life of One's Own.*

NAVARRE SCOTT MOMADAY (1934–), an American Indian author, is professor of English at the University of Arizona. He received the Academy of American Poets Prize for his poem *The Bear* and the Pulitzer Prize for his novel *House Made of Dawn.*

KARY B. MULLIS (1944–) is a particularly inventive biochemist who received the 1993 Nobel Prize in chemistry for his invention of the polymerase chain reaction (PCR), an enormously useful biochemical tool.

DAVID OGILVY (1911–), an acclaimed British advertising executive, authored *Confessions of an Advertising Man; Blood, Brains and Beer; Ogilvy on Advertising;* and *Leisure Interest: Gardening.* He is in the Advertising Hall of Fame.

LAURENCE OLIVIER (1907–1989) was the world's leading tragic and comedic film and stage actor of his time. He was also a director and producer of films and theater companies. He won three Emmy Awards, the 1948 Academy Award for Best Actor for his role in *Hamlet,* the 1955 British Academy Award for *Richard III,* and a Special Academy Award in 1978.

IRVING OYLE (1925–), a physician, is the author of *The Healing Mind* and *The New American Medicine Show: Discovering the Healing Connection.*

RAINER MARIA RILKE (1875–1926) was a prolific author of prose and verse who wrote in German and French. His important works include *The Notebook of Malte Laurids Brigge; Sonnets to Orpheus; Duino Elegies;* and *Letters to a Young Poet.*

MURIEL RUKEYSER (1913–1980) was a multifaceted writer who wrote more than a dozen books of poetry; an important biography, *Willard Gibbs: American Genius;* and several books for children. Her books of poetry are both mythic and personal, and they protest economic and political injustices in the United States and the world.

MAURICE SENDAK (1928–) is a writer and illustrator of more than one hundred children's books, and he has been a set and costume designer for stage and film productions. He has received numerous *New York Times* Best Illustrated Book Awards, the Caldecott Award, the American Book Award, and the Hans Christian Andersen International Medal. His most famous work is *Where the Wild Things Are.*

MARY WOLLSTONECRAFT SHELLEY (1797–1851) was an author of novels, poetry, short stories, plays, travelogues, and literary criticism, and editor of her husband Percy Bysshe Shelley's complete works. She is most famous for her visionary, sometimes nightmarish novel *Frankenstein, Or the Modern Prometheus.*

IGOR STRAVINSKY (1882–1971) was a Russian composer of ballet, opera, and film scores, and one of the most important composers of the twentieth century. He was first known for his score for *The Firebird,* and he became famous for his collaboration with the producer Diaghilev on the riot-inspiring *Rite of Spring.* He held the Chair of Poetics at Harvard in 1939 and published *The Poetics of Music* in 1942.

PETER ILICH TCHAIKOVSKY (1840–1893) was a leading nineteenth-century composer of symphonies and classical ballet scores. He wrote the music for *Swan Lake, The Sleeping Beauty,* and the *Nutcracker.* He is especially known for his sixth symphony, *Pathétique.*

PAMELA L. TRAVERS (1906–1996), a novelist and essayist, became famous as the creator of the *Mary Poppins* series of children's books.

VIRGINIA WOOLF (1882–1941), a British novelist, essayist, and biographer, is noted especially for her feminist essay *A Room of One's Own* and her novels *The Waves, To the Lighthouse,* and *Orlando.*

WILLIAM BUTLER YEATS (1865–1939) was a poet, playwright, and Irish patriot. He received the Nobel Prize for Literature, and honorary doctorates from Trinity College and Queens, Oxford, and Cambridge universities. He founded the famous Abbey Theatre in Dublin, where many of his plays were produced. Among his noted works are *The Countess Kathleen* and *The Tower.*

FRANK ZAPPA (1940–1993) was an iconoclastic musician, composer, and producer who drew inspiration from doo-wop, jazz, blues, and the modern symphonic works of Stravinsky, Varèse, and Webern. He hit the pop charts with *Don't Eat the Yellow Snow, Dancin' Fool,* and *Valley Girls,* but is best known for his extremely challenging, angular compositions in both rock and orchestral music, his innovative guitar playing, and his irreverent lyrics.

about the editors

FRANK BARRON is professor emeritus of psychology at the University of California, Santa Cruz. He has been a Guggenheim fellow, holds an honorary Doctor of Science degree from La Salle University, and has been a fellow of the Center for Advanced Study in the Behavioral Sciences. He has received many awards and honors, including the Richardson Creativity Award from the American Psychological Association in 1969 and, most recently, the 1995 Rudolph Arnheim Award. His other books include *Creativity and Psychological Health*; *Scientific Creativity* (with C.W. Taylor); *Creative Person and Creative Process*; *Artists in the Making*; *The Shaping of Personality*; and *No Rootless Flower: An Ecology of Creativity*. He is married to Nancy Jean, singer, painter, and mother of three children, Frank Jr., Brigid, and Anthea.

ALFONSO MONTUORI, PH.D., is associate professor at the California Institute of Integral Studies. An Italian citizen, he was born in Holland and lived in Lebanon, Greece, England, and China. While living in England he performed as a professional musician, recording several albums with his own band. His publications include *Evolutionary Competence*; *From Power to Partnership* (with Isabella Conti); and *Social Creativity* (with Ronald E. Purser). Montuori is associate editor of *World Futures* and series editor of *Studies in Systems Theory, Complexity, and Human Sciences* at Hampton Press. He is married to jazz singer Kitty Margolis and lives in San Francisco.

ANTHEA BARRON has many interests, including landscape design, herbology, mathematics education, intaglio printmaking, dance, music, and poetry. She lives in Santa Cruz, California. This book is her first publication.